# PAKISTAN ADRIFT

ASAD DURRANI

# Pakistan Adrift

*Navigating Troubled Waters*

HURST & COMPANY, LONDON

First published in the United Kingdom in 2018 by
C. Hurst & Co. (Publishers) Ltd.,
41 Great Russell Street, London, WC1B 3PL
All rights reserved.
© Asad Durrani, 2018
Foreword © Anatol Lieven, 2018
Printed in India

Distributed in the United States, Canada and Latin America by
Oxford University Press, 198 Madison Avenue, New York, NY 10016,
United States of America.

The right of Asad Durrani to be identified as the author of this publication is
asserted by him in accordance with the Copyright, Designs and Patents Act,
1988.

A Cataloguing-in-Publication data record for this book
is available from the British Library.

ISBN: 9781849049610

This book is printed using paper from registered sustainable
and managed sources.

www.hurstpublishers.com

چلتا ہوں تھوڑی دور ہر اک تیز رو کے ساتھ  پہچانتا نہیں ہوں ابھی راہبر کو میں

I drift a little with every fast current, but have yet to find my direction.

Mirza Asad-ullah- Khan Ghalib
Nineteenth-century Indian poet

# CONTENTS

# CONTENTS

## PART THREE
## THE OVERVIEW

# ABBREVIATIONS

| | |
|---|---|
| AJK | Azad Jammu & Kashmir (the part administered by Pakistan) |
| AIG | Afghan Interim Government (the Mujahedeen government in exile, formed after the Soviet withdrawal from Afghanistan) |
| ANP | Awami National Party (ethnically Pashtun and based in Pakistan's North-Western province) |
| BB | Benazir Bhutto (Prime Minister of Pakistan, 1988–90 and 1993–96) |
| BSA | Bilateral Security Agreement (between the US and Afghanistan signed in 2014) |
| CGS | Chief of the General Staff |
| CMI | Corps of Military Intelligence |
| COAS | Chief of the Army Staff |
| CJCSC | Chairman Joint Chiefs of Staff Committee |
| CSCE/OSCE | Conference (Organisation) of Security and Cooperation in Europe. |
| CSD | Cold Start Doctrine |
| DCC | Defence Committee of the Cabinet |
| DGMI | Director General of Military Intelligence |
| DGMO | Director General of Military Operations |
| DGISI | Director General of Inter-Services Intelligence |
| DL | Durand Line (Pak-Afghan border, established after an 1893 memorandum of understanding between Mortimer Durand of British India and Afghan Amir Abdur Rahman Khan). |

# ABBREVIATIONS

| | |
|---|---|
| FWO | Frontier Works Organisation (a civil works agency of the Pakistan Army) |
| GDR | German Democratic Republic (the former East Germany) |
| GIK | Ghulam Ishaq Khan (President of Pakistan 1988–93) |
| IB | Intelligence Bureau |
| IHK | Indian-Held Kashmir |
| IPI | Iran-Pakistan-India (a pipeline project, now on hold, and very likely to drop the second "I") |
| ISI | Inter-Services Intelligence |
| ISPR | Inter-Services Public Relations |
| JATM | Joint Anti-Terror Mechanism |
| JIC | Joint Intelligence Committee |
| JCSC | Joint Chiefs of Staff Committee |
| JKLF | Jammu & Kashmir Liberation Front |
| KKH | Karakorum Highway |
| NDC/NDU | National Defence College (now a University) |
| NGG | The New Great Game |
| NLC | National Logistics Cell |
| MFA | Ministry of Foreign Affairs |
| MI | Military Intelligence |
| MNS | Mian Nawaz Sharif |
| MOU | Memorandum of Understanding |
| MQM | Muhajir (now *Mutahidda*) Qaumi Movement |
| NDS | National Directorate of Security (Afghan Intelligence Service) |
| NDC | National Defence College |
| NLC | National Logistics Cell |
| NRO | National Reconciliation Ordinance (promulgated by President Musharraf in 2007 to provide immunity from prosecution to eminent politicians against corruption) |
| NSAG | National Security Advisory Group |
| PM | Prime Minister |
| PML | Pakistan Muslim League |
| PML (N) | Pakistan Muslim League, Nawaz (Sharif) Faction |
| PMO | (Indian) Prime Minister's Office |

# ABBREVIATIONS

| | |
|---|---|
| POF | Pakistan Ordnance Factories |
| PPP | Pakistan Peoples' Party |
| SCO | Shanghai Cooperation Organisation |
| THK | Tehreek-e-Hurriyat-e-Kashmir (formed by resistance parties in IHK in 1991) |
| VCOAS | Vice Chief of Army Staff |

.

# FOREWORD

It is an honour to be asked to write the foreword to this book by Pakistan's foremost military intellectual. General Asad Durrani's combination of memoirs and reflections is among the most important works to have emerged from the Pakistani Army since independence. Its dry wit and wealth of anecdote also makes it a pleasure to read, and its wryly perceptive take on the failings of both civilian and military government in Pakistan distinguishes it from most self-serving memoirs by former leading figures. General Durrani was in the best of positions to observe those failings. As a junior officer, he served in the wars of 1965 and 1971; as a senior officer, he was commander of both Military Intelligence and Inter-Services Intelligence. He worked in senior roles during the governments of Zia ul Haq, Benazir Bhutto and Nawaz Sharif, and casts a cold eye on all of them.

This is a highly enlightening, necessary, but also, in many ways, depressing memoir. Writing on Pakistan—by both Pakistanis and Westerners—has a longstanding tendency to veer wildly between prophecies of imminent doom and belief in miraculous salvations. For liberal Pakistanis and most Westerners, this salvation was supposed to come from some mixture of "democracy" and obedience to the latest ideas of the World Bank. We were told repeatedly that if Pakistan underwent a regular transition from one elected government to another, then it would provide some sort of magic key that would unlock the country's hidden capacity for political, social and economic reform. In 2013, the first such transition occurred—and no miracle has taken place. Equally, the hopes of many Pakistanis that military government would transform the state have been repeatedly disappointed.

On the other hand, the portrayal by so many analysts of Pakistan's imminent demise have also been repeatedly proved false. Despite all its weaknesses, Pakistan has proved extraordinarily resilient in the face of the many dire challenges that it has faced. Contrary to the great majority of expert predictions, the army and state eventually defeated the Pakistani Taliban insurgency that began in 2004 and for a while seemed to be sweeping more and more of the country. Terrorism, of course, remains a permanent danger—but that, alas, is now true of many countries. Asad Durrani's book provides some of the clues to the sources of this apparently mysterious resilience.

Among these has been the unity and discipline of the Army. General Durrani's book is not propaganda for another military takeover of government. On the contrary, as well as highlighting the terrible mistakes of particular military rulers, it is a soldier's warning of how military rule both fails to solve problems and corrupts the soldiers. As Durrani writes:

> The Army's takeover of political power, whatever else it may have done to the country, never did any good to the service ... After the putsch of 1999, [Musharraf] had all the country's resources at his disposal, but since he mainly trusted the military, he planted members of the armed forces in many important civil institutions, and thus undid most of the good work done in the previous years to cleanse the armed forces of the unmilitary traits... When serving generals started falling for prime land offered at bargain prices and their palatial houses were built by government contractors, one knew that the fish was now rotting from its head.

This also helps explain why—despite the firm belief of most observers—large numbers of Pakistani officers and their commanders have always opposed the idea of military rule, and are willing enough to live under civilian rule as long as civilians respect certain essential "red lines". These relate to national security as the military understands it, but also to the control of the military by the military, especially the promotion and appointment process. Anyone who thinks Pakistan would be better off if civilian governments appointed their military cronies to senior positions along political lines should take a close look at the history of neighbouring Afghanistan—one among many other countries around the world where a divided military has led to catastrophe.

A source of endless interest at elite parties in Pakistan is to guess the identity of the next Chief of Army Staff (COAS) and what his political agenda will be. General Durrani's memoir brings out how pointless this exercise usually is. As he repeatedly highlights, the Pakistani Army is first and foremost a corporate body, whose officers (when serving) are loyal to and shaped by the institution, a feature rooted in the fact that as well as an institution, the military is "a way of living, often with its own way of dying".

Only when a COAS seizes power as leader of the country do his personal views become of key importance. The same is true (with certain qualifications) of commanders of Pakistani intelligence, though not necessarily of all their staff.

For a former ISI commander, General Durrani's views of that institution are notably—and informedly—sceptical. This includes a strong critique of exaggerated Pakistani fears of Indian influence in Afghanistan. A leitmotif of General Durrani's book is indeed the repeated failures of political manipulation by the Pakistani military and its intelligence services, whether at home or in neighbouring Afghanistan. Repeated attempts to run Pakistani politics from behind the scenes through loyal proxies collapsed as the proxies freed themselves from the military and pursued their own (often disastrous) agendas. As for Pakistani attempts to manipulate Afghan affairs, the best that could be said for them is that such attempts on the part of the USSR and the USA have proved even more disastrous. As he and many others have emphasised, Afghan realities and the Afghans themselves are singularly recalcitrant to any attempts at outside control, including from their paymasters. Thus, at the time of writing, former President Hamid Karzai—a figure entirely created by the USA—is touring the world telling people that the USA destroyed Afghan democracy and established the Islamic State terrorist movement in Afghanistan.

At the same time, General Durrani makes absolutely clear the reason why American hopes of Pakistani military action against the Afghan Taliban have always been completely illusory, no matter how much US pressure may be brought to bear:

> ...as a policy [Pakistan] does not use force against any Afghan group except in self-defence, not only because it has to live with them long after the foreigners are gone, but also because it believes that it must

one day bring all of them to the negotiating table. That again is a mission that cannot be aligned with the American interests and those of its clients in Kabul.

As to General Durrani's portrayal of the Pakistani political elites, it is a bleak one, but hardly bleaker than their record deserves. He brings out how again and again the distrust that permeates Pakistani political society often makes it impossible for Pakistani leaders to take actions that would be in their own interest—let alone that of the country—because an opponent might thereby gain some small benefit. The chronic inefficiency and repeated crises that result generate the (empty) dream of regeneration through military rule.

Since General Durrani completed his military and diplomatic career, a new outside actor has attained great potential economic and political importance in Pakistan: China, with its offer of investments in the China–Pakistan Economic Corridor, dwarfing anything that the USA has provided since the 1980s or even the 1960s. It remains to be seen whether China can bring about a transformation of the Pakistani state, or indeed whether it has any desire to do so. As General Durrani's account makes clear, anyone embarking on this project had better do so with eyes wide open.

Anatol Lieven
*Georgetown University Qatar*

# PREFACE

It was a short stint: a mere eighteen months as the head of Pakistan's premier secret service, the ISI. Before that, I was the Director-General of Military (Army) Intelligence for about two years. My tenure in Intelligence barely accounted for a tenth of my service in uniform, though it left me with the label, or the burden, I have had to carry for ever after. As a former chief of the legendary ISI, I was asked, beseeched, cajoled, and even coaxed to write a book. I do not know if any of my predecessors or successors were similarly pestered, but I do know that it was a legitimate request. A stint in Intelligence at that level provides a perspective that can usefully be shared with posterity. That it has not been done often enough in Pakistan, is, perhaps, for both good reasons and bad.

The sensitivity of the job would be an obvious reason, or at least provide a convenient excuse, not to write a book. I believe, however, that unless the holders of these posts were, for reasons of state policy, forbidden to put their experience on paper, it is not reason enough. There will always be confidential matters, which might have to be excluded, or even recorded, but not made public until the appropriate time. When I decided to undertake this project, exposing official secrets was certainly not my main purpose. Since leaving service, I have spilled a few beans, so to speak, but not once have I been cautioned or charged with indiscretion. For most, want of the discipline that writing requires was a greater impediment. What is more, most of our intelligence chiefs stayed too short a period in the job to be able to hold their own on the subject. I, too, was there very briefly, but I still believe, perhaps out of vanity, that I might have something of interest to tell the general reader.

There were other factors I had to consider before taking the plunge into authorship. Since there is so much I have to relate that did not work out well, by being overly critical of individuals and institutions I could come across as wallowing in nihilism, or, alternatively, get carried away by a messianic desire to tell the truth, and go overboard with it. The converse could also happen. As an act of atonement, one might take on more than one's fair share of blame, and the book would then read like a confessional account. And, if overly Socratic, one could end up confessing to self-doubt all the time. The narration would then be a slightly wishy-washy or, at best, confused chronicle. Former "spooks" carry another piece of baggage as well: the credibility deficit. Who would be willing to believe that those who once lived in the shadows were now coming clean?

What still tempted me to run the gauntlet was that I had had some experience of wielding the pen.

My first published work was the result of a an act of rebellion. A junior officer, I was unhappy with the military practice that required me to write an essay every now and then, and at times to also write on behalf of my seniors. I responded by recording what I saw as the chemical analysis of an archetypal soldier. Taking a few digs at some military quirks was not likely to get me any exemption from further compulsory writing, but I did expect to feel lighter after telling others further up the hierarchy what I thought of them. To my great surprise, the chain of command—which for a subaltern terminated somewhere at the brigade level—seemed quite pleased with this "juvenile creativity". But to keep me in my place, and to make sure that I did not get too big for my boots, the piece was published only when I had achieved the exalted rank of major.

The lesson that I had to learn time and time again, in the army and elsewhere, was that rank and status mattered more than substance: the same story, when told by a senior officer, had more impact. The same story, when told by a senior officer, had better effect. After I got my second star, someone in the Psychological Warfare Directorate dug up an article that I had once contributed to the NDC journal and had it published in a newspaper. If that gave me ideas about ever becoming a writer, then it is the only coup, to my knowledge, that the Directorate ever pulled off.

To rise in the military hierarchy, one had to practise and often preach the military art. That included, to my great discomfiture, the science of military writing. Not till I became the head of the Army's Training Branch, however, did I muster the courage to protest, albeit meekly, about adhering to the letter too strictly. Such writing was intended to train the mind, not the spirit. The exercise of writing, quite apart from the time and effort that we had to spend to fit the paper to the prescribed layout, often forced our thinking into a strait-jacket. Mercifully, I no longer have to stick to any format; whether the soul is also now free, it is for the reader to judge.

The dilemma, of whether one should merely present the narrative, or also attempt a post-mortem, was probably the most acute. A worthy academic advised me to leave the latter task to the readers, presuming that all or most of them would want to draw their own conclusions. Even if that were so, besides placing the view from the vantage point at a certain perspective, some reflections on my part can do no harm. Moreover, these events took place decades ago, and, as such, the context must be explained. The book therefore is both descriptive and deductive, with no claim to be the last word. Having been trained in the art of hard-nosed assessment, I have tried not to make too many value judgments, complain about missed opportunities, and have attempted to avoid wishful conclusions. Being only mortal though, and having been at times part of the decision making process, one also knows that some of those failings are hard to avoid. To make up for this inevitable human failing, the penultimate chapter is devoted entirely to my mistakes.

Readers expecting a former head of the world-famous ISI to reveal many sensational plots will be disappointed. I do not believe that our establishment, civil and military, or, for that matter, our political leadership, went around crafting deep designs. A few of those who worked with us certainly had ambitions which were not always in the country's best interest. At times, they even tried to realise them through unsavoury means, but I am not aware of any entire institution that collaborated to pursue an underhand agenda. That external powers had the ability to strongly influence our decision making is also a great exaggeration—beyond creating a bit of mayhem and confusion, there was not a great deal outsiders could do. The perception that nothing of any significance happened in Pakistan without American blessing was our own contribution to this mythic relationship. Those amongst us who jumped onto their bandwagon for favours or in the belief that the country's best interests were served by collaboration or compliance, must have contributed to this misconception.

My account, therefore, is an attempt to describe how most of what happened in the country was the outcome of our own decisions (though these were indeed influenced by circumstances), and not because of a hidden hand at the wheel. In a few forums, when I tried to make this point, some members of the audience walked out in disbelief.

Lastly, since it is solely my personal account, I am entirely responsible for its veracity, or for the lack of it. Of course, there is no claim that the narrative, as laid out in Part One of the book, is the whole truth. In fact, I have made no claim that I have always known the truth—only what I believed to be the truth. Part Two is essentially my assessment, developed over a long period of time, of some of the major subjects that I had to deal with, or of the events that I witnessed. In Part Three, I have tried to defend my argument, as well as concede my inadequacies, and have indulged in some reflection. So structured, some recapitulation became unavoidable, for which I seek the reader's indulgence.

Asad Durrani
Rawalpindi

# INTRODUCTION

It was like any other flight from the Gulf. The PIA aircraft that landed at Islamabad Airport in the small hours of 13 May 1993 held mostly Pakistani expatriates, and consequently conveyed more hand luggage than the hands on board could carry. The government had recently revised the baggage rules and many of the passengers were obviously worried. I was also on that flight and just as restless. But as the Commandant of the National Defence College (now a university)—the post I held at that time—things like excess baggage did not trouble me. In fact, I had good reason to be at peace. After some high-pressure assignments, I was in an academic environment again and was gratified to lead what was arguably the top think-tank in the country.[1] Was this edginess a premonition of sorts or had I started enjoying myself too soon? Both, as it turned out.

Something must be the matter. An eerie feeling surrounded me as I walked into the VIP lounge. Instead of the odd member of the personal staff who normally received the Commandant, almost all the officers of the College headquarters were present. And there were some others too. A former colleague of mine, probably summoned for this very purpose, broke the bad news. This was to be my last day in uniform. I had been compulsorily retired three years before the stipulated period of service for a Lieutenant-General. No one in the reception line dared venture a guess, but I found out in good time that the accusation was that I had been "dabbling in politics". It was not too inappropriate a charge and it brought to an end a not unsuccessful career. The irony is that I was the one who had, only a few years ago, passionately argued

1

that the Army must never get involved in politics. Now I had done it myself and done it blatantly. How did this come about? This book might provide an answer—my answer.

The countdown ended where it had begun: at the NDC.

The first thing that one learnt in this institution was that, within its four walls, one was fairly free to give one's opinion. The majority would also get away with it, most of the time.

In May 1986, we, a group of budding national strategists, gave our opinion to Zia-ul-Haq, the country's military ruler. Though an elected Government headed by Prime Minister Mohammad Khan Junejo was already in place, we pleaded with Zia to restore undiluted democracy in the country. We must have been too forceful in our emphasis on the famous ideal that democratic institutions must be allowed to evolve and mature without interruption and intervention. The President-General was known to have a patient ear, even on such matters, but on that day, he threatened us. As an immediate response, he merely mumbled something about our ignorance of ground realities. But he did not work very hard to conceal his true message for us, "Many a zealot was reformed after a brief sojourn in Siberia". I was not sent to Siberia, but as the chairman of the presentation, I was denied the post recommended by the Defence College and sent to cool my heels in the (professional) wilderness. My dabbling in politics started only when Zia-ul-Haq's ended.

Some two years later, in August 1988, when Zia's plane tumbled from the skies, I was back in the mainstream commanding a brigade at Kohat (a garrison town in the North-West), but still reflecting on "ground realities". I was soon to learn more about these. Within forty-eight hours of the crash, I was out with my brigade to deal with one more aspect of the fallout of his era.

Even before Zia-ul-Haq and the Iranian Revolution, Kohat was one place where Shia-Sunni sensibilities had to be watched carefully. With the arrival of the Afghan refugees, the sectarian balance in the nearby Kurram Agency, so delicately maintained over time, tilted against the Shias. Already ill at ease with his Islamisation, the community had much grievance against Zia, the architect of our Afghan policy and also of the new ideological orientation. Only a few weeks before the fateful crash, Allama Arif-ul-Hussaini, a prominent Shia leader from the area, had been assassinated. His followers suspected that the General was responsible; it is possible therefore that some of them from a small sectarian enclave near Hangu (between Kohat and our border with Afghanistan) fired a few shots to celebrate his exit.

The Sunni tribes on the hills heard the shots before the local administration, which only learnt about it when a tribal *Lashkar* (militia) arrived in the area to teach their religious rivals that such occasions were not for rejoicing. It was, perhaps, not so much that anyone in the area was so sensitive to gunfire, or so infatuated with Zia and his Afghan policy (even though many of them benefited from it). In the sectarian context, this was a classic case of 'بغزِ‌ءعلی' *rather than* 'حُب 'معا ویا' (hatred of the Shias rather than love for the Sunnis). As soon as the officialdom found out what had happened it asked for military help.

Armies do not like to join such battles right at the outset. In the belief that they are the 'instrument of last resort', they prefer it if all other options to defuse a crisis are exhausted first. As we moved to meet the *Lashkar* at short notice, I too cursed the civilian agencies for not doing their bit. In hindsight though, the civil bureaucracy's early passing of the buck—whether done routinely as the more convenient option or with a great amount of foresight, since the available paramilitary forces might have failed to save the vulnerable community—turned out to be the right course. There was a lesson there for all of us: call the fire brigade in time. Before another incident could occur, the famous "Triple One" came in.[2]

The operation itself was a tame affair. When the tribesmen learnt that we meant business, they went back to the hills, leaving a message behind: *if only the Army had looked the other way, they would have taken care of the "common enemy"*. Zia, if memory fails us, was, in the first place, the Army Chief. These tribesmen were not the only ones unaware that state institutions functioned in complex ways. I, too, had much more to learn but only after crash-landing in the corridors of power. It took what proved to be a rollercoaster ride of nearly three decades, for me to get there.

When Ayub Khan took power in a military putsch in October 1958, I was happily pursuing academics at the prestigious Government College in Lahore. Soon thereafter, a few of us, in our youthful exuberance, tried to defy security personnel tasked with keeping the railway platform free for a train carrying some members of the military top brass. A policeman put the fear of martial law into our hearts, reminding us that "under the new order, one could be hauled up on any charge, even if it were trumped up". To escape this hanging sword, I had to get onto the right side of the new regime. I am not sure if this was the thought, or if it was the near-zero chance of heading the country after doing a Masters in science, that made me apply to join the Army soon thereafter. In the end, it was probably more the promise of getting a regular commission after only a year's cadet training if one was a graduate. But just in case the Army did not see a future General in me, I also enrolled for post-graduate studies at the renowned Institute of Chemical Technology.

With the prospect of further education firmly under my belt, I was not desperate to acquire an officer's cross-belt or, in due course, a General's cross-swords; ultimately, it was probably this that helped me to wear both. While appearing before the selection board at Kohat, I was asked at the final interview who I thought were more important for the country: politicians or soldiers. I took the liberty of choosing the former. With the military now firmly in control, it seemed like a foolhardy response. The selection board, however, was large-hearted and I got away with this impertinence—but have kept wavering on the subject ever since. By a strange coincidence, I was again in Kohat (on my way to Bannu where I was posted), when in March 1969 Yahya Khan imposed martial law. Something didn't seem quite right, but it gave me my first taste, or illusion, of power over civilians. For the next few months, I was heading a summary military court and taking to task anyone carrying an unlicensed weapon—the Army's pet procedure to restore law and order in the country. The problem was that in the two districts under my jurisdiction, Bannu and Dera Ismail Khan, this covered almost everyone. Of course, only those who were on the wrong side of the law (or its enforcers) were charged and produced before me. I don't think it did much good for law or order, but it did help the civil administration to show khaki rule in a bad light. That the Army lets itself be duped every time it assumes political power, I was to learn much later. That, as a cog in the military machine, one was contributing to such a design became a pretty discomforting thought.

Mercifully, when Zia took over in July 1977, I was commanding troops in an operational area and thus unable to contribute to any design, evil or divine. That, however, was not to last forever and during the 1984 Referendum, I (now a Brigadier) along along with my command, gave a collective thumbs-up to his heavenly right to lord over us for five more years. (Indeed, only the Lord in Heaven could cut it down to four.) Armed with the sanctity of being an elected President, in the following summer Zia invited the heads of the diplomatic missions in Islamabad to Murree, a hill station nearby, for a day of fun and frolic. I was assigned to entertain them, probably because as a former Defence Attaché it was assumed that I would be familiar with diplomatic norms. I was indeed—if not with the norms, then with the practice. On such occasions, the diplomats would rather relax than be encumbered with protocol. To acknowledge that the entertainment had been a success, Zia gifted me a prize, claiming to have bagged it in the gala; it was not his, he picked up someone else's. The man never gave away anything that he believed belonged to him, rightfully or wrongfully, as the regime he had installed under the new order was to find out only too late.

Soon after, I was at the NDC, evolving national strategies, telling the military rulers not to adulterate democracy, and being told in return that I had learnt nothing. I think Zia was right. I only discovered it after his death.

PART ONE

THE VIEW FROM A VANTAGE POINT

1

# INTO THE CORRIDORS OF POWER

The military ruler at the head of a political regime must wear many hats. This was also the case with Zia. There was a time when he was simultaneously the President, the Chief Martial Law Administrator, the Chairman of the Joint Chiefs of Staff Committee (CJCSC), and the Chief of the Army Staff (COAS). In due course, he took some of them off, and ended up wearing just two: that of the COAS, which had helped him keep or shed all the others, and that of the President, the post that all our coup-leaders need for legitimacy, and one they seek even by rigging referenda. After his departure, the Constitution required the Chairman of the Senate, Ghulam Ishaq Khan, to be the Acting President. Khan understood power politics in Pakistan better than any other person, living or dead. He therefore made the first move, and invited General Mirza Aslam Beg—who as the Vice Chief of the Army Staff was now the COAS and Zia's military heir—to wear the late President's political mantle. With wisdom that matched Khan's, Beg suggested that it was time to restore civilian supremacy. Ghulam Ishaq Khan gratefully accepted.

Three months before his plane crashed in the desert, Zia had dismissed the government headed by Mohammad Khan Junejo that had been elected under his own aegis. After his death, the decision was challenged in the Supreme Court and it seemed likely that the apex court—now that Zia was no more—would reverse the dismissal. Beg, however, believed in making a clean break from the past and therefore pre-empted the possible U-turn. He summoned Waseem Sajjad, the acting Law Minister, and told him to ensure that the ensuing elections were not foiled. Political power continued to flow from the barrel of the gun, but there were, nevertheless, good reasons, once the transition was over, for Beg to be hailed as the Godfather of the new democratic order. Had it not been for him, the elections Zia had promised for November 1988 might not have been held, and not only because the General had leaned on the superior judiciary.

In the only general elections held under Zia in 1985, the candidates were not allowed to contest under party flags. This was his ploy to keep the PPP—whose founder Zulfiqar Ali Bhutto he had toppled and hanged—out of power. The Party took the bait and boycotted the elections. Its Chairperson, Benazir Bhutto, often regretted this decision, quoting some political Gurus who said that *in politics no space must be surrendered without contest*. However, those who stood as independent candidates and were elected, grouped themselves according to their political orientation. There was, therefore, a good case to let the elections planned for November 1988 be held on a party basis. The Acting President accepted the logic. The PPP, with its claims of victimisation and repression by a military regime, was now the hot favourite to win. The political heirs of Zia, led by Mian Nawaz Sharif (to be Prime Minister many times thereafter), were therefore desperate to have the elections scrapped or postponed. It is interesting that they did not plead with Ishaq Khan; having been a close associate of the deceased President and often his de facto deputy, he was expected to be more sympathetic to their cause. Instead, they knocked on the Army Chief's door. Khan's proclivity to say 'no' in such matters was not the only reason. The Army was believed to be the true guardian of Zia's legacy. To their utter dismay, the new Chief was hell-bent on ushering in a new democratic dawn.

Soon after assuming his new office, Aslam Beg, once my Corps Commander, inducted me into his team as the Director-General of Military Intelligence. I had not served in Intelligence before but, as in many other countries, the heads of agencies are outsiders, and are expected to introduce some fresh air into this secret world. I now had the privilege of attending a forum that was, in due time, to gain worldwide fame, the Corps Commanders' Conference. A briefing on the general elections was usually the first item on the agenda. In view of a likely PPP win, a small but vocal group was pretty nervous. The progress reported by General Hamid Gul, then the Director-General of the ISI, on the evolution of an anti-PPP alliance, the IJI (*Islami Jamhoori Ittehad* or Islamic Democratic Alliance) provided some solace, but not very much. On one point, the Conference was in agreement: democracy as enshrined in the Constitution had to be restored in letter and spirit. If, however, despite all efforts (though these were not strictly in keeping with the spirit of democracy), the PPP won the elections, it was not to be prevented from forming the next government. The creation of the IJI was also rationalised as being good for democracy: "two nearly equal parties, presenting a viable alternative before the electorate, would do the system a world of good". Some of us really believed this.

With Hamid Gul and his team taking care of the Army's political management, Military Intelligence and myself were mercifully left to do our primary work. But the vantage point I enjoyed did help me gain some insight into the country's politics. My first impressions, even though I could make sense of them, were rather unsettling. The military apparatus was poorly suited to command political matters, and even less so to make political assessments. By a strange coincidence, the ISI's forecast of the election results added up nicely—it was wrong about both Sindh and Punjab, but by the same margins in opposite directions (the PPP fell short of the ISI's estimates in Punjab, but gained nearly by the same number in Sindh). Another line swallowed by quite a few was that once in power, the PPP would wreak revenge on the Army for having hanged its founding father, Zulfikar Ali Bhutto. Much later, we discovered that it was the Army's own creations that were far keener to cut it down to size.

There was universal consensus on the management of elections: these had to be free and fair. The Army, though not involved in the actual conduct of the elections, was very keen to live down the last eleven years of military rule, especially the Presidential referendum of 1984, which had been till then the most heavily rigged electoral exercise in our history, and the only one to involve the Armed Forces. The Acting President certainly had a soft spot for the IJI, but he also knew what was expected of him, which was to be seen as being above board. The election machinery quickly grasped the mood and acted according to the book. The results, by and large accepted as fair, led to more commotion.

No party or alliance emerged with a clear majority. Out of 213 seats in the National Assembly, the PPP won 92 and the IJI 54. Despite the large gap, the IJI attempted to get its leader in Parliament nominated as the Prime Minister and claimed that it could prove its majority on the floor of the house. Under a certain constitutional provision still in force, the President could have facilitated that. But Ghulam Ishaq Khan, true to his calling, was not about to do something so blatant in its partiality. In any case, it would not have worked without the support of the MQM, a party representing the majority of immigrants from India. It had won 13 National Assembly seats in the southern province of Sindh and had already tied with the PPP to rule over the Province. These were all the mundane reasons that led the President to invite Benazir Bhutto, the leader of the PPP, to form the first elected government after Zia's death—and not because the United States persuaded him to do so, as many later speculated.

Once this decision was taken, Beg invited Bhutto to Army House. Some eyebrows were raised but, at the time, it was the sensible thing to do. Benazir needed to be assured of the Army's support. In return, she would not meddle in the military's professional affairs. Both these pledges were made. I believe these were also intended to be kept, but it did not quite work out that way.

2

# BENAZIR BHUTTO IN THE TROIKA

When Benazir Bhutto became the Prime Minister of Pakistan in November 1988, it was widely acclaimed as an earth-shaking event. It was not only the surprise of seeing a woman, and a young one at that, being elected the leader of a conservative Muslim country. It was also hard to believe that there could be such such happy endings in real life. It was like a fairy tale: a popularly elected leader is removed from power by a military dictator and hanged, but then his young daughter returns after years in exile and, with the help of the downtrodden people, takes back her father's mantle. In the real world, however, hardly anyone lives happily ever after. Bhutto, in any case, did not believe that a workable arrangement with the Establishment was possible, and that was despite the fact that a fair number of persons, not necessarily enamoured of her and her party, wanted to see the lady survive to complete her term. In a country with Pakistan's political history, an elected assembly completing its term was considered a milestone on the road to democracy. When it came to BB, she also had the sympathy of the masses for all that she had endured. Contrary to some impressions, her gender usually worked in her favour. In an opinion poll conducted in one of our formations (an unusual procedure, I might add), the majority said they had nothing against a woman becoming the head of the government in our Muslim country.

13

Shortly after Benazir was sworn in, the Chinese Ambassador called on the Army Chief and told him that the Prime Minister needed Beg's help. Armed with the knowledge of thousands of years of statecraft, the Chinese had enough foresight to suspect that the viciousness of the opposition and her own inexperience and feudal mind-set provided a recipe for disaster. Little did the Ambassador know that help was already being offered to her.

The first paper sent to the PM's office from the Army Headquarters proposed the formation of a National Security Advisory Group (NSAG). Mindful of the sensitivity of civilians to the idea of a National Security Council (NSC), which they regarded as the perpetuation of military rule by other means, the proposal did not adopt the guise of another name. Essentially, it recommended that, though it was up to the Government to take decisions, it would be well served by a body of experts, working under the Prime Minister to suggest different options on national security policy. The paper did, however, suggest that representatives from the major opposition parties should also be included. Its main argument was that this arrangement, besides creating a 'memory bank' involving individuals who had played important roles over the years, would dissuade the parties of the Opposition from exploiting critical issues for political ends, provided they were kept on board. From the military top brass, only the Chairman of the Committee of the Joint Chief of Staffs (the most harmless four-star General) needed to be invited, and that too only if seeking advice on defence matters. This paper never saw the light of day.

A few days before I assumed office as the Director-General of Military Intelligence (DGMI), an ethnic clash broke out in Hyderabad, a city in the southern province of Sindh, claiming nearly a hundred lives. A review of the situation was my first assignment. A coalition between the Pakistan People's Party (PPP) and the Muttahid Qaumi Movement (MQM), representing the old and the new Sindhis respectively, seemed a good idea to bridge a critical divide. When it actually happened, after the elections, we all heaved a huge sigh of relief. But the arrangement was too good to last beyond the traditional honeymoon period of a hundred days. Within a few months, Sindh was again in turmoil. This time, the mission to help Benazir Bhutto was led by the President.

In March 1989, Ghulam Ishaq Khan started a process of consultation. One of the groups that he invited when he was in Karachi consisted of myself, the Chief of Army Staff (COAS) and the Director-General of the Inter Services Intelligence (DGISI). We all agreed that the situation was serious enough to merit the sustained involvement of the Prime Minister, who needed to send the right message. If she were to spend the next few days in the province, she could help to steer and oversee the reconciliation process with her party's estranged ally, the MQM. BB made it very clear what she thought of this piece of Presidential advice. After the meeting, she got into her plane and headed for Islamabad. And it was not to oversee the other operation that was stuck at that time, the one around Jalalabad.

The date by which the Soviet forces had to withdraw from Afghanistan was 16 February 1989. A few weeks before the deadline, Victor Yakunin—then the Soviet, and after the collapse of the Soviet Union the first Russian, Ambassador to Pakistan—called on General Beg. The DGMI is usually present on such occasions. Essentially, he came to seek our help to prevent their retreat from turning into a rout. Indeed, a large number of the Mujahedeen had taken positions north of the Hindu Kush to ensure that the Soviets did leave—and did not, as some anticipated, hunker down in areas controlled by allies of theirs, like Rasheed Dostum, and thus achieve their minimum goal of a North-South divide of Afghanistan. Interestingly, the favour he solicited was veiled in a threat: "Right now, Najeebullah [of the People's Democratic Party of Afghanistan (PDPA) who headed the regime installed by the Soviets] is extending his hand of friendship towards you. Let us hope it will not turn into a fist!" The hand that mimed this change, of course, belonged to the Ambassador. Whether the arrogance that made it difficult for him to ask politely was a Russian trait or that of the ego of a big power, I do not know, but Yakunin was assured that the resistance forces would not disrupt the Soviet withdrawal.

For the Mujahedeen, however, there was unfinished business. The regime installed by Moscow was still in place, though it controlled only Kabul and some big cities and hardly any of the countryside. To mop up these Soviet remnants, the ISI persuaded the Mujahedeen to form a coalition of seven major resistance groups, the "Afghan Interim Government" (AIG). To claim legitimacy, it was required to secure a foothold within Afghanistan. The city of Jalalabad in eastern Afghanistan seemed ideally suited for this purpose, but when it failed to fall, the

ISI, as the sponsor of the strategy, paid the price. Our Afghan policy and its conduct I will discuss in detail later, but some reference to it throughout the book is unavoidable, since it so deeply impacted the balance of power within our country. The failure at Jalalabad, for example, provided the civilian government with a chance to snatch control of the ISI from the Army.

Bhutto was understandably uncomfortable with someone like Hamid Gul in charge of this formidable entity. The General was not only one of the better-known survivors from the Zia era, but also the self-proclaimed godfather of the right-wing Islami Jamhoori Ittehad (IJI). The creation of the IJI had, the PM believed, robbed her of an absolute majority in the National Assembly, and what was worse, deprived her party of the mandate to rule the crucial province of Punjab, which she could not forgive. The failure at Jalalabad was just the right opportunity to remove him from the country's top intelligence job. In his place, she appointed (retired) Lt Gen. Shams-ur-Rehman Kallue. It was the first time that this post was taken by someone not on the active list of the Army.

The selection of the DGISI is indeed the Chief Executive's prerogative and according to the rules of business, he (or even she) does not have to belong to the Armed Forces. The Army's claim on this post is based on the argument that since the bulk of the personnel in the ISI come from the Army, its head should be a serving General. The real reason, of course, lies in the Army's larger than life role in the country's polity. General Beg had put up, as was the practice, a panel of officers from among whom the PM could choose the new DGISI. So he was obviously miffed. Those who used to argue that, to get even for her past indignities, BB would try to defang the Army once she came to power, were now in full cry. A running battle between the Government and the Army high command followed, rapidly engulfing the Presidency. The deadly combination of the distribution of power in the system and our reluctance to abide by its constraints made this inevitable.

Zia's party-less polls had not only kept the PPP out of power, but also drained the real power out of all political institutions. Eager to enjoy symbolic power, the House elected in 1985 gave the President, now elected in a referendum, the power to unilaterally dissolve the National Assembly and elected governments, as well as to choose service chiefs.

This was the famous Eighth Amendment to the Constitution. Ishaq Khan had inherited these powers, which made the President an important pillar of the new power structure, with the Prime Minister as the chief executive, and the COAS as the prime arbiter, being the other two. This power trio was popularly known as the Troika.

In its original Russian sense, the troika was a chaise driven by three horses in unison. Our arrangement was designed to rein them in. The Army Chief now did not have to break loose and take the country with him. If the Prime Minister ran amok, he or she could be pre-empted or prevented from doing irreparable damage. The President, in any case, had nowhere to go. This did not look like a bad idea, considering our previous and also our subsequent experience. Had it worked, it would not have had the mobility of a troika but could have enjoyed, at least, the stability of a tripod. It was workable, provided the three of them accepted the limits of their power, and more important, could withstand the pressure from their cohorts to test these limits.

*The Army made the first move*

The Government has the right to make or review policies. After the Soviet withdrawal and the Jalalabad fiasco, its decision to have another look at our Afghan policy was, therefore, quite in order. Indeed, the Opposition, even before the review, used to shout from the rooftops that the rollback and the sell-out of our nuclear programme and other core issues were BB's real agenda. But the pressure that General Beg had to withstand came from within the fold in uniform. Some of them had too much faith in the old policy (it had got the Soviets out, after all), the others had none at all in the new government. And so they pestered the Army Chief to have this review business nipped in the bud.

General Beg acted rationally and in mid-1989 a review was carried out. I was a member of the team that included our top expert on Afghanistan from the Foreign Office, Ashraf Jehangir Qazi (see the chapter on Afghanistan). Besides preparing me for my assignment as the DGISI, which was to come a year later, the exercise helped us reconsider some critical assumptions. The trouble, however, started when Beg persuaded the Prime Minister to let him be the chief coordinator of the Government's Afghan policy. The Government felt humiliated, not because it could not snatch control of our Afghan policy from the Army, which it might even have been quite happy about, but because it lost a crucial round in the turf war.

Of course, BB was not going to give up. Soon thereafter, she tested the ground by suggesting that although the President could appoint the CJCSC—the post held by Admiral Iftikhar Ahmed Sirohi at that time—deciding when the incumbent retired was the prerogative of the Prime Minister. No one had ever told GIK that what he thought of as his domain was no longer his and got away with it (as the Prime Minister was going to learn a few months down the line). In this case, there was another, graver, reason that Bhutto was not going to get her way. Aslam Beg was convinced that the removal of Sirohi was only a test case for the real thing: his own retirement. Had the time come to give the lady a taste of her own medicine?

Benazir had always believed that in the provincial phase of the 1988 elections, she had been robbed of victory in Punjab. The suspicion was understandable. In the national elections, the PPP had secured a majority of seats in the province. In the provincial round that followed three days later, her edge vanished. The party, and at times Ms Bhutto herself, complained of selective rigging of the vote (in 22 seats, she once claimed). I do not believe that this discrepancy was because of any foul means. The three-day gap had been used to spread the word that it was time for the Punjabis to wake up and take note of how the Sindhis were united behind one of their own (BB, an ethnic Sindhi, had bagged all the seats where her community was in a majority) but the people of Punjab remained divided. A small number were convinced by this exhortation and that helped to swing a crucial number of seats, which had been won narrowly by the PPP in the national round, in favour of the IJI in the provincial round.

There was another possible explanation for the swing. People may well vote for one party at the federal level and for another at the provincial, depending on the issues or on the individual candidate in the area. That, however, has seldom happened in Pakistan. The provincial card that the PPP had so often played to its advantage worked, this time, against it.

The PPP's clean sweep in rural Sindh may have cost it the province of Punjab but it won the Party an unlikely ally. The MQM, which in the meantime had emerged as the main representative of the Urdu-speaking émigrés from India, won in the major cities in Sindh. In order not to be left out of the provincial government, the party that was once created to countervail the PPP forged an alliance with its nemesis both at the provincial and the federal levels. BB thus had a comfortable majority at the Centre; but, for her party, in Sindh it was an alliance of inconvenience. The MQM's price for this shotgun wedding was a list of fifty plus points, which no one, least of all the PPP, could fulfil. The baggage of the past and the nascent political culture made mutual accommodation nearly impossible. The communities that the former rivals—now allies—represented went on the warpath. Any concession that the Prime Minister was seen making to the MQM would be at the cost of her loyal following in Sindh. Less than a year into the alliance, the MQM was already thinking about fresh choices.

I never found General Beg to be particularly fond of the MQM, and certainly not of its methods. He was also discreet enough to keep himself away from its politics. The MQM, on the other hand, wanted him to be known as one of them, as the seniormost *Mohajir* (migrant) in the country's hierarchy and a member of the so-called troika. In any case, the party was always susceptible to his nod. I do not know if he gave any such nods to the MQM, but its decision to part ways with the PPP came at a time, early in September 1989, when both Beg and Altaf Hussain (the MQM leader) seemed to have concluded that parting ways with Bhutto was now inevitable. The loss of an important coalition partner reduced the Government's majority in the National Assembly to twelve. The Opposition led by Ghulam Mustafa Jatoi decided that the time was now ripe to wrest power from the PPP through a motion of no confidence. This was the first serious political crisis that BB had to face, and it was also my first serious brush with the country's politics.

Since the ISI was now headed by someone out of uniform and appointed against the wishes of the COAS, it was not available for the Army's political work. I was asked by Beg to assess the no-confidence motion's chances of success. I do not know if he also gave a similar task to two officers of the ISI, Brigadier Imtiaz (who later headed the Intelligence Bureau when Nawaz Sharif succeeded Bhutto) and Major Aamir. While trying to persuade some PPP legislators to vote against

19

their party, both were trapped in a sting operation setup by one Brigadier Rao Akhtar Khan, an outstanding army officer who had not been promoted by Zia because of his family links with the PPP, and who was now a joint secretary in the PM's office. In this operation, code-named Midnight Jackal, he was assisted by Major Masood Sharif (retd.), the de facto head of the Intelligence Bureau (and its de jure head during BB's second stint) and a pal of the Prime Minister's spouse, Asif Ali Zardari. The case was then handed over to us. After due process, both Imtiaz and Aamir were retired from service. During the interrogation, Aamir tried to suggest he had been acting on Beg's instructions. There was no way to know if this was true.

After meeting some politicians from both sides, it looked unlikely to me that the no-confidence motion would be carried. It was a sobering experience. Bhutto's supporters in Parliament knew that the mighty Army wanted it to succeed and also that the wielder of the Eighth Amendment had blessed it. But none of them was willing to run the gauntlet to vote for the motion. In the end, it was the ruling party that walked away with one member from the other side (Mr Anwar Aziz), and the motion fell short by 13 votes. BB had won against the other two, supposedly more powerful, members of the troika. It was a pyrrhic victory because it soon led to another round of confrontation, this time with the President. The old man on the Hill never forgot anything, least of all a slight.

As the head of Military Intelligence, and later the Inter Services Intelligence, I met the President many times. He was indeed very knowledgeable. His long and varied career was an asset, and so was his remarkable memory, which some compared to that of the proverbial elephant. But what really made the difference was his ability to remain focussed (for example, despite immense pressure he never let our nuclear programme be derailed, of which more later). Often, when we were mired in our many intractable issues, his subtle Pashtun sense of humour and grasp of Persian and Urdu poetry provided welcome relief. But he also had his blind spots. That he did not like Ms Bhutto was well known, a dislike that was exacerbated because of the lady's disrespect for decorum (in a briefing session in the GHQ, she mocked him more than once). Even so, it surprised us when he embroiled himself in a squabble with the Prime Minister that he could well have lost.

# BENAZIR BHUTTO IN THE TROIKA

Some time at the end of 1989, I was asked by General Beg to see the PM and dissuade her from taking a contentious matter to court. Apparently, the President had disregarded some of her recommendations for appointments to the higher judiciary. She probably had a good case there, and, having defeated the no-confidence motion on the floor of the house, was now raring for a constitutional showdown. Air Chief Marshal Hakeem-Ullah, the Chief of the Air Staff, was also there on the same mission. A compromise formula was worked out and BB agreed to stand down in the hope that her gesture would help get both the Army and the President off her back. But that is not how politics works anywhere. How it did in Pakistan, I was soon to learn.

During one of the sessions at the PM's secretariat, I stole a few minutes with BB and asked her if she was willing to seriously consider a hint dropped by General Beg (he did that often, to the chagrin of the Government and at times also of the Army), that in view of these recurring conflicts between the various power centres the country would be better served by a national government? If I had any idea about a politician's paranoia, I would not have been so taken aback by her reaction. She could not believe that I had asked this question without being deputed to do so by the Army Chief (on another occasion, a similar assumption on her part was to cost me dearly). And I could not understand, initially, why she kept repeating: "What's in it for me?" I finally stumbled on the right answer: "In a national government, Prime Minister, you could destroy your opponents from within". There was a fleeting flicker in her eyes. But if the Army was making the suggestion, there could scarcely be anything in it for herself, her thoughts might have run. My memory ran back to General Zia's retort when we exhorted him to restore undiluted democracy, "You chaps haven't got a clue what politics is like out here". I was getting a taste of power play. It might not taste good, but it certainly was addictive.

At the turn of the year, there was a godsent pause in these running battles. Mrs Asif Zardari was expecting a child. In the true chivalrous tradition of our society, her antagonists waited till the baby was safely delivered. Never before had the head of a Government delivered a child in office and, according to cynics, this was the only thing the Chief Executive delivered whilst in office. The storm that followed this lull was unleashed by the MQM in Karachi on 7 February 1990. Scores of people were killed. The countdown for the end of BB-1 had started.

During the next few months, the supporters of both the MQM and the PPP clashed many times, mainly in Karachi and Hyderabad. Sindh, however, was not the only area on fire during that period.

Earlier that year, there was the sudden eruption of an uprising in Indian-held Kashmir against the occupation. Unlike some of its fore-runners, the uprising did not seem to be petering out. Instead, the struggle expanded in its intensity and violence. One sensible decision that the Prime Minister took was to task the Foreign Office, the ISI, and the MI to brief the political parties, even those outside Parliament, on this development. (Had the NSAG penny dropped?) Most of the participants, especially those considered a "security risk", credibly assured us that the briefing would be treated as confidential. How fool-ish of us to have branded some groups in the country "traitors," simply because they were not on our side. It was equally naïve of us to believe that all those who were briefed on sensitive matters, because of the offices they held, would not trade them for some nebulous gains when it was expedient. We learnt that at great collective and individual cost.

When Rajiv Gandhi, the then Indian Prime Minister, visited Islamabad in 1988, we learnt that BB assured him of cooperation against the Sikh uprising then raging in the Indian Punjab. (She once conceded that she had helped India bring the Sikh insurgency under control. It was also confirmed to me years later from a foreign source.) Since the unrest in the Indian Punjab had a direct bearing on the Kashmiri freedom struggle, which stood to suffer if the Sikh movement collapsed, the Prime Minister had obviously acted without consulting all relevant organs of the state.

A few months later, during the PM's visit to the US in June 1989, she was given an unprecedented briefing by the CIA on our nuclear programme. She was reported to be shocked and stated that she had not been adequately briefed on the subject at home. Some of us gave her the benefit of doubt since feigning ignorance under the circum-stances was the sensible thing to do. However, on her return, it became quite clear that the Prime Minister would rather have our nuclear agenda rolled back. (A Wikileaks cable confirmed this assessment. In May 1998, when Pakistan was dared to respond to the Indian nuclear tests, Ms Bhutto, then in Opposition, confided to her American inter-locutors that contrary to her public stance, she did not support a Pakistani response in kind.)

BENAZIR BHUTTO IN THE TROIKA

We now had a dilemma. On Kashmir and on our nuclear programme, there was near consensus in the country. And both were likely to be compromised under the then political leadership. The Army Chief therefore requested the Prime Minister to visit the GHQ for an exclusive briefing on what we regarded as our core security issues. She accepted, but when she arrived at the gate of the GHQ I was informed that Robert Oakley, the American Ambassador, was also in her car. I had to quickly warn the presenters of the brief to drop the "exclusive" part. It was obvious that the Prime Minister wanted the Americans to be in the loop on these sensitive issues. More doubts arose about her commitment to the country.

In March–April 1990, India undertook a military build-up on our eastern borders. We were pretty certain that the Indian forces had left some essential war fighting echelons back in their cantonments. Clearly it was a political move in reaction to the uprising in Kashmir and not for something more serious (which in any case would not have created any strategic effects and only intensified insurgencies both in Punjab and Kashmir). We therefore decided against mobilising our troops. But then those who solely depend on satellite imagery can be very imaginative. In the US, they saw fresh military concentrations on the Indian side (true), and detected nuclear-tipped missiles moving out of our air bases (probably trucks carrying construction pipes). William Gates, the then Deputy National Security Advisor to the US President—later the director of the CIA and Secretary of Defence—was rushed to the region to persuade the two countries to back off from a nuclear Armageddon. The American assessment of the ground situation may have been faulty, but the mission did result in the Indian forces going back to barracks and, of benefit to us, reinforced concerns that Pakistan might actually be in possession of nuclear weapons.

Much was made of the Prime Minister's absence from the country when Mr Gates dropped in. Actually, this was further proof that the country was not in a state of panic because of the Indian troop movement. There was no big design behind it. She was on one of her fortnightly out-of-area sojourns to recover from the rigours of Pakistani politics, and perhaps met the US emissary while still abroad. However, she missed the fireworks—probably by design—of her provincial government's raid on the *Pucca Qila*, an MQM stronghold in Hyderabad.

The timing was curious. Not only was the Prime Minister out of the country, but so were the COAS and the Karachi Corps Commander. And it was for the first time, during this phase of unrest in Sindh, that the provincial administration did not coordinate a major operation with the Army.

How the military was to be employed in aid of civil power to combat ethnic warfare in Sindh had become a contentious issue between the Government and the Army High Command. The Government wanted the Army to operate under Article 137 of the Constitution, that restricts the latter's room for manoeuvre. General Beg asked for more freedom of action under Article 242, declaring that his troops would not "chase shadows". The Government did indeed have the prerogative to decide. But when we got a list of miscreants to round up that had only MQM names on it, it became clear that the ruling party wanted to hound its political opponents with the Army's help. Understandably, the GHQ decided not to oblige. In fact, it intervened to scuttle the police raid on the *Pucca Qila*. Soon after, some time in June, both the President and the Army Chief agreed that BB now had to be shown the door. The method and the timing were to be decided by the President.

In mid-July, I learnt purely by chance that some of the President's men were working full steam on the dissolution of the National Assembly. When I informed General Beg, he seemed a bit dismayed. It had been less than two years since the democratic process had been restored, with much fanfare and all round applause. As the acclaimed godfather of this restoration, he had hoped that Ishaq Khan might first try something less drastic than invoking the much dreaded Article 58.2(b) that empowered the President to send the Government and the National Assembly packing. After a brief meeting with GIK, he confirmed that the die had been cast.

The Government too got a whiff of what was brewing. To pre-empt the possibility, it asked the President to call a session of the National Assembly. Dissolving an assembly in session is not the 'done thing', and so the idea was to have a session in full swing—hopefully before the President was ready with his decision—and then to drag on till help came, not from any divine quarter but from the source BB had more faith in. On at least one previous occasion, in the autumn of 1989 when the no-confidence motion was being debated, she had sent an SOS asking President Bush (senior) to 'save democracy' in Pakistan. She had to be reminded that such motions were part of the democratic process.

On 6 August, the air in Islamabad was rife with rumours that the President was all set to dissolve the National Assembly and dismiss the federal Government. His lack of response to the PM's request to summon the National Assembly must have reinforced this inkling. BB called Khan at about noon and asked him if he was going to do so. His response that he would not act unconstitutionally should have made her suspicious. Bhutto, however, had too much faith in her own destiny and was apparently relieved. Some others were not. One of her federal ministers, Khawaja Tariq Rahim, rang me to ask why he could not see any tanks outside his office. Obviously, these people had no idea how softly the Army, with all its experience, could carry out such tasks. This, in any case, was no coup-d'état (though, in Pakistan, even these can be carried out without heavy weapons). A few khaki uniforms posted at critical points served the purpose. The President made the announcement at 1700 hours that afternoon.

Soon after her dismissal, the deposed Prime Minister went all guns blazing for Military Intelligence, holding it responsible for the downfall of her Government. I, as its head, was obviously caught in the crossfire.

Some of the reaction was understandable. There is a fairly widespread paranoia in the country, not only amongst the politicians (and not entirely misplaced either) about the agencies, and that almost always means 'intelligence agencies', especially those manned by personnel in uniform. These invisible hands are the usual suspects when no others are obviously involved. They are not always innocent, but rarely as guilty as alleged. When a civilian government is toppled, especially with the actual or perceived backing of the Army, the ISI takes the flak first. In this case, the ISI, headed by Bhutto's nominee, could not be targeted and had, in fact, played no part in her removal. So MI was the prime suspect. Some of our reports, which were rather critical of her party's conduct, had been shared with her office too. The discussions at my meetings with politicians, including a few from the PPP, reinforced this impression.

After a few days, she moved her sights to the President. If she was advised not to target the Army for too long or she found out who was really behind the move, I do not know. But the fact is that, notwith-standing all that the MI did, or General Beg said, at the end of the day, it was the President's call. He also took charge, assisted by some of his former associates, Roedad Khan, Ijlal Haider Zaidi, and Rafi Raza, of the next steps, such as the selection of caretakers, and the framing of corruption cases against the ousted PM and her consort. His office and experience eminently qualified him to do so. My task was to liaise between the Presidency and the GHQ.

But there are, indeed, no perfect solutions.

If anyone believed that the job of the caretaker regime was to hold fair elections in the ninety days it had under the law, that belief (or the believer) had no place in the interregnum. Ghulam Mustafa Jatoi, the leader of the opposition in the dissolved assembly, was made the care-taker Prime Minister. The foremost criterion for inclusion in the interim setup was how deeply one was committed to preventing Benazir's comeback. The only competence that counted was a person's perceived ability to keep her at bay. Nothing else mattered. The stark-est example was the selection of Jam Sadiq Ali as the Chief Minister of Sindh. Going by the aforementioned standards, he must have been the best choice. The PPP lost its power base. In the bargain, we handed over the soft underbelly of our nation (Sindh) to the grubbiest man alive, and got it back, further softened up, only when he died (of cir-rhosis of the liver). To put the fear of the "hidden hands" into the hearts of the PPP supporters, I myself, now a proclaimed offender in BB's eyes, was handed the stewardship of the ISI, the country's premier intelligence agency. The worse was still to come.

If the idea was to save the country from its worst security sce-nario—the return of Ms Bhutto—then the Army was not leaving it to the bungling bureaucrats or blundering politicians. Generals Beg and Hamid Gul taught them the art of strategic thought. Some sessions which I attended were devoted to psychological warfare. It was yet another sobering experience.

Benazir's election victory in 1988 was quietly celebrated by a good number in the military hierarchy. The reasons varied, from disaffection with Zia's regime to a desire for genuine democracy, even to hoping and giving her a sporting chance. After all that she and her party had suffered, some took it as divine retribution. Her performance in office, or the lack of it, overjoyed her opponents but made many of us nervous. People like me, who had witnessed her gaffes from close quarters, convinced ourselves that there was no hope that she could be saved from herself, and therefore she had to go, before the country was irreparably damaged. For all these reasons, I should have been happy to see the pack stacked against her. The pack that I saw at these strategy sessions depressed me.

They were some of the best-known names in the country, from fields as diverse as politics, bureaucracy, journalism, academics, and business. The ultimate stratagem that this conglomerate came up with was based on two ideas. The first was the assumption that the PPP, after twenty months in power, must be awash with money, so funds had to be found for the bankrupt IJI, and the other intention was to deprive Benazir Bhutto of any coverage in the media. One of the wizards present wanted the chief of the state-run TV sacked for showing an uncomfortably large crowd in the five minutes devoted to the PPP's election rallies. That the IJI usually got half an hour was no consolation to him. The quest for money to finance the IJI's campaign led to an unsavoury episode.

A couple of weeks before the October 1990 elections, General Beg called me to say that some businessmen from Karachi who had suffered under the PPP regime had joined hands to raise money for the IJI. Due to the shortage of time and because the donors would not trust any channel other than the Army, would I provide some help? Under certain circumstances, the DGISI could have refused such a request from the Army Chief and I believe General Beg would have understood that it did not fall under our normal charter. But these were not normal times and nor was I personally averse to seeing the People's Party bite the dust. Without any involvement of the ISI in this murky operation, I arranged the collection of money from one Younas Habib, a banker in Karachi, and some 70 million rupees were distributed. Since this episode later created plenty of commotion in the country, I have covered it in some detail in Chapter 8.

The ninety-day interregnum was a very busy period for me, and not because of any activity related to the ensuing elections. A few days before the dismissal of Bhutto's government, Iraq had invaded Kuwait. The assessment of this crisis was one of my first engagements when I moved into my new office on 20 August, and Mr Ahmed Badeeb, the special emissary from Prince Turki al-Faisal (who headed the Saudi Intelligence Agency, DGI, for 22 years) was my first visitor. In addition, there was the on-going engagement with Afghan affairs. I was mercifully spared from much involvement in extra-curricular affairs, except for the distribution of funds. At times, I was called upon to give the ISI's assessment of the likely election results. Once again, it was wide off the mark. Despite the unified strategy of the opposition and concerted efforts by the establishment, in our assessment the PPP would suffer only marginally. However, when the results were announced, from 92 seats in the 1988 elections, its tally was reduced to fewer than 50. After the elections, BB alleged some sophisticated rigging. Except for a seat in Jacobabad, where the loser, Mr. Soomro of the IJI, was declared the winner after the third count, and that too with his nephew posted as the Assistant Commissioner, I had no first-hand knowledge of any serious misdeed. But there was certainly something fishy about the way an infamous former spook was conveying the actual results to a select group well in advance of the Election Commission's declaration.

The Pakistan Muslim League (PML) was by far the largest component of the IJI and so its leader, Nawaz Sharif, who had his power base in Punjab where the IJI had won comprehensively, was the obvious choice to be the next Prime Minister. Mr. Jatoi, the caretaker PM, though he did not have much following in or outside the new assembly, made a faint effort to secure the presidential nomination. Once again, Ghulam Ishaq Khan did not exercise his prerogative (this was the last time it could still be done), as that would be clearly arbitrary. He also remained unmoved by the thesis that another Prime Minister from the South might console the Sindhis, who had had three of theirs—Zulfikar Ali Bhutto, Mohammad Khan Junejo, and now Benazir Bhutto—sacked in a row. Since he was party to all three decisions, he might have concluded that it was time to test the process minus the ethnic card, under a person who was not from Sindh.

There was another mission I had to carry out during this period. Since Indian-held Kashmir was in the throes of an uprising, the President's office and the GHQ decided that our part of Kashmir needed political stability, which was best achieved by a compromise between the two major parties. Raja Mumtaz Hussain Rathore from the AJK People's Party was at that time the Prime Minister of Azad Kashmir, duly backed by the PPP government recently dismissed by the President. Sardar Abdul Qayyum Khan, a former President and Prime Minister, had the support of the other mainstream party in Pakistan, the Muslim League. In the interests of the Kashmir cause, I had to persuade Mr Rathore to let Sardar Qayyum be elected as the new President and thus help build a grand alliance. Rathore agreed and kept his part of the bargain. Qayyum, though elected on this understanding, got rid of the Prime Minister soon after his patron party came to power in Islamabad. The Pakistan Army was never a match for the shenanigans of some of our politicians.

3

# THE KING AND THE KINGMAKERS

Mian Nawaz Sharif's claim to the post of Prime Minister was unexceptionable, but his credentials were not. As the Chief Minister of Punjab he had used political patronage generously and there were genuine fears that he would continue the practice in his new assignment. As a self-confessed follower of Zia's mission, and having actively lobbied to stall the elections of 1988, his commitment to democracy was also suspect. No one had any doubts about his excessively limited attention span—three minutes at most, provided the topic was of interest (therefore excluding all affairs of state). One impression he did start to dismantle, however, without any loss of time, was that he could be dictated to by the civil and military establishment, merely because he had been helped into office by them. The two nominees of the President—Ijlal Haider Zaidi, the Advisor on Defence Affairs, and Sahibzada Yakub Khan, the Foreign Minister—were bundled out in quick succession. Just in case Aslam Beg and I, Asad Durrani, respectively Chiefs of the Army and the ISI, had had any illusions about our exceptional role in the power matrix, Mian Sahib was not similarly impressed. He believed the kingmakers must be got rid of as soon as possible, failing to learn from his predecessor that one did not have to pick all one's fights right at the outset. With some unintended help from General Beg, he was soon on the warpath.

I went to Saudi Arabia in September 1990, ostensibly to call on my counterpart, Prince Turki-al-Faisal, but in fact to meet General

Schwarzkopf. He was the overall commander of an expeditionary force being assembled on the Arabian Peninsula to evict the Iraqi occupation forces in Kuwait, if necessary by force. As the CENTCOM (Commander US Central Command), the General had visited Pakistan a few times and knew some of us in the military hierarchy. I requested Prince Turki to facilitate my call on him but he was reluctant. I still managed to see Schwarzkopf who, besides briefing me on the crisis that was brewing, also mentioned that the Saudis were sensitive about the two of us meeting. What I learnt was still worth the displeasure of my host, who indeed conveyed it in his own princely way. It became quite clear that Washington was preparing and raring for war, but also that the CENTCOM understood that it would have grave implications for the region. On my return, Igave my assessment to Beg, who in the meantime had been struck by a strategic blitz.

Soon after Saddam's invasion of Kuwait, the General had persuaded the Interim Government to provide a brigade to Saudi Arabia as a gesture of solidarity with the Kingdom. By his own account, he was having second thoughts towards the end of September, because of anti-American sentiments in Pakistan on one hand, but more likely under the influence of his informal advisors (the equivalent of a "kitchen cabinet"). Typically for him, he adjusted his arguments to suit his fresh objective, which was to be seen as a crusade against American imperialism.

He went around propounding the thesis that when nations decided to resist, like the Afghans had done and the Iraqis were all poised to do, they became invincible. He also predicted that if the US imposed a war on Saddam, the Iraqi leader would "set the desert on fire". (Eventually both happened: the war, as well as Saddam's pyrotechnic display at the Kuwaiti oil wells). He had also convinced himself that the US would see the writing on the wall, having read some of it from close quarters in Afghanistan, and back out of any military adventure.

Beg was not amused by my assessment of what the US and the Saudis were up to, and entrusted one of his inner circle to prepare a counter-narrative. A presentation was scheduled during a high-level military meet held close to Gujranwala, a city in central Punjab. Though the top brass would normally be briefed by the DGISI on such subjects, under the circumstances, it was more convenient if Major-General Agha Masood, the Commander of the Air Defence Command, could convey "the good news" that the Americans would soon be rolling back their war plans. To spread good cheer among the general population, the media were also invited. The event was planned for 17 January 1991. I rang General Beg up the night before the event to give him the bad news. The US led war against Saddam Hussain had started, with the bombardment of Baghdad. When he asked me about the Iraqi response, I had to report, "nothing so far". In his presentation, General Masood conceded that his belief that there would be no war was misplaced. The Kuwait war came back to the ISI.

A few days later, Mr Ijlal Haider Zaidi, the Advisor for Defence Affairs, forced a meeting of the Defence Committee of the Cabinet (DCC) on a reluctant Prime Minister who had no stomach for such complex subjects. Matters got worse during the discussion, when differing views were expressed. General Beg maintained his view that the US would bite the dust in this war, while the rest believed that the dice were heavily loaded against Saddam. On such occasions, a difference of opinion is not unusual. In fact, no real discussion is deemed to have taken place unless an opposing view is expressed. But for someone who was used to hearing only one opinion, usually his own, it was nothing less than an affront, and for that show of nerve alone, Nawaz Sharif was not going to forgive General Beg. The more urgent matter, however, was that because of a dissenting opinion, and that too from a heavyweight like the Army Chief, the Prime Minister was forced to take a decision. A committee was constituted to mull over the issue and it came up with the right "non-decision". The PM would visit a few countries (not Iraq or the US), and seek support for a resolution of the conflict. This was of help to neither Iraq nor Sharif.

When he returned, the Prime Minister was very disappointed that no section of the press was waiting in the reception line in order to be enlightened about his peace mission. They had chosen instead to listen to the Army Chief, who by now was openly propounding the Beg Code, aptly labelled "Strategic Defiance". The time had come to take the bull by the horns. Nawaz Sharif requested the President to sack the General with immediate effect.

Beg had undoubtedly acted improperly. Expressing his views in the DCC or discussing doctrines in military circles was in order. But publicly adopting a collision course with the Government was not. He later apologised to the Prime Minister for the embarrassment he had caused, but the ill will continued. When the President was found unwilling to retire the General prematurely, the PM persuaded him to name the new army chief three months before Beg was to complete his tenure. That, Nawaz Sharif believed, would make him a lame duck COAS. Suffice it to say, our politicians never did understand how the military functioned.

General Beg was an enigmatic army chief, who had assumed office in unusual circumstances. Bringing democracy back to the country's polity came with the job and he relished the role, as he did the self-assumed part of guiding the fledgling system. He also embarked on a mission to restore professionalism in the post-Zia army and ensured that he got due acknowledgement for this. "Offensive-Defence", being the only sensible concept, had been our doctrine all along. That he came to be seen as its guru was more a PR coup. He launched this order along with "Zarb-i-Momin"—perhaps the largest exercise involving troops in our history. It created the right ripples, even across our borders, and did bring the focus back to the Army's primary mission. Beg was also the godfather of *glasnost* in the Army. With a microphone in his hand, he was, in our books, a security risk. At times, I wished I could downgrade his security clearance, but there was an positive side to this proclivity as well.

He was sufficiently familiar with the psychological element in warfare and politics, and was adequately equipped to employ it. For two years, as his chief intelligence aide, I was present during most of his meetings with foreign top brass, and he had many of them eating out of his hand. American Congressman Stephan Solarz was a well-known critic of Pakistan, especially of our nuclear policy (BB bestowed upon him one of our highest awards, which we found incredible). He entered Beg's office with a twenty-strong entourage and at his most hostile, but emerged full of bonhomie. "General, you are a man after my heart," declared the un-friendliest man we knew in the West. Similarly, Mr J N Dixit, one of the most competent, if not the friendliest, men from the east, was clearly stumped when, on his first call as the Indian High Commissioner, the General invited him to send military observers to Zarb-i-Momin.

The trouble was that his favourite technique of communicating in signals had equally begun to affect him. He actually started to believe that he was ordained to lead us all to a new epoch, guided of course by his strategic vision. Nevertheless, one instrument that he was not going to use to realise his mission was that of a military takeover. The ceremony that marks an army chief's formal handing over of command to his successor—which had not taken place in Pakistan for a long time—was more important to him than the "My Dear Countrymen" address that ushers in a fresh military era. However, the aura that General Beg had created kept many, even some within the Army, on tenterhooks until his last day in uniform.

The way he handled his succession, successfully illustrates the paradox that was Beg. As is the norm, he sent three names of his recommendation to the President. (It was indeed for the President to select one of them or ask for additional names.) GIK selected Asif Nawaz Janjua, who had been Beg's last choice. Well before this process though, Beg moved Janjua, who had not served in GHQ in a senior rank, to the coveted post of Chief of the General Staff (CGS). Beg's rationale was sound. Asif Nawaz may not have been his favoured successor but wanted him to be adequately equipped, just in case the job came to him. When it did, Beg was so upset that he refused to treat him as the Chief-Designate. At one stage, Janjua started to suspect—and he told me in so many words—that Beg would rather take over the country than hand over the Army. The outgoing COAS softened his stance when I told him about his successor's discomfiture. That may have calmed Asif Nawaz, but not Nawaz Sharif, who addressed the nation a few weeks before Beg was to retire and conveyed his fears about the future of democracy in Pakistan. Mercifully, it went largely unnoticed. These were the blessings of an era when the media still retained its sanity and the country had only one TV channel that no one took seriously.

When Asif Nawaz took over as the Army Chief on 16 August 1991, there was an audible sigh of relief in the PM's camp. A minor matter still had to be taken care of: what was to be done with the incumbent DGISI? Understandably, I was regarded as Beg's man. He had brought me in as the DGMI and he was the one who, during Jatoi's interim government, had a hand in my appointment as head of the ISI. With him gone, there should have been no problem dispensing with me. The DGISI, in any case, serves at the Chief Executive's pleasure. General Asif Nawaz, suspecting that the PM would be uneasy with a "Beg loyalist" in this sensitive and powerful job, had already told me that it was time I commanded a division. Like the politicians who often guessed incorrectly how loyalties and affiliations worked or did not work in the military, we too were completely off the mark, at least about Mian Sahib's logic on this subject.

Though a little surprised at Sharif's sudden display of warmth towards me after the new COAS took office, I ascribed it to his post-Beg exultation. It took me a while before I understood the real reason for his newfound affection. Asif Nawaz, always in a hurry to put events behind him, and anticipating the likely change had suggested a panel of names for the Prime Minister to choose my successor from. Having suffered the Beg-Durrani axis for almost a year, Sharif was in no hurry to take on another Army-ISI nexus. His solution was for me to remain in office but also to be mindful that the new chief was not very agreeable with this arrangement. This package was conveyed to me with plenty of finesse.

Nawaz Sharif's opening shots were indeed disarming. He told me that he did not think that the ISI heads should be changed too frequently (true), and that both the Kashmir and the Afghan issues were hanging fire (true again), so therefore I should continue. Having been told by the boss that I was needed, even indispensable, I should have been gratified, but for the caveat. Sharif wanted me to tell the Army Chief, "who was eager for a change", that the division command could wait. As any military professional would know, it is not done this way. Mercifully, Asif Nawaz, the thoroughbred infantryman with his ear close to the ground, sensed the Prime Minister's reluctance to accept his nominee and told me that it would be better if I stayed on. I was to regret this decision.

General Asif Nawaz, God bless his soul, was a man of sterling soldierly qualities. Too impatient and sensitive for his own good, he had a sharp tongue and a heart of gold. Above all, he played straight and expected others to do likewise. Political gamesmanship, in which the Army Chief in Pakistan is an important actor, has other rules.

When he was designated to head the Army, I told him in a lighter tone that he would now be a member of the Troika. He retorted by saying that once he was in office, the Troika would make way for a "diarchy". He did believe that the affairs of the state had to be taken care of by the President and the Prime Minister. Being their mutual choice, he seemed comfortable with this bargain. And being the man that he was, he did not relish playing either a balancing or partisan role in the uneasy relationship between the two top guns that was now coming to light.

Nawaz Sharif was never very comfortable with the rules of business that restrained his style. In a cabinet meeting on law and order, the interior secretary, Mr Jamshed Burki, pointed out that the Constitutional deadline to free the judiciary from executive control was already long over, and therefore something had to be done. The PM wanted that very provision to be quashed. In a crowd of more than sixty persons, only Ghulam Haider Wayn, the then Chief Minister of Punjab, had the courage to advise caution. "Rein in the politicians and the bureaucrats, and not the Bench", was his plea. The law was not changed, nor did the judiciary get its promised freedom.

Late in 1991, the PM's office initiated a proposal that the Afghan Cell, traditionally chaired by the President, should henceforth be placed under the Prime Minister. Ishaq Khan agreed and Sharif chaired the next meeting of the Cell in January 1992. As per the SOP, the Foreign Office had drafted a working paper that recommended Pakistan's endorsement of a UN sponsored peace initiative for Afghanistan. Some of the Prime Minister's close aides had convinced him that giving the UN the lead role would deny his government the credit for the (inevitable) Mujahedeen rule. Before the conference, he asked me to oppose the MFA's proposal. Since the Ministry had consulted the ISI on this issue, I had to express my regret that I could not. When the PM found no support from any of the participants, not even from the Army Chief who was at his (briefest) best; "II agree with all the others", he glumly agreed. Siddique Kanju, the Minister of State for Foreign Affairs, soon thereafter briefed the press. Back in his office, Sharif called Professor Rabbani, leader of the Jamaat-e-Islami of Afghanistan, and told him that the Government's declared policy was for the birds, and if Rabbani and Hikmatyar who headed the other large party, Hizb-e-Islamai, came together, they would get complete backing from the Prime Minister. Rabbani dropped into my office on his way back to Peshawar to tell me that he would rather work with the rest of the AIG. When the President learnt about this episode, he used a few adjectives for the Prime Minister that I had never heard from him before.

Once, when Prince Turki al Faisal, my Saudi counterpart, was in town, Sharif insisted on meeting him alone. The Prince obliged him but in his own subtle way conveyed to me that the confidential meeting was about Sharif's business interests in the Kingdom and had nothing to do with the business of the State.

Soon after he assumed office, Sharif was warned about the Army's favourite recipe, the NSAG, which recommended consulting the opposition when formulating national security policies. Obsessed with unbridled power, he was of course not going to give this proposal a second thought.

Given his disposition, it was inevitable that his relations with the other two pillars of the Troika would continue to be on the boil. Even in his second term, he remained ill at ease with a defanged president and a laid-back COAS. To add to his woes, Sharif had to contend with a President armed with the dreaded Eighth Amendment, and someone like GIK, too, who was known to throw his considerable weight around and had plenty of experience of palace politics. Sharif's remedy was to reach out to the Army Chief to win him over for his camp: it backfired.

Asif Nawaz, who on assumption of office wanted no part in the country's power politics, was now raring to get the PM's hide. "I can't do business with this Prime Minister of yours", was his opening salvo as I entered his office. Amused at the puzzled look on my face, he elaborated. He and his wife were invited to the Sharif family house in Lahore and asked to accept a BMW as a token of friendship. That obviously got his goat and his inability to contain such sentiments led to plenty of commotion all around.

A serious deficit that most of our leaders suffer from is their propensity to be influenced by a small, often loose, coterie of henchmen. This creed survives and thrives on information coups, insidious schemes, and conspiracy concoctions—anything to justify their indispensability. Their exaggerated, often fabricated, accounts keep the boss on edge, and by taking care of these non-existent threats they ensure their continued existence. In the process the threats become real, because the other side reacts in the same vein.

The PM's camp responded to Asif Nawaz's expressions of discontent by threatening to do a "Gul Hassan" on him. (In 1972, Zulfiqar Ali Bhutto had sacked General Gul Hassan, the then COAS, accusing him of "Bonapartism".) Not to be outdone, the Chief blurted out his view on the subject at a Formation Commanders' conference in February 1992. All those present, over a hundred of them, froze. A few eyes turned towards me. Luckily, I was too numb to show any reaction. Afterwards, when I asked the Army Chief what led him to this indiscretion, he—not yet fully cognisant of its implications—responded with his trademark nonchalance, "I just wanted to get it out of my system". Perhaps he did, but in the process he had shaken the bigger system to the core.

Like his instincts, Asif Nawaz' calculations were also infantile, or, to put it more kindly, simple and down to earth. "In a Troika, two must prevail against the third", was his political doctrine. Though not universally true (his successor persuaded both the President and the Prime Minister to step down), in the situation obtaining at the time, it was pragmatic thinking. By supporting Ishaq Khan, who was not too happy with Nawaz Sharif, the General believed that the latter could be shown the door. He did not contemplate a military takeover for which the ground situation was unfavourable. Sharif and his gang, on the other hand, understood his outburst in the GHQ Auditorium as an ultimatum from the Army. It was time to test the credentials of the DGISI, who had been kept in his post for just such an eventuality.

I flunked the test.

Indeed, Mian Sahib had received a thorough account of the episode from some or many of the large number present. But he, rightly perhaps, expected me to talk about it and give my assessment. I, on my part, wrongly perhaps, saw this as a low, sneaky way of doing business and unlikely to help matters. I insisted that the PM and the COAS thrash it out in a bilateral meeting. The PM finally agreed. "Whatever you say, sir", he said ironically, conveying his displeasure. He sent for the Army Chief to tell him that he did not want me in the ISI any more. I was in the interior of Balochistan when this decision was conveyed to me by Asif Nawaz.

This was not to be the last time I would lose my job while being away from the headquarters and without even the formality of a farewell chat with the boss. In this case, however, there was a good explanation. My successor, Lt Gen Javed Nasir, at that time the Chairman of the Pakistan Ordnance Factories (POF), was told to take over the same evening in order to prevent me from getting up to any mischief. (These civilians never understood the way military functioned.) Javed Nasir was traced and found in a mosque in the middle of a *chilla* (a religious ritual). He reluctantly turned up in the morning to say hello and went back to the POF to wind up his charge. I returned from Balochistan after three days and started preparing to hand over mine. When Nawaz Sharif learnt about this process that was to leave me in charge of the ISI for another two weeks, he was alarmed. My successor explained to him that I did not pose any threat to his Government during the handing/taking over period. In the first week of March 1992, I left the ISI to take charge of the Training and Evaluation Branch at the GHQ.

The change in the ISI made Asif Nawaz unhappy on two accounts. Only a few months previously, when the Prime Minister suggested that events in Afghanistan warranted continuity in the ISI, he had agreed to leave me in place. Now that events were moving rapidly—the regime in Kabul collapsed in mid-March—Nawaz Sharif had forced the change. Secondly, he did not like Javed Nasir. Like a good old soldier, he appreciated my refusal to report on him to the Prime Minister but was so upset with these developments that he wished I had done so. I am glad I did not. Do it once, and you will be required to do it again and again.

The next event to further widen the gulf between the Army and the Government, this time with the President's involvement, was the Army action against the MQM. As the Corps Commander in Sindh, Asif Nawaz had had some difficult moments, from the Hyderabad massacre of September 1989 to the 1991 carnage in Karachi, and the raid on Pucca Qila. The fascist ways of the MQM and Altaf Hussain's messianic hold over the masses had him worried. He was quite excited when the organisation's former militant aces, Amir and Afaq, broke ranks with the leadership to form a splinter group (the Haqiqis). He believed, rightly, that the personality cult of the *Pir* (the saintly status that some of Hussain's fans had conferred on him) could only be weakened from within.

On 19 June 1992, the Army, with the help of Haqiqi informers, raided some MQM facilities reportedly used for the detention and torture of dissidents and rebels. The results were very revealing and, within hours, many of their leading members were detained or went underground. Since neither the Prime Minister nor Sindh's new Chief Minister, Muzzaffar Ali Shah, were fond of or even comfortable with the MQM, their coalition partners, the operation had the tacit nod of the federal and the provincial Governments. It was, however, stopped in its tracks by Ishaq Khan, the President and the Supreme Commander, in this case acting primarily as the country's last defence against Benazir Bhutto's return to power in Sindh. He quickly grasped that the MQM's loss was inevitably the PPP's gain. Once Nawaz Sharif understood the implication, his conclusion was equally obvious: that the operation had been Asif Nawaz's plot to topple his government.

Both Asif Nawaz and I could not empathise with Nawaz Sharif. It probably had something to do with the military temperament. To Mian Sahib's credit though, he never asked me, when I was the head of the ISI, to do any political work for him (only once did he suggest that the ISI could counter the reports about the involvement of the Sharif family in the Cooperatives Scam that was then creating ripples). In that sense, the Agency remained largely apolitical during his first tenure, except for the DGISI himself. At some stage, I established contact with BB (needless to say that she was overjoyed) and in due course told Asif Nawaz about it (he too was delighted). The idea was to assess any changes for the better that the lady may have undergone when out of power. One could argue that it was none of our business, but then one also knows that we had made it our business. I continued these contacts even after leaving the ISI. Sharif learnt about it at some stage and complained to Asif Nawaz, who asked me to be more careful. He did believe, though, that if BB created trouble on the streets, GIK, already pretty disappointed with Mian Sahib's rule, might be persuaded to dismiss his government. BB quite liked the idea and started to plan a long march to Islamabad in late 1992. The attempt was effectively scuttled by the administration by blocking all routes leading to the capital. The Army was also asked to come to the aid of civil power and, being a legitimate request, it did provide help against a movement that had its chief's tacit support. Such are the contradictions in a system that does not follow its natural course.

A few months later, Asif Nawaz suffered a massive stroke and died within hours. (He did once mention to me that he was not too well and would be having a medical check-up after his return from a trip abroad.) On 8 January 1993, a Friday (that in those days was the weekly holiday), the General got onto the treadmill after breakfast and collapsed while exercising. The death of an army chief in Pakistan is a tectonic affair even in normal times. This one happened when the three pillars of political power were in a state of critical imbalance. The events that followed were as illustrative of the genesis of Pakistani politics as perhaps at any other time.

Selecting an Army Chief in Pakistan is like launching a boomerang. If not done perfectly, it can do immense damage, even to the launcher. Zulfiqar Ali Bhutto in 1976 and Nawaz Sharif in 1999 went deep down the ladder to find someone who they believed would be beholden to them and spare their throne, never understanding, as civilians, the way the military functions. They both regretted it later. GIK was also in for a surprise this time, even though he would not have to pay with his life like Zulfikar Ali Bhutto, or go into exile like Sharif did a few years later.

Selecting Asif Nawaz' successor was indeed the President's prerogative, but Sharif understandably wanted a say in the matter. His experience of dealing with the two previous Army Chiefs, Beg and Janjua, was not particularly reassuring. (That it did not work out with anyone who followed might have led him to do some introspection in his days in exile.) He asked the President to take a consensual approach. GIK agreed to listen, but without any binding obligation. However, when Sharif blurted out in frustration that he would accept anyone but Farrukh Khan (whom he believed to be an Asif Nawaz devotee), the President thought that the Prime Minister could be accommodated. I have reasons to believe that Waheed Kakar was GIK's first choice and he was using Khan's name merely as a red herring. Though not very happy with the President's decision, Sharif had to swallow the less bitter pill. For his ungrateful reaction, Ishaq Khan gave the PM one more black mark, and also informed Kakar that he was not in Sharif's good books.

Benazir Bhutto was absent from the country at this crucial time. Farooq Leghari, then her deputy and later the President of Pakistan, asked me to contact her and persuade her to return. I did that (this conversation was tapped either by the ISI or the IB). I also informed Kakar, without giving any details, that I was in contact with BB and that

Asif Nawaz had known about it. The new Chief told me to sever the connection and I had to comply, but I suggested that I would do it gradually. Soon thereafter, I took over as the Commandant of the National Defence College.

Kakar was also not the "takeover type", but he did believe that, as the Army Chief, he had a political role. In March 1993, having been hardly two months in office, he told me that he was trying to effect a patch-up between the President and the Prime Minister, who were once again on the warpath. I expressed my doubts if it would work since the two were too different as personalities to find a common working ground. Another colleague of mine, Major-General Mahmud Ali Durrani, Chairman of the POF, who was Zia's Military Secretary for many years and knew both GIK and MNS reasonably well, also tried to reconcile the two. I wished him all the worst luck in this endeavour. Nawaz Sharif made a clumsy effort and conveyed to the President that he was prepared to bury the hatchet and that, if the President too were a bit more accommodating, the ruling party would support him if he sought another term as the head of state. The PM's younger brother, Shehbaz Sharif, broke the news to some of us during a dinner at the PM's house, and looked not too pleased at the idea. I do not know what his reasons were, but thought it a bad idea too. Anyone could have seen through the feint—the strategy was to disengage to regain breath and then reposition to resume battle. (He made a similar move in his second tenure when he offered Musharraf the additional office of the CJCSC, and then tried to wield the axe.)

Ishaq Khan, even if he wanted to be re-elected, could not have lived with the perception that he had bargained for the office. The President now felt obliged to let the Government know that he was not satisfied with its performance. In the belief that Nawaz Sharif was now on a weak wicket he decided to go public with his charge sheet. It was now the Prime Minister's turn to show that he was the elected leader of the country. He made his famous *"I will not take any dictation"* speech on 17 April 1993. The President, duly provoked, invoked Article 58.2(b) for the second time and dismissed the government on 18 April, in what was clearly seen as a riposte. Desperate to combine all anti-Sharif forces, GIK swore-in an interim government of more than sixty members which included Asif Zardari. This was the man against whom the

President had used every trick in the trade in an attempt to to cast him away for life. Such were the incongruities of a system that was neither parliamentary nor presidential.

The dismissal, like all the previous ones, was challenged in the Supreme Court, but unlike any of them, was reversed while the dismissing authority was still in office. GIK's case was indeed weak and he had obviously acted in a fit of rage, but whether the Court's decision was based on the merit of the case or influenced by the Army's non-partisan posture is difficult to judge. The fact is that this time no Law Minister was summoned by the Army Chief and threatened with consequences if the apex court dared to reverse the order of the President, to whom he was beholden for the ultimate military rank. This is one lesson the civilian leadership never learnt: an Army Chief, regardless of how and by whom he has been appointed, draws his strength from the institution.

These were bad days, not only for GIK, who had played his trump card and lost, but also for myself. When I called BB on the telephone, she assumed that I had the Chief's sanction. Indeed I did, but that Chief in the meantime had died. She returned to the country after Sharif's dismissal and went straight to see Kakar, who obviously denied any knowledge of it and soon thereafter issued my retirement orders. Confronting the offender is an option but the Chief did not have to exercise it.

After the Supreme Court restored Nawaz Sharif and his government in May 1993, some of his advisors suggested that in this moment of triumph it was his call to make a gracious gesture towards the President and seek at least a working relationship. It was good advice and, if accepted, might have prevented the unsavoury turn of events.

I am not sure how the provincial governments that were also dismissed on 18 April were to be restored after the decision of the Supreme Court, but there was certainly a complication in Punjab. The anti-Sharif interim Government there had apparently hijacked the majority of the Assembly members—who in the process earned themselves the unflattering label of *lota*, the name of a round-bottomed vessel that because of its unstable configuration is used, pejoratively, for those who switch sides to achieve sleazy ends—and refused to step down. For the Sharif brothers, the control of Punjab, the base of their power, was more important than to rule at the centre. Having caused enough discomfiture to Ms Bhutto during her premiership, they knew the nuisance value of *Takht Lahore* (the throne of Lahore). To regain control, they did something outlandish: they asked the Rangers (a para-military force that operates under the Ministry of the Interior) to evict the provincial Government. Having used the land mafia, *"qabza group"* in the vernacular, to oust occupiers over the years, it was a familiar way out for the Sharif family.

The officers in the Rangers are all from the Army. The commanding Major-General therefore referred the matter to the Army Headquarters (naturally, because what Punjab is for the Sharifs, the GHQ is for all those who wear khaki). Kakar was obviously reluctant to have army officers employed as political bouncers. The deadlock led to another military intervention, though of a different nature.

The Army Chief's previous attempt to bring about reconciliation between GIK and MNS had failed. He tried again and proposed to the Prime Minister that to break the impasse the latter might consider seeking a fresh mandate from the people both at the Centre as well as in the Provinces. He also suggested that these elections be held with all officeholders remaining at their post. Nawaz Sharif, after consulting his team, agreed that another electoral exercise was now the best option—but only if held under an acceptable caretaker arrangement with all the incumbents, including the President, out of the way. Three years previously, almost to the date in 1990, he was the beneficiary of GIK's political and executive clout. He was now obviously reluctant to be at the receiving end.

The President must have been disappointed when Kakar, the man he had selected earlier that year to arguably the most powerful post in the country, approached him with Sharif's formula, but then he had enough experience and sense not to challenge the army chief. During his term, he often advised people not to waste time speculating about what the Army might do. "When these chaps decided to act, they are not likely to consult you or me", was his favourite observation on the subject. After the judicial reversal of his act of 18 April, he was, in any case, no longer his old fighting self. When I called his Military Secretary to get an appointment, I was told I could come any time. There was no queue outside the Hill.

It was a sad end not only to an illustrious career, but also for a person who had made his mark both at home and abroad. After the Soviet forces withdrew from Afghanistan, the US resumed its pressure to have our nuclear programme scuttled with a vengeance. All the organs of the state agreed that GIK was the best person to formulate and execute our counterstrategy. Bartholomew was the special emissary of the American government sent to put the fear of what was now the sole superpower in our hearts. He got such a mouthful from the President that he whispered audibly to his Ambassador: "I cannot take it any more".

He also kept us on track in our policies towards the two neighbours: India and Afghanistan. "UNSC resolutions on Kashmir provide us the *locus standi*; so don't give them up, but by all means find other ways to manage the issue", was his advice to all who cared to listen. He understood the complexities of the Afghan issue well enough not to obstruct the efforts of General Beg, and then of Nawaz Sharif, to explore fresh ideas. Many years later, as Ambassador in Saudi Arabia, I learnt that he was still remembered for having helped formulate a few financial codes that the Kingdom gratefully adopted.

As DGISI, I was once summoned to brief him on a certain dispute amongst the two Pashtun tribes of Balochistan (I think these were Suleman Khel and Mando Khel). When I finished with my ten-minute script, he went on for half an hour to explain the genesis of the issue that he had learnt about over the years. On another occasion, he made the military top brass look sheepish by proving to them, simply with his back-of-the-envelope calculations, that their "modest demands" were in fact far from affordable. Indeed, he had some blind spots, and whether the ignominious end that he met was because of them, or he had simply overplayed his hand, is a matter of individual judgment.

Before bowing out though, he still had to help resolve one major issue—that of the interim setup.

An essential clause of the compromise formula facilitated by the COAS had prescribed that the acting Head of the Government would be selected by mutual agreement between the President, the Prime Minister and the Leader of the Opposition, Benazir Bhutto. After failing to agree on some of the proposed names, Mr Sartaj Aziz, a member of Nawaz Sharif's team, suggested Moeen Qureshi, a former vice-president of the World Bank. GIK and BB agreed. (That was how we got an imported Prime Minister, and not because anyone exported him.) I had to watch this election from the sidelines, except for an odd glimpse provided by some of my old contacts amongst the politicians (protecting names, as far as possible, is a time-honoured rule in the Intelligence game).

Both the major parties, the PML led by Nawaz Sharif and the PPP, had a few factors going for them. The former had swept the previous elections, won an unprecedented battle in Court in May, and was confident of its standing in the crucial province of Punjab. However, its vote bank was less than intact since one of its factions, once loyal to former Prime Minister Mohammad Khan Junejo and now led by Hamid Nasir Chattha, had broken away to join the PPP. Another ally that it lost was the Jamat-e-Islami (JI), which, unlike in 1990 when it had been part of the Sharif-led alliance, decided to contest under its own flag.

A chance conversation provided me with a little insight in the tactical wisdom of our common voter. During the run-up to the elections, I asked a group in Rawalpindi how they would vote. They said their heart was with the JI, but since it could not win that constituency, they would vote for Nawaz, as otherwise Benazir's party might take the seat. That seat was carried by the Sharif-led League, but since the hard core JI voters still voted for their own party, the PML lost in constituencies where its edge over the PPP was marginal.

The PPP indeed benefited from both the losses suffered by the League and possibly from the perception that this time around it was the Army's preferred choice. Most of the assessments gave the party an edge. (BB still panicked when in the middle of the campaign, her brother, Murtaza Bhutto, returned from exile. Was it because the son might have had a greater claim on the father's legacy?) It won the elections in a tight contest mainly because of the factors mentioned above—let us say, it had a better alliance strategy. The PML, since it led in the earlier results, had reason to suspect foul play, but the reversal was probably because the League won largely in the urban constituencies, where the results came in early. All in all, it was one of the fairer elections in our history and the PML leadership accepted it in good grace. I also benefited from the outcome. Back in the Prime Minister's office, Benazir Bhutto decided to make up for her part in my premature retirement. In consultation with the Army Chief, I was nominated to be the country's envoy to Germany.

4

## IN THE LAND OF THE TEUTONS

I arrived in Germany in May 1994 to take up my Ambassadorial assignment. It was not my first sojourn in the Federal Republic. In 1975, I had attended the German General Staff Course as an exchange officer, and then in the early 1980s had done a stint as Defence Attaché. That was probably the reason that I got the job. How well I acquitted myself is not for me to judge, but I believe I learnt a great deal.

My new superiors at the headquarters, the Ministry of Foreign Affairs, were obviously none too pleased. The Ministry had learnt to live with governments of all hues usurping some of their prize posts like Washington, London, even Paris and Riyadh. This was, however, the first time a political appointee had crash-landed in Bonn. I still do not recall if the Ministry ever gave me any cause to complain. On the couple of occasions I expressed dissatisfaction with the performance of an odd individual in the mission, he was quietly removed. The problems that I faced were largely chronic: there was not enough information from home; of what there was it was never timely; and most of the visitors who came were simply on a jaunt.

Transition from the military to a non-military environment required patience and good humour. I often had to recall a piece of advice given by my Corps Commander when I was moved from the command of an artillery formation to an infantry brigade. He cautioned me about a gunner's propensity for quick action and told me to learn to relax, because the infantry takes its time. The problem is that the "lateral-entrants" are constrained to prove that they can do the job at least as well as the core clan, and, consequently, they are in a hurry. As an Ambassador, I only had two or three years to learn the ropes and make a mark. And there was the additional pressure of living up to the traditions of a "soldier-diplomat".

The host government and the people there treated me well. My knowledge of the country and the language was, of course, helpful. What also came in handy were a few lessons from the past. I used to fondly recall visits by some of our delegations that I conducted as the Military Attaché. Whenever the guests showed interest, the hosts went out of the way to accommodate them and provide information—even pretty sensitive information in the occasional case. A group of doctors were especially well-treated. The commanding officer of one of the three big military hospitals came only to say a few words of welcome and invite questions, as was the norm. When he realised that this was a serious group, he called his adjutant and told him that all his appointments for the day be postponed, because he would like to be with the Pakistani delegation all through their visit. A Defence College contingent also made a good impression, primarily because its leader, when thanking his hosts, was generous in his remarks and quoted profusely from German military history. The Germans, of course, take their speeches seriously and make them virtually at the drop of a hat. Never at loss for words and always obsessed with their language, they often lamented that German lost the battle to become the lingua franca of the US to English by a single vote. Though I had never heard this story anywhere else, I would still console them by saying English was no more than an offshoot of German.

The term of my Ambassadorship, 1994–97, was an interesting period to study a country in transition. Having reintegrated its eastern part, the former German Democratic Republic (GDR), in 1990, the new *Bundesrepublik* had by then overcome its euphoria (in any case, a very un-German trait), and was going through the pangs of transformation. It was indeed the decline and the subsequent dissolution of the Soviet Union that had made the reunification possible. When it became obvious that the Soviet empire was imploding, the East Germans tore down the iron curtain—the Wall that physically separated the two parts of Berlin. Thereafter, it was essentially a matter of negotiation between the Russians and the Germans with the US playing the facilitator's role. Moscow did extract its pound of flesh, at times on issues too trivial for a superpower, even one in decline. Germany, for example, had to construct barracks for the Soviet troops returning home. More painful for the Germans was the abdication of any claim over the territories once called "East Prussia", now part of Poland and the Russian Federation. Then there were the financial costs.

In 1990 when I was the DGMI, Hans Engel, the German Defence Attaché in Islamabad and a former graduate of the Staff College, Quetta, came to give me the good news that Germany was to be reunified. He said it was only a matter of 50 billion DM (about $25 billion), adding, "We have the money". I wished him and his country all the best. He returned a few weeks later to say that someone at home had made a "minor mistake". The cost of the reunification would now be 100 billion DM, but there was still nothing to worry about because they had the money. I think I know why he never came back to update me on the subject. When I got there in 1994, the Federal Government was spending 150 billion DM every year in its eastern parts, with no end in sight. And that was in addition to the monetary compensation. Before the reunification, the East German Mark, though officially at par with the Deutsche Mark, was not more than a quarter of its value in the open market. In a grand and generous welcoming gesture (probably after plenty of hard bargaining behind the scenes), Bonn agreed to pay at par for the East German Mark. Overnight, most from the former East, called "Ossies" (Easterners) for years to come (just as our Muhajirs and settlers have retained their label over the decades), became rich many times over. Did that make them happy?

When I led the NDC delegation on its annual *"badeshi yatra"* (foreign tour) to Germany in April 1993, we were briefed on how the Ossie armed forces were being absorbed into the *Bundeswehr*. No officer above the rank of Lieutenant-Colonel was retained, and the selected ones from among the rest were demoted two ranks. The rationale was sound. It was because of the inflated rank structure in the disbanded army and a more centralised system of command. And then it struck us: the social divide between the two people might be more difficult to bridge than the physical, and more complex to handle than the administrative or the economic integration. Many a wise man and woman cautioned time and again that the condescending reminders made by the "Wessies"(the former West Germans) to their less fortunate compatriots, that but for the former's generosity the latter would still be poor and backward, were extremely unwise. This, they argued, would erect a new wall, one in the minds of the people, and more durable than the one that the Ossies had demolished in 1989.

De Gaulle had once said he loved Germany so much that he was happy there were two of them. On both sides of the divide, old and new, one found a good number unhappy with the now united Germany. The most famous amongst them was the late Günter Grass, a Nobel Laureate and an iconic name in literature. I believe his main concern was that a united Germany would again be too big for its boots. Others had more mundane reasons. Some from the (former) West complained about the economic cost of unity and how it was hurting their life style. The Easterners, too, had much to groan about. The feeling of being treated as the lesser Germans despite their proud Prussian heritage was indeed the most grievous. A "Wessie" diplomat saw me talking to another diplomat from the former East. Deeply concerned that I might get an unflattering view of the German Foreign Service, he made it a point to let me know that my previous interlocutor was not yet up to the mark. It just so happened that the lesser diplomat had already admitted that he was new to this snooty club. The ones from the East were paid less than their counterparts from the "Bonner Republik" (the former West Germany). The human gulf seemed almost unbridgeable. I did come across some Easterners who would rather have remained under the Communist system. Though enjoying more freedom now, they still missed the security of jobs, food and children's education that they had got so used to. The unemployment rate in the eastern part was, and continued to be, much higher than in the western.

The sentiment against foreign workers, who by accepting low wages had subverted the job market, was thus stronger among those from the erstwhile East. Before my arrival in Germany, an incident had caused much uproar. In Rostock, a former GDR port city on the Baltic, some unemployed youth had burnt down part of a building that housed migrants from Africa. Still clinging to my habits as a "spook", I, as the new Ambassador, went undercover to discover the truth. Travelling by public transport and carrying a rucksack, I asked the people on the streets: "You folks seem among the friendliest I have met—what did you do to those poor foreigners?" Everyone in listening range was keen to explain, speaking of "misguided youth", "not enough information", "not yet functioning administration", but "we are trying our best to make amends". No one who apologises for a mistake has ever been any the worse for it. The politicians have the luxury of doing it all the time, except when in power.

The Communist Party of the defunct GDR was indeed still around but under another name, the Party of the Democratic Socialists (PDS). In keeping with the Prussian tradition of loyalty, it still had a committed following. During my time, the Party was not in power in any of the five new states created in the former East, but it did have its representatives in many provincial assemblies and, in due course, also in the Bundestag. It made sense therefore for the other parties—especially for the big players like the CDU and the SPD—to retain the option of an alliance with the new entrants. It would also have helped to bring the PDS voters into the mainstream of national politics. The SPD, being left-of-centre ideologically, had a better chance to do so. To pre-empt this nexus from becoming a reality, the Christian alliance (CDU/CSU) relentlessly crucified the old Communists to ensure that the rival SPD, obviously sensitive to its vote bank in the West, kept its distance. A CDU minister admitted in a private conversation that though bad for national integration, the policy was good for party politics. I was reminded of a similar remark back home: "This government policy may be good for the country, but for us in the Opposition politics comes first—and hence we must run it down".

Expediency in politics is short-lived. Not long thereafter the PDS did make a coalition with the SPD in one of the states. (Our major parties have also in the meantime agreed to sign a 'charter of democracy', even though it is meant only to keep the Army at bay.) Roman Herzog was elected as the Federal President in 1994. While addressing a group of veteran diplomats, he adjudicated (after all, Herzog was once the Chief Justice of the Constitutional Court) that immoral politics was not Realpolitik.

Soon after assuming office, President Herzog decided to visit Pakistan (and two of the Central Asian States). It was planned for the first week of April 1995. The dates were cleared by the MFA after due consultation, but soon after I was informed that a meeting with the Prime Minister might not be possible since she had decided to leave for the United States a little earlier than previously foreseen. My pleas with her staff made no difference. The earlier departure was to provide Benazir Bhutto enough rest before she took on those who wielded the most power in the world. My trump card was to ask the DGISI (Lt Gen Javed Ashraf Qazi at that time) to put some unworldly fear in her heart. Finally, she was persuaded to delay her departure by a few hours. Roman Herzog reciprocated the gesture by slightly advancing his arrival in Islamabad. BB called on the German President, appeared at the state banquet hosted by President Leghari in honour of the esteemed guest (where she brought her children along, much to the astonishment of the protocol conscious Germans), and flew off to the Promised Land.

The German President is a titular head of state. The Constitution, called the 'basic law'—no doubt for some very Teutonic reasons—gives the following as his job description: "to represent the Federation abroad". Like in any parliamentary system, it is basically the ruling party which decides who will be the President. All the same, as the highest office in the state, it is not a post for a party or a family loyalist (as happens in our own case), and great care is exercised to field a person of stature. At least in two cases, I heard a genuine expression of acceptance from the opposition. When Richard von Weizsäcker, Herzog's predecessor, was elected to this office, the Opposition candidate Hans-Joachim Vogel, after losing the contest, generously conceded that the President was "head and shoulders above the rest". I presented my credentials to Weizsäcker (it was a solemn occasion, but I noticed a slight smile on his face when he heard me recite the prescribed text in German). To benefit from his insight, I had to wait till he retired from the office. During that meeting, he said that he was now entrusted with the task of suggesting reforms in the UN system. (I believe some others were too, just to ensure that the mission-oriented German did not rock the boat.) I was also told that our former caretaker Prime Minister Moeen Qureshi and an Indian diplomat were also in his group, which was supposed to turn the world body around, and that he had a hard time keeping the two South Asians on board. He was quite generous with his time and a meeting scheduled for half an hour lasted till the patience of his staff ran out.

Roman Herzog had won against Johannes Rau, an iconic figure from the SPD, then in Opposition, and received the ultimate compliment. At an opportune moment, Rau publicly declared that he had no regrets because he lost to someone who was doing full justice to his office. No wonder that in due course, Rau himself made it to the exalted post. Herzog was a professor of constitutional law and a thinker. In the address I cited above, he also stated that theses like the "clash of civilisations" could become self-fulfilling prophecies. "The concept of nation state had run its course," was another of his formulations that raised many eyebrows. His speeches were later compiled into a couple of volumes. For his visit to Pakistan, he specifically invited Professors Annemarie Schimmel and Michael (Mohenjo-Daro) Jansen, both well known for their services to Pakistan. In another goodwill gesture, he asked the German hockey team to be flown in for a friendly match against our national team on the day he would be in Lahore. There were good reasons, therefore, to look forward to this visit.

It went off well. We were the usual warm and chaotic hosts. Pakistan has its charms and an infectious ambiance that usually positively affects a visitor. The hockey match in Lahore between the two best teams of that time mercifully ended in a draw. Diplomacy won. The visit to Lahore Fort topped off with spectacular fireworks and soothing Sufi music was the visit's high point. *Traumhaft* (like in a dream), was what the accompanying Minister of State was heard saying, almost in trance. Professor Schimmel was extremely helpful and along with Professor Jansen kept the Chief Guest and his entourage briefed on the country's rich heritage. Befittingly, she celebrated her birthday in Lahore, a city that had adopted her and that she had grown to love. The President awarded her with a peace prize on their return.

From the official meetings too, the guests drew all the right conclusions. Herzog was too well briefed to be impressed by the oratory of Leghari, whose introductory remarks went on for half an hour in a meeting scheduled for 45 minutes (Herzog was getting visibly impatient), or by BB's boast that Pakistan had bagged $20 billion in investment in her first year back in power (those were the days a "Memorandum of Understanding" was all that counted). I was not present when it was the turn of Nawaz Sharif, the leader of the Opposition, to meet the German President (this was according to his wishes), but I have reasons to believe that he mainly asked for more German investment and support for our Kashmir cause. Herzog had to reiterate time and again that as someone familiar with international law he knew that the Security Council resolutions on Kashmir remained valid, but since he saw no way to get them implemented he could only advise other means to resolve or at least to manage the dispute. Moreover, Germany was in no position to provide any concrete help. On the question of investment, the President could only promise that he would ask the German entrepreneurs to visit Pakistan. It would then be up to them to take the mutually beneficial course.

I was rather dismayed when a visit to the Northern Areas was cancelled at the last moment. Weather-wise, April is usually a safe month for air travel in that region, but we were told that though we could be flown in, flying out might pose a problem, and so they would rather not risk a trip with such important passengers. The Germans too might have been disappointed but still appreciated that we were so careful. To fill the empty schedule for the day and to correct the impression about our cautious conduct, they were driven to the Taxila archaeological sites. The road rage on the highway reduced some of them to seeking forgiveness for their sins.

I had known better days in the Pak-German relationship. It may have started with Ayub Khan striking the right chord with Conrad Adenauer, the first Chancellor of the Federal Republic after the Second World War. I suspect though that it also had something to do with the German fascination with the Hindu Kush, the Karakorum, and the region's cultural heritage. They call Nanga Parbat the German Peak, probably because of the many Germans who came to conquer the mountain and perished on it. There was even a railway engine at the Kabul museum that Germany once gifted to Afghanistan in the hope of building a railway line in that country. What helped too was the fact that during the Cold War both our countries were on the same side. That also explains our close military relations right from 1949 when the Federal Republic came into being. Under German license, we had started manufacturing two of our important weapon systems, the G3 Rifle and the Machine Gun 1A3 (MG 42 of the WW2 fame). Before the Indo-Pak War of 1971, German officers came to Staff College Quetta more regularly than we went to the *Führungs-Akademie* in Hamburg. After the 1965

War, Germany provided us with nearly a hundred F-86 Sabres (mercifully none of the F-104 Star fighters that they had modified and which were crashing at the rate of one every week). After the Soviet invasion of Afghanistan, as the Defence Attaché in Bonn, I had more access to information than any of my non-NATO colleagues.

Post 1990, it was a different story. It was not only that the Germans were now embroiled with the aftermath of the reunification, but also because with the end of the Cold War they could build upon *Ostpolitik*, the Look-East policy of their late Chancellor Willy Brandt. Because of Germany's historical affinity with Eastern Europe it made sense to reach out to the countries there even though they were at that time in the opposite camp, the Warsaw Pact. In fact, this fence mending might have helped bridge the Bloc Divide. After the collapse of the Soviet Union, Germany was thus well placed to go east; except that it alarmed the two major European powers: the British, the chronic balancer of power, and the French, already a bit worried about the Great Merger (no more two Germanys). That may well have been the motivation behind the fact that in the Yugoslavian crisis, both the British and the French supported the Serbs, the only people in Eastern Europe with a history of successful resistance against the Nazis. Germany's close relations with their rivals, the Croats, reinforced this nexus. The worst sufferers in this turf war were indeed the Bosnians. One reason that Britain was against Europe integrating too deeply was the fear that it would make the 'German Bloc' (Germany and its eastern neighbours) too strong—even though the idea of a United States of Europe was first floated by Churchill. Widening (expansion), on the other hand, had the advantage from the British point of view—as I luckily learnt from one of their illustrious diplomats—that it would make deepening less likely.

Germany's relationship with Pakistan, now that we were no longer a frontline state against the common adversary, the former Soviet Union, was indeed adversely affected. Economic relations suffered not only because of increasing German interest in their immediate east, but also because by then the East- and the South-Eastern Asian countries, "the dragons and the tigers", had become attractive partners. The first casualty was the formation of the Pak-German chamber of commerce for which some of our German friends, jocularly called the "Pakistan lobby" by their colleagues, had worked long and hard. The more important reason I suspect was the situation back home. It always is. And, it had little to do with the security environment in our region.

No serious potential investor ever asked me about our tensions with India or about the law and order situation in Pakistan. Questions or reservations were always about feasibility: an economically viable proposal, information about physical and human infrastructure, labour laws and laws providing protection to foreign investment and, most importantly, the credentials of local partners (who remained reluctant to provide information about their tax returns). Our Board of Investment in those days used to churn out feasibility reports on an industrial scale, some even in (broken) German. These were regarded as inadequate and unprofessional. The only policy of that time creating interest, was about the private power projects. Lack of transparency, however, kept most of the entrepreneurs at bay. Only Siemens made a bid at one stage. All the same there were a few bright spots, even a sound basis, on which to build economic ties. Siemens and some other big concerns especially in the chemical and pharmaceutical fields (Hoechst, BASF, Bayer, Merck and Schering) had their presence in Pakistan and most of them were making good money. The country specialist of the Deutsche Bank—bowled over by what he described as the ingenuity of our artisans, Sialkot being his favourite destination—used to tell his management that the problems in Pakistan were temporary and the country '*hat es immer geschafft*' (had always made it through).

The experience of two business houses provided an interesting comparison. Otto Versand based in Hamburg was at that time the world's largest mail order firm. According to its executive director, Dr Otto, they imported annually 10 Million Deutsche Marks worth of goods from Pakistan, mainly children's apparel. They sent a salesman to Karachi in June 1996, a particularly hot month with street violence at its peak. On his return, I was told that on this trip he had placed orders worth twice the normal sum and the firm was now thinking of opening a permanent office there. On the security situation, he had nothing to report because he was just minding his own business. Our Consul-General in Hamburg and the owner of a big corporate empire, Dr Schnabel, encouraged by this story and to show allegiance to the country he represented, decided to follow the successful trail. In Karachi, his man reported to the German Consulate where he was given a paper. This was the standard advisory dispensed by all missions in troubled times, primarily to cover their back just in case something happened. When he read all the "Don'ts" he took the next flight home. The moral of the story: if you mean business, avoid your diplomatic mission. This sounds like a stretch (indeed it is) but one did notice that a seasoned Pakistani businessman went straight to the customer. Our mission, if it had done its job, was more useful to a newcomer.

Industrial and trade fairs are a part of German tradition, mainly because of the country's pivotal location in Europe. It hosts more than half of them held worldwide. In the 1990s, Pakistan took part officially (with the Ministry of Commerce and the Embassy involved) in nearly a score of them every year. At the Textile Fair, our representation was indeed of a high order. In other sectors where our products like surgical instruments, leather goods and sports gear, had already established a sound market, no state sponsorship was needed. The manufacturers, therefore, made their own arrangements. Visiting these fairs one could tell the difference between genuine entrepreneurs—usually Memons, Khojas and other traditional business families—and those who were there courtesy of the Ministry. The former were busy with clients while the joyriders kept cribbing. The episode starkly highlighted the difference in outlook between our salesmen and their Indian counterparts.

The Frankfurt Book Fair is the world's largest of its kind. Pakistan had not taken part for many years. This was seen as a sign of declining scholarship back home and therefore some abnormal efforts were undertaken to resume participation. Many rules had to be circumvented to ensure that our publishing houses made an appearance in 1996. The participants were grateful to the Embassy for its efforts and expressed their resolve to participate regularly. They even accepted our offer to leave their samples at our consulate in Frankfurt. As a rule, they could not sell them at the Fair. On the last day though, many of them do. And that is precisely what our booksellers did. They sold all their books, and no literary baggage was left in the Consulate or carried back home. On the other hand, I had selected a book from an Indian stand, to be paid for and collected by a member of my staff. It was also delivered on the last day, with compliments from the Indian publisher and a note saying it was an honour for them that the Ambassador of Pakistan had visited their stall.

The German institutions divide the world as they deem fit, and not necessarily after forging a national consensus. Their Foreign Office had placed us in the Asia-Pacific group that extends from Pakistan in the west to Australia and New Zealand covering the eastern flank. But for trade relations, we were part of the Near East (what we call the Middle East). No longer a frontline state, one had to make the best of the new world order. Claiming to be a bridge between multiple regions, I enjoyed the hospitality of both the clubs. There may have been another reason as well. We were told that the focus had shifted from traditional to economic diplomacy and the performance of the Ambassador would be judged by the quantum of foreign investment and bilateral trade that he or she could generate. Of course, one often had to be economical with the truth in the line of duty, but it was not easy to pull wool over the eyes of those who were expected to put their money where *my* mouth was. In any case, there was no way to bring the others around, when our own entrepreneurs were either reluctant to invest or abandoning ship. We were taught at the NDC that foreign policy succeeded only if it was in tandem with domestic policy. It is the home base that matters, always and every time. A foreign mission can certainly make a difference but only within the overall national framework.

The goodwill that I found amongst the academics and the experts who had worked on Pakistan was hardly surprising. Amongst them, one noticed a fascination with our past, its versatility, and its culture. Some of them had spent a lifetime researching in our remote mountains and deserts, and written books—one even on Lahore's Master Plan (and lately on the evolution of Islamabad). Anne Marie Schimmel became a household name in Pakistan. Dr Ruth Pfau, founder of the Karachi Leprosy Centre, was another familiar name. She would start missing Pakistan if she spent more than a few weeks in the country of her birth. Professor Jansen led the research and rehabilitation project on Mohenjo Daro in Aachen University for a number of decades. Professor Hugh van Skyhawk preaches inter-faith harmony around the world but cannot have enough of Pakistan. Whenever there is an explosive clash of ideologies here—and that is often—he rushes to plead tolerance. No wonder he is so popular, and not only with our state security apparatus.

The late Professor Jettmar, one of the many whose contributions have been acknowledged by the government of Pakistan, pioneered a project on rock carvings in our northern areas. His successor, Professor Hauptmann, established a centre in Heidelberg and has documented his work in several hefty volumes. Dr Waseem Frembgen writes books, one of them on everyday life in Pakistan; teaches in our universities; and organises exhibitions in Germany (his modified name suggests that he might have converted to Islam). Professors Scholz and Kreuzmann used to bring groups of students from their universities, Berlin and Erlangen, on study tours, at times to some godforsaken places (the former dreams of spending a month lying on a woven cot in Bhera, a village in Punjab, listening to bells around a bullock's neck.) And indeed it was the late Hermann Schaeffer who during Z A Bhutto's tenure ventured into Hunza and wrote his famous treatise about a "people without disease" (he gave most of the credit to eating apricots). To venerate this connection, his son, an ophthalmologist, gave me a special prescription for my spectacles.

Many others returned from their assignments in Pakistan and joined friendship societies to promote understanding about our country. Mr Schanzmann represented Siemens long enough to be baptised *Shah Zaman*. After retirement, as one of the two vice presidents of the Pak-German Forum (the other, Dr Saeed Chaudhry, wrote his thesis on Kashmir, and is now the president), he used to squeeze an annual donation of 10,000 DM from his old company. I did not expect that a people with such refined, almost snobbish, sense of art would fall for our painted lorries. Called "truck art" or "art on wheels", one found images of our truck paintings compiled in book form. A lady, Dr Anna Schmidt, raised a couple of hundred thousand Deutsche Marks and spent nearly a year buying and bringing one such truck to Germany (this may have been the only locomotive that moved in the reverse direction). A wall in the Hamburg museum had to be broken to get this monster in the display hall. "Flying horses of Pakistan" was how this exhibition was advertised, probably because of the most popular picture displayed on our mobile galleries. (Yes, a flying mare had snatched this honour from Ayub Khan's portrait.)

Dr Hein Kiessling headed the Hans Seidel Foundation in Pakistan for a decade and a half, and now he is one of our defenders in that part of the world. He understandably believed he was amply qualified to take the ultimate plunge and to write a book on the ISI. (After reading it, I thanked the Almighty who alone is the all-knowing.)

During my tour of duty, I stumbled upon a group that must be the only one of its kind. As early as the 1960s, some Germans went back after spending a few years on various development projects in Pakistan. Some of them had a problem reintegrating in their own society and became homesick (Pakistan, in this case, had become home). This must be a typical German sickness and perhaps also a German obsession since they insist that everyone must integrate in his or her adopted country. Their solution too was vintage German: they formed a club. Ever since, they get together every year with their families for a couple of days. A hall is rented, a big Pakistani flag hangs on the wall, spicy meals are cooked, and they talk about the good old days. In the meantime, some others from the neighbouring countries, also returnees from Pakistan, have joined them. They keep the whole affair very private and I got invited for an evening almost by accident. Not knowing their customs, I was the only one in a suit. All the others, including women and children, most of whom had never visited Pakistan, were in Shalwar Qameez. I never heard from them again.

Germans may be the only people who faithfully believe in Murphy's Law: "whatever can go wrong, will go wrong". Many of them may never have heard about it, and indeed Murphy was no Teuton, but their historical experience has taught them to look extra carefully at the worst-case scenarios. After the demise of the Soviet Union, when most of the West was in a festive mood, a former officer of the German Air Force, Colonel Niemoeller, who was once the administrative head of the *Bundessprachenamt* (the Federal Institute of Languages) and later a business tycoon, was thinking of shifting his fortune to Latin America. He had convinced himself that Vladimir Zhirinovsky, a populist Russian politician who enjoyed doing NATO-bashing, would find a way to take revenge on the capitalist West.

A comparison with the relaxed Pakistanis was very educative. A new golf course, close to Bonn, had no legal recourse to deny the right of passage to locals who used to cross through the area now covered by the links. Of course the administration had worked out some safety drills to prevent injuries from flying golf balls. But whenever I asked if anyone passing through was ever hit, the stock German retort was: "not so far, but this year someone will certainly be". In similar situations, our likely answer would be: "Inshallah, no one would ever be".

And the contrast with their neighbours with their French neighbours' *laissez-faire* attitude was no less enlightening.

My French colleague from my Military Attaché days was previously the commander of the Franco-German Brigade, a concept that was less about operations, and more of a symbol of the two countries trying to bury an antagonistic past. After an unusually busy period, the General said that for a day they wanted to do nothing but waste time. When the German adjutant heard his commander's desire, he immediately took out a pen and paper and said, "Great idea Sir, now what is the plan?" The message was clear: with that mismatch between the two nations, the "interoperability", NATO's mantra to integrate national armed forces was not enough to bridge the temperamental gap.

I was indeed very grateful to an old colleague from my attaché days who once walked up to me and said (and that was before we went overtly nuclear): "Don't ever give up your nuclear programme. All this talk of a nuclear umbrella or other guarantees is pure humbug". Another comrade in arms was Dr Folker Flasse. In 1971 we were both students at the Staff College in Quetta. He too got bitten by the Pakistani bug. After shedding the uniform, he helped the city administration of Berlin to cope with the federal capital shifting from Bonn. Because of him, we used to have a priority call on attractive real estate offers. He is now running a charity foundation with *Schwerpunkt Pakistan*, and has been deservedly decorated by our Government.

It is not easy to strike the right chord in Germany, but when it happens the results can be very gratifying. During my ISI days, Mr Willy Wimmer, the then Parliamentary Secretary of Defence, visited me and we have remained in touch ever since. He was very helpful during my Ambassadorial stint and once explained to me the idea behind the OSCE, the executive arm of the Helsinki Process (he was one of its vice-presidents). It was actually quite akin to the classic concept of a Council of Elders, or of wise men. When clans or countries were stuck with intractable disputes and the instrument of force had run its course, persuasion through trusted arbitrators might be a good option. In January 2007, both of us made a joint call on President Hamid Karzai to assess if the Afghans were still receptive to their traditional instruments of conflict resolution. He is now a rebel with a cause: *détente* with Russia. He would make a good team with another General with a "spooky past", Michael Flynn, with whom I did a programme on Al-Jazeera, and who was honest enough to concede that Pakistan, like the US, was pursuing its national interest in Afghanistan.

My interest in Afghanistan brought me into contact with another wise man whose insight was very helpful. In the early days of the present phase of the Afghan War, I visited Dr August Hanning, at that time the President of the BND (the German foreign Intelligence agency). Since the ISI and the BND go back a long way, the empathy was perfect. It helped me fine-tune my assessment, and Dr Hanning thought I could usefully contribute to a high-profile German documentary on the state of the post-9/11 world. Indeed, both of us continue to exchange views about the mess we were once part of.

And how could I have said no to an unusual request by a German lawmaker who was refused a visit to Peshawar by their Embassy in Islamabad? Elke Hoff was the last German Parliamentarian still standing for Afghanistan. She was asked to cover herself well and get in the back of my SUV, and I drove her to Peshawar and back. Neither the Embassy nor my wife were much amused, but the lady got her wish before her party, the FDP, was voted out of the Bundestag.

My favourite politician in Germany was Egon Bahr, an iconic SPD figure who reached the ripe age of 93 because he never spared anyone. "All German Chancellors were American agents," he once thundered. I asked him not to be too harsh on the poor blokes: "They probably did it for good of their country, I know people back home who would sell their soul to the devil for a pittance."

So strong is the place of cultural relations in German diplomacy that, from Bismarck's days, their Foreign Office has a dedicated office to deal with the area. Foreign Minister Kinkel used to ask the German entrepreneurs to donate money to promote the country's culture. "Our products would find the right price only if our ideals too were admired," was his punch line. Amongst many other activities, this office spreads German values through a chain of Goethe Institutes. In 1997, a former head of its Karachi bureau, Dr Scherer, mobilised a quarter of a million Deutsche Marks to celebrate 50 years of Pakistan. I was asked if the PIA could help by flying Pakistani artists free of cost or on discounted tickets. Luckily, Mr Tiwana (who was later, sadly and wrongly, targeted by the Musharraf regime) headed the Airline at that time. He allowed them to travel at a fourth of the normal fare. The events were a resounding success.

Because of our rich heritage and the once close relationship between the two countries, we did have a cultural agreement. Making good use of it would have been nice except that I could not do much to promote cultural relations with my host country. The few times that I tried, our artists could not make up their minds or asked for exorbitant fees. Good galleries are booked years in advance and (the late) Ismail Gulgee would not confirm a date even weeks in advance. And when Adnan Sami conveyed how much it would cost us to hold his concerts, we almost included it in our bid for the next year's development aid. Their Indian counterparts on the other hand were flown free of charge by their airlines and performed gratis.

Mercifully, there was one development that impelled me to do something for which I had the right background. In July 1995, a group that called itself *Al-Faran*, allegedly an affiliate of the militant organisation, Harkat-ul-Ansar, abducted some Western tourists in Indian-held Kashmir. A German national was amongst them. This created a furore in the country of my accreditation. Details coming out, mostly from the Indian sources, were however quite dubious. Having studied such acts in the past, it was not too difficult for me to explain to my hosts that it was more likely to be a "false-flag" operation. The German media carried my version with its ample intelligence credentials quite prominently. The Indians protested that I was misusing my diplomatic status. To its credit, the German Foreign Office told me that it had nothing against us expressing our opinion publicly. The hostages were never recovered. In 2012, Adrian Levy and Cathy Scott-Clark, a husband and wife team, in their book *The Meadow*, more or less supported our version.

Relations between the Pakistani mission and our community in the country depend upon many factors: the size of the community, its status in that society, the environment in the host country and, indeed, on the Ambassador and the attitude of the mission staff. At its peak, probably in the mid-1980s, the number of our compatriots in Germany was about a hundred thousand, the majority of them seeking asylum. Grounds varied according to the situation at home. The first batch, though fluent in Punjabi, pretended to be Bengalis escaping persecution by the Pakistani Army. Then came the Ahmadis, after the sect was declared non-Muslim. They were followed by those who claimed to be PPP activists being hounded by Zia-ul-Haq's regime (many of them failed the test when asked to describe their party flag). Essentially, most of them were in search of greener pastures. In due course, the Germans and the others saw through the game. The asylum laws became stricter, and the procedures got streamlined. During my period, the official figure of Pakistani nationals in Germany was about thirty-four thousand. The majority of them were (probably) Ahmadis, since the host government considered their claim to be more genuine.

Despite their suspect credentials, the expatriates maintained good relations with the Embassy and were always ready to play their part, be it to raise donations, organise functions, or cheer for our sportsmen. The only problem was that a small number of them wanted to be recognised as community leaders or favourites with the Embassy. Groups affiliated with the political parties at home, especially when their party was in power, were a real pain in the neck. Some of them would even threaten the Embassy with consequences if it did not behave. A circular from the MFA indicated that the threats were not always hollow. The rank and file however, as in Pakistan, were hard-working and loyal to both countries.

During Herzog's visit, President Farooq Leghari had told him that he considered his powers to dismiss the Government under Article 56.2.b of the Constitution as undemocratic. But the Article could only be got rid of by a two-thirds majority in Parliament, and since the main Opposition headed by Nawaz Sharif was not playing ball (perhaps in the hope that one day it might come in handy to get rid of Benazir Bhutto),it was proving difficult to do so. In November 1996, both Leghari and Sharif must have thanked their stars that the provision was still alive. Bhutto was sent packing for the second time, this time from a flank that she had covered in the belief that along with control of Punjab and goodwill of the Army, it would ensure her perpetuation in office regardless of any misrule.

In Germany, there was plenty of goodwill for Ms Bhutto when she started her second term. As Ambassador-designate, I was part of her delegation when she visited Germany in early April 1994. Except for the large number of freeloaders, the visit had touched all the right chords. Her speech to the prestigious Foreign Policy Association was remembered for a long time. That made her lack of performance in office all the more disappointing. When General Waheed Kakar, the Army Chief, visited Germany during my tenure, I told him about my hosts' opinion of our Government. I believe he conveyed this message to the Prime Minister on his return. I also had an opportunity to talk about it when I called on President Leghari some time in mid-1996. He had his own charge sheet against BB. Of course, I never found out the actual grounds on which Leghari dismissed the government headed by his former leader and benefactor. President Herzog, when told about the dismissal of her Government, said he was not surprised.

A non-service Ambassador, also called a "political appointee", serves on contract, initially for two years (in my case, it was extended to three). One of its clauses reads something like: *"If the government that had appointed you is no longer in office, you are deemed to have resigned"*. I was promptly reminded of the clause, but also told to remain in the post while the new interim government headed by Mairaj Khalid decided my case. Shortly thereafter, I was informed that I could continue and complete my tenure. In February 1997, when Nawaz Sharif was elected for to be the Prime Minister for the second time, the contract was terminated and I was given three months' notice to pack up.

It was an invaluable experience, which provided me was a perspective on my country and an opportunity to look at the post-Cold War world from the vantage point of Central Europe. It did not seem to have become a unipolar world. After the demise of the Soviet Union, Europeans looked all set to create an entity that could play a more independent role in international affairs. If only they knew how.

5

# THE VIEW FROM THE GALLERY

When I returned from Germany in the middle of 1997, Nawaz Sharif was in the saddle for the second time. No longer muffled by any service constraints, I decided to indulge in a bit of public discourse. In the belief that the past amply qualified me to do so, besides some pen-pushing, I joined a few talking circuits—which were more in fact like circuses, moving and performing from place to place. It was fruitful activity all the same as it kept me abreast with events and trends. It also meant that there was no real break from the past, especially when asked: "What did you do when you were at the wheel?" And one could also reflect and review. In the process, many of my ingrained convictions had to be revised, a few rather reluctantly. Some were reinforced: for instance, that people in power pursue ever more power, not necessarily as a means to perform, but as an end.

Nawaz Sharif was elected with a huge majority, often described by his camp as "the heavy mandate". In that he was heavily helped by President Leghari, who not only dissolved the government headed by his former guru, Benazir Bhutto, but also marshalled all instruments of state to deny her a level playing field in the run-up to the elections of January 1997. (GIK did the same after dismissing BB's first government.) Leghari deluded himself, as had the kingmakers of 1990, myself included, that in return, Nawaz Sharif would be eternally grateful. Sharif may have twice been the beneficiary of the Eighth Amendment, but in 1993 he had a close shave from its cutting edge. With the required majority in the Parliament, there was no doubt that he would get rid of it. That he did so in such indecent haste, over a weekend, left the President red-faced. Those familiar with Mian Sahib's obsession with total control were, however, not surprised, just as they were not when he took on the higher judiciary. A desire to tame the adjudicative arm of the state is a trait shared by most of our leaders, military and political.

Bhutto in her first term nearly went to court to reclaim her right to select judges for the Supreme Court. Sharif was reluctant to let even the lower judiciary be free from the executive's stranglehold. (I have described both the events in earlier chapters.) I just happened to be around when Benazir, in her second incarnation as the chief executive, summoned someone known to be a master of the craft. She asked him how best to defang Sajjad Ali Shah, whom she had elevated out of turn as the Chief Justice, but who was now becoming too big for his boots (or shall we say, wig). I have no idea what advice was given or if she pursued the matter any further, but when Nawaz Sharif got his chance he not only got rid of the same Chief Justice, but also of Farooq Leghari who had vainly hoped that even after the loss of his power base, the PPP, and the real instrument of Presidential clout, the Eighth Amendment, he could still hang on to his office.

A three-way battle between the President, the Prime Minister, and the Chief Justice was waged in and out of court at the end of 1997. I was present in the Supreme Court when Sajjad Ali Shah restored presidential powers to dissolve the government, inviting Farooq Leghari to oust Nawaz Sharif. Khawaja Asif, an ace bouncer of PML (N) who was later in the vanguard of the assault on the apex court, threatened the Chief Justice that the latter would have to pay for it. That all three of them—the President, the Prime Minister, and the Chief Justice—subsequently tried to invoke the Army's help amply illustrates the place of the man on the horseback in our country's polity. When the first two pleaded with the Army Chief, Jehangir Karamat, to disentangle them, one might have been amused if it was not so pathetic. There was no comic relief however when Sajjad Ali Shah too appealed to Karamat to provide him security and was stonewalled. With the Army staying out of the equation and the state apparatus firmly under the Prime Minister's control, the President and the Chief Justice had no choice but to quit. In due course, Sharif was to add another scalp to his collection, that of Jehangir Karamat. All these victories were to prove pyrrhic eventually, but the Prime Minister did acquit himself in glory when he had to take a momentous decision a few months later.

*Nuclearisation of South Asia*

Old habits die hard and old soldiers remain obsessed with their units and pet projects. In December1995, Narasimha Rao, the Indian Prime Minister, when faced with a few domestic problems hinted that he might order another nuclear test (the first had been in 1974). As Ambassador in Germany, it might not have been my business, but if it was about India and nuclear power, I could not resist giving my "expert" opinion. I sent home a telegram, which is a foreign mission's primary tool to justify its existence, and one, since it reaches all the right quarters, that can be quite effective. The essence of that wire was that if India did carry out another test we would have no choice but to respond in kind, and the window of opportunity to do so would not remain open for too long. This unsolicited advice was probably not necessary. There was enough consensus on the subject in the corridors of power and Prime Minister Bhutto had therefore directed that some preparatory work, like on the test sites in Baluchistan, should be started. It helped reduce our response time when the need arose a couple of years later.

In March 1998, Atal Bihari Vajpayee, the leader of the BJP, was elected Prime Minister of India. Even before the elections, the party had declared that if voted to power it would carry out nuclear tests and claim the status of a nuclear weapon state (NWS). Providing timely warning of threats is one of the primary functions of Intelligence. Soon after the BJP came to power in India, I published an article, "Get ready for the Big Bang", published in *The News*, an Islamabad daily. The thrust, indeed, was the same as that of the telegram. In May, India exploded four devices. The cartel of the five recognised nuclear powers was obviously not pleased. Countries like the US were, however, now more concerned about Pakistani response. Our ability to produce a nuclear bomb was generally known, and so was our constraint to admit our possession of the capability. For the purpose of deterrence, a reasonable doubt that we might have this capability adequately served the purpose (in nuclear parlance it is called ambivalence), as it had done in the previous two decades. But when India brought its bomb out of the basement, ambiguity alone was not going to achieve the range of objectives a nuclear power seeks, or fulfil some of the conditions that give credibility to its deterrence.

To start with it, it was a matter of status. A perceived nuclear capability would not have qualified us for the membership of the club of recognised nuclear countries. India, after its tests, could at least make a bid. More importantly, it was now a psychological issue. By going overtly nuclear, India had broken a taboo and dared us to follow suit. At stake was the belief in our nuclear programme. In the late 1970s, when I was an instructor at the Staff College, Quetta, we were on our weekly shopping trip in the city. It was not too difficult for a shopkeeper to make out that I belonged to the military fraternity. He asked my wife to wait because he had an urgent message for me. If it was true that Pakistan was making an atom bomb, he would be willing to live without sugar (there was a sugar shortage in the country at that time), but could we make sure it was not a scam. For two decades, we had consoled the nation that their sufferings were not in vain and one day we would be a nuclear power. Despite gross provocation, if we now failed to prove that we had in fact become one, people would have lost any remaining faith in the State of Pakistan.

Then there was a less familiar technical point as well. Deterrence is not only about a physical possession. It must be accompanied by the will to use it. If we were now deterred from testing because of any economic or political concerns, no one would ever believe that we could muster the courage to use it in face of graver consequences. Indeed, there was a cost to be paid in case Pakistan carried out tests. Besides the wrath of the international community, especially that of the US, it would face economic sanctions, like those already imposed on India.

During the fortnight following the Indian explosions, Pakistan was subjected to immense pressure to prevent it from responding in kind. Bill Clinton, the US President, made a number of calls to Nawaz Sharif and offered some incentives to dissuade him from nuclear testing. A healthy domestic debate was of course expected and took place, at times with astonishing outcomes. At a public forum organised by the Institute of Regional Studies under the aegis of Mushahid Hussain, the Minister of Information, four out of five retired three-star generals were not in favour of Pakistan following suit. I have reasons to believe that the Service Chiefs gave only the defence point of view and asked the Prime Minister to take the final decision, as it was more than a military affair. On the other hand, our traditional "doves" in the foreign office, led by Foreign Secretary Shamshad Ahmed, were raring for a bang. Sharif's decision may have been influenced more by politics than strategy but he still takes the credit for not wilting under external pressure as well as from his core constituency, the business community. On 28 May, he told the nation that Pakistan had carried out five nuclear tests and had thus catapulted into the exclusive club of nuclear powers.

Some celebrations were indeed in order, especially because it had been a long time that the people had not had much to rejoice about. Amidst all the chest thumping and the euphoria about Pakistan now having become an invincible fortress, some in the government circles and what passes for the country's strategic community had to quickly think of how best to cope with the new environment. Living with the nukes became a matter more serious than surviving as America's ally with the greatest number of sanctions against it. Luckily, many on the Indian side too were seized of the matter. Given the history of mistrust and acrimony between the two countries, a nuclear launch, in panic or by mistake, could plunge the region into a terminal conflict. Luckily again, only a year before, both India and Pakistan had evolved a sound framework, nicknamed the Composite Dialogue, to resolve their disputes. Careless management had made it cease in its tracks but the spectre of a nuclear conflict was soon to bring the two sides back to the table.

The nuclearisation of the subcontinent had evoked, quite expectedly, different reactions in the rest of the world. People and countries that genuinely wished us well were delighted. No overt salutations were exchanged, but some of them expressed their sentiments in private conversations and, at times, through the media. During my Ambassadorship in Germany a couple of years before this, some of my old friends, especially from the military, often whispered in my ear that we must, at all costs, pursue our programme. A few of them even warned against succumbing to American pressure and accepting the ruse of an international nuclear shield. Later, as the country's envoy to

Saudi Arabia, I met a large number who said that they prayed for the safety of our nuclear assets, which they considered one of the very few Muslim achievements of modern times. The self-proclaimed "free world" slavishly followed their leader, the sole surviving superpower, and slapped all sorts of sanctions on the two nuclear upstarts. Australia, probably the most loyal amongst them, spewed out the shrillest screams. "These dirt-poor South Asians have no right to such possessions", declared Prime Minister John Howard, and threw out our Senate delegation led by its chairman, an act that added to the glee of the Pakistani masses who always take sadistic pleasure whenever our globetrotting and good-for-nothing elite suffers humiliation.

It was obvious, though, that countries like India and Pakistan could not be left in isolation for too long. Efforts to constructively engage with us were soon afoot, starting with offers to share with us the experience and expertise of those who had handled this lethal arsenal for decades. It sounded reasonable to learn from them the art of nuclear confidence-building and of security against pilferage and accidents. It, however, soon dawned on both countries that the West was more interested in securing ingress, and their entrepreneurs in selling out-dated equipment, than in helping us to prevent a nuclear holocaust, which in any case would be best done through a mutual covenant.

Jahangir Karamat was professionally an outstanding Army Chief. When I joined Aslam Beg's team as the DGMI, he was already there as DGMO. Both of us had worked together on a number of projects including the review of Pakistan's Afghan policy in 1989. Another paper that we jointly produced was on how best to handle the country's core security issues. With the title, "National Security Advisory Group", it was sent to successive Prime Ministers. All of them applauded the idea when in Opposition but would turn a deaf ear once in power. In October 1998, Karamat in a talk at the Naval Staff College, advocated this concept and, untypically for him, got the gist released through the ISPR (Directorate of Inter-Services Public Relations). It was obvious to his old colleagues that he did that as a last resort. Having failed to convince the Government that the suggested body was not meant to give any special role to the military, he was now giving a public message that in our environment some institutionalised decision-making on vital issues was sorely needed. Indeed, he had a good idea about the furore it would create and as soon as Nawaz Sharif expressed his displeasure, JK, as his friends called him, sent in his resignation. The Prime Minister nominated General Pervez Musharraf as the new chief of the army staff. Oddly, whenever the political leadership went down the seniority list to select an Army Chief they thought would remain subservient out of gratitude, they came to regret the decision. Zulfiqar Ali Bhutto, in fact, paid with his life for his mistake.

In the meantime, Vajpayee, probably the most astute Prime Minister India has ever had, was contemplating how best to manage relations between the two nuclear twins. In February 1999, he undertook the famous Bus Yatra to Lahore. Amongst much fanfare and euphoria, Nawaz Sharif received him and the bus at the Wagah border. The service chiefs, quite appropriately I think, decided to pay their compliments when the guest arrived at the Governor's House in Lahore. Both sides signed an agreement to frame and execute a safety regime and, as the icing on the cake, agreed to revive the dormant Composite Dialogue. It now seemed reasonable to assume that perfect conditions to turn a new page in the history of Indo-Pak relations had been established. Within a few weeks though, one was wondering if the two countries were fated to remain at loggerheads.

## The Blunder at Kargil

The Line of Control (LOC) in Kashmir that delineates the Indian and Pakistani controlled territories, though lawfully violable, was still observed in peacetime by the two sides as a working boundary. North of Srinagar, it runs from west to east between the Northern Areas of Pakistan and Indian Held Kashmir (IHK). In the Karachi Agreement of 1949 that was signed by the two countries to suspend hostilities pending a plebiscite in Kashmir, this line was labelled as the Cease-Fire Line (CFL). A vital supply route on the Indian side ran at places perilously close to the hills dominated by Pakistan. In the Kargil Sector (a large township on this route), its use was almost impossible during hostilities. In both the 1965 and the 1971 wars, India pre-empted and occupied features on the Pakistani side to overcome this disadvantage. India had to vacate them after the 1965 round because of the terms of the truce. Post 1971, however, it could retain them and the new CFL was renamed the LOC (Line of Control).

Pervez Musharraf was obsessed with the idea of restoring the status-quo-ante, or perhaps pre-empting another incursion by India like the one in the Siachen Glacier back in 1984. As the DGMO in Benazir Bhutto's second stint, he sounded out the idea to gauge the Prime Minister's reaction, but was told that its political management would be problematic. Soon after becoming the Army Chief in October 1998, Musharraf persuaded Nawaz Sharif to give him a chance. It is quite possible though that he did not reveal the scale of the operation and Sharif, never too fussy about finer details, did not ask about the implications. Given his lack of focus, it is also possible that he forgot to tell the Army Chief to call off the operation when Vajpayee was planning his peace bus journey. Musharraf indeed had no excuse not to remind the Prime Minister.

The presence of a large armed body on the Indian side of the LOC in the Kargil Sector was detected in the first week of May 1999. In normal times, it would have been acclaimed as a feat of the Kashmiri freedom fighters (as was indeed proclaimed by the official military sources), and one might have got away with it—except that these were no longer normal times. Firstly, it did not gel well with the peace that was supposed to have broken out in the subcontinent. And, now that the two countries had shaken the world order with their nuclear impunity, for the rest of the world, "two rogue nuclear states were all primed for an Armageddon". Hardly a voice from within or outside the area showed any understanding of this venture. Before the month was out, it became quite clear that the hills of Kargil would have to be vacated. While we were struggling to work out how to do so, the Indians had put in place a brilliant counter-plan.

"Battle" and "Manoeuvre" are the two classic components of strategy. The Kargil heights were not easy to recapture by physical means. That task was therefore to be accomplished by an exterior manoeuvre, primarily to be conducted through the US exercising its considerable leverage to pressure Pakistan to call off the exercise. It was obvious, however, that for political and psychological reasons, the mission must be seen to have been accomplished by military means. Confident in their assessment that the battle would be restricted in space, Indians concentrated overwhelming ground and air resources against the incursions. Having declared that only the Kashmiri Mujahedeen had gone across the

LOC, we could only provide limited help to our troops and, indeed, no air support at all. By the time the hostilities ceased in the first week of July, the Indians had retaken some of the positions—in all fairness because of some valiant efforts by their troops, who repeatedly attacked against the grain of the ground and suffered heavy casualties.

I kept myself abreast with the developments courtesy of my old colleague, the late (retired) Lieutenant-General Iftikhar Ali Khan, then the Defence Secretary, who always took time out to brief me on the various aspects of this operation. I believe that the decision to withdraw from the captured posts was taken as early as the end of May, but it was not clear how best to go about it. The simplest way seemed to be putting a falsehood—that the infiltrators were Kashmiri freedom fighters—to good use. Since the irregular troops (those not in a military's orbit) do not retain ground, the area taken across the LOC could be quietly vacated. It was also possible to restore the status quo ante by mutual consent. I was told that soon after our presence was detected, Vajpayee had asked Sharif to clear the violation. He had recently decided to call for early elections and was heading a caretaker setup. If Kargil kept hanging fire, his chances of re-election could be severely diminished. Sharif's visit to Beijing in the middle of June offered yet another opportunity. Reversing the course on the advice of friends like China (who did express this desire) would have placated most of the hawks in Pakistan.

I am not sure why none of these options was used and why the Prime Minister ultimately took the decision that was seen to combine the worst of all options. He imposed his presence on the US President on 4 July and was told to sign a withdrawal order on the dotted line. In return, Clinton offered to make some conciliatory noises. India had reason to celebrate it as a victory and Vajpayee sailed through the crucial elections. It may also have helped India build on its evolving relationship with the US. After the Cold War, both countries were mending fences, with merely a minor hiccup after the Indian nuclear tests in May 1998.

For Pakistan, the Kargil enterprise was an unmitigated disaster. When it ended, there were no gains to show, only losses. More importantly, so soon after demonstrating its nuclear capability, it initiated an act that in theory might have provoked a nuclear exchange. Paradoxically, the operation was launched precisely with the opposite idea, in the reasonable belief that under the nuclear overhang a limited conflict like Kargil was unlikely to escalate—since all relevant powers would try to keep it below either country's perceived nuclear threshold. The assumption, though a bit risky, was sound enough to give Indians ideas that in due course were to form the bedrock of their declared strategy against Pakistan. These were concepts like Limited War and Cold Start, both of which had their rational and irrational elements.

## The Coup of 1999

Kargil cost Nawaz Sharif his job. As the Chief Executive, he indeed had to take the ultimate responsibility, but then, politics is primarily about taking credit. Realising how damaging the episode was for his political future, he tried to defend his trip to Washington as 'the humble pie he had to eat to save our troops hopelessly stuck in Kargil'. Hardly anyone bought that line and it obviously did not endear him to the Army. Sometime in August, Musharraf called me to his office, probably as part of a consultative process, to discuss the dilemma. I have reasons to believe that he and his team had agreed that a military takeover under the circumstances was not a viable option—unless of course there was a good enough *casus belli*. Sharif could be counted upon to provide one.

Always uneasy with those who gave an opinion different to his—one only has to recall his discomfiture with Beg's doctrine of "strategic defiance", and displeasure with Karamat's pleadings to form a national security council—there was no way the Prime Minister could have endured an estranged army chief for too long. Within weeks of the Kargil comedown, he started sounding out if Musharraf was amenable to being kicked upstairs to become the Chairman of the Joint Chiefs of Staff Committee, a harmless post in our military hierarchy. Musharraf threatened to hit back. Sharif then tried a stratagem that had already backfired on a previous occasion. During his first stint, when he had problems working with Ghulam Ishaq Khan, a president armed with the powers to dismiss his government, he tried to disarm him by offering support for a second term. Khan did not rise to the bait. This time around, it might have worked if Mian Sahib had been more receptive to good advice and kept his natural instincts in check. (According to

Iftikhar Ali Khan, both Shehbaz Sharif, the Prime Minister's younger brother, and his close confidant, Chaudhry Nisar, often pleaded with Sharif not to fiddle too much with the military.)

Musharraf seemed quite gratified when he was granted the additional charge of the CJCSC, but he too had received enough advice from his inner circle of friends and, unlike the Prime Minister, he took it. He was warned that Nawaz Sharif never forgot a slight and would remove him at the first available opportunity. He and his colleagues had therefore prepared a contingency plan to topple the Government if and when that happened. Sharif did not let them wait for too long. After attending to some official business in Colombo, Musharraf was to return on 12 October 1999. Soon after the PIA plane carrying him and his wife was airborne, the Prime Minister announced his removal from the office and appointed Lieutenant-General Khawaja Ziauddin, then heading the ISI, to succeed him. Sharif must have assumed that the few hours in which Musharraf would be incommunicado with his command were enough for the nominated Chief and his handpicked team to take firm control of the Army. This, however, was not to be, since the "counter-coup" (as the military described its move when it reacted to Sharif's "coup" against the Army) gave the newly installed Khawaja no chance. The PM's team did attempt to delay Musharraf's arrival probably to gain more time, but with the situation on the ground having got out of Government control, it did not matter. Musharraf assumed the leadership of the coup when the plane landed in Karachi around midnight.

The impression that the military coups in Pakistan are generally hailed as a good thing can be understood. Firstly, there are always a good number of sufficiently estranged factions who are happy to see the last of the Government, or have lost patience with the inadequacies normally inherent in a civilian rule. There may be a larger number who might be unhappy with the coup but are unsure if they can mobilise the street against the Army. What probably bolsters this impression more than anything else is the sudden quiet and order that replaces the lively disorder that is part of Pakistan's political landscape.

Musharraf's putsch was genuinely welcomed by large sections of society. The heavy mandate with which Nawaz Sharif had won in 1997 had turned his head. His "victories"—the removal of Chief Justice Sajjad Ali Shah, the resignation of President Leghari, and the triumph over the powerful Army when Jehangir Karamat resigned—gave him the illusion of invincibility. His tit-for-tat response to the Indian nuclear tests, though popular, had also contributed to pump his ego, but his decision in its aftermath to freeze foreign exchange accounts was indefensible, especially since he had reportedly allowed some of his cronies to withdraw their holdings before the freeze came into effect. At the time of the coup, Mian Sahib had thus lost the goodwill of the majority. This helped Musharraf to make a good start and he quickly built upon this positive wave by presenting himself as a man of action, all set to root out the ills of corruption and bad governance.

The team he collected looked good and his speedy crackdown against the big guns suspected of financial misdoings won him all-round applause—giving people much-needed hope. Unlike our earlier coup makers, Musharraf had no qualms about deeply involving the military in civil affairs. Consequently, the resentment amongst civilian cadres and an adverse effect on our military culture was bound to occur. Viewed from the perspective of an old soldier, Musharraf was also guilty of ignoring some fundamentals of military precept and practice.

Though not exclusively the military's domain, scholars of warfare still take pride in the study and evolution of strategic thought. They believe, rightly in my opinion, that the principles of strategy developed by the military thinkers were universally applicable. To illustrate, battle and manoeuvre, alluded to earlier in this chapter, are the two major components of a war strategy. For success, each is employed in turn to create a favourable environment for the other. Their non-military equivalents are force and persuasion. Used in tandem, they achieve the desired objective. This elementary principle was lost sight of when the new military strongman and one of our former colleagues, known for his intellect and scholarship, Lt. Gen. (retired) Tanwir Naqvi, embarked upon reforming the administrative structure of Pakistan with a missionary zeal.

I was present when, soon after assuming the title of the country's Chief Executive, Musharraf spelled out his vision before a large gathering of Islamabad's civil and military elite. While he and his cabinet would take care of the tactical battle, the mundane business of governance, Tanwir Naqvi would manoeuvre the government to the people's doorstep. The idea was neither a new one nor a bad one. Devolution of power, political and administrative, besides being one of the favourite themes at the National Defence College, has often been discussed and at least once before—during BB-2—earnestly considered by the government. The new team looked serious, except for a fatal flaw. The battle to be waged by a highly centralised dispensation under a military ruler was unlikely to create conditions conducive for the manoeuvre that was to usher in the era of subsidiarity in the country. How far the system that descended upon the country on 14 August 2002 was technically sound, and if the right combination of force and persuasion was used to get the minimum level of acceptance for the reforms from the general public and the establishment, or whether a gradual approach to devolve power would have been better, are facets best left to the experts of civil administration.

After receiving his commission in the Army, Musharraf had joined a formation of which I was a part. He quickly made his mark as a smart and confident young officer. During our days in service, our paths crossed often enough to develop mutual respect. Now that he had the ultimate authority in the country's hierarchy, he offered me the Ambassadorship to Saudi Arabia. His intention was to make use of my familiarity with diplomacy and to have someone from the military fraternity to represent Pakistan in a country of strategic significance and with proven ties with our armed forces. I accepted the offer, but to suppress the feeling of guilt, since I had no claim to this post, I consoled myself with the thought that it must have been a divine calling or yet another chance to seek salvation. The real reason for my acceptance, of course, was the lure of another high-profile assignment.

Before leaving for the Kingdom, I did get a glimpse into the thought process of the new power elite. My assessment was that in the run-up to the inevitable transfer of power to an elected government, there would be no referendum to have Musharraf legitimised as the President, and unlike with the earlier military regimes, this time there would be no formation of a 'King's Party'. Eventually, both took place. I might have misread their thoughts; more likely, this regime had drifted into the mould of its military predecessors.

# 6

## IN THE HOLY LAND

Pak-Saudi relations are indeed special and strategic. The reasons are historic, pragmatic, and sentimental. They go back to the period before the Kingdom became oil-rich and began to be wooed and pampered by all and sundry. The Muslims of the subcontinent, even when some among them were the rulers, were a minority in their own country and therefore drew strength and solace from the belief that they were part of the larger *Ummah*. The holy cities of Mecca and Medina were their spiritual centre. Some of them left their homeland to be near the fountainhead of faith and not because they were in search of a better worldly life. Émigrés generally work harder than the natives. When fired with missionary zeal, they invest heart and soul. So it was with many who migrated from areas that are part of today's Pakistan. When the Kingdom was founded in 1932, this diaspora had already established itself as a useful part of the community. Their contribution was recognised and rewarded. The first head of the Saudi State Bank, Anwar Ali, was a Pakistani, as were most of the physicians with the Royal Family. There was, for a period, even an ideological affinity. In 1979, Maulana Mawdudi, a renowned religious scholar from Pakistan, became the first recipient of King Faisal's International Prize for services to Islam.

Once the Kingdom was found blessed with phenomenal reserves of black gold, it could pick and choose expertise and products from all around the globe. Its newfound infatuation with the more advanced and powerful countries obviously affected the quality of its relationship with Pakistan. In the meantime, even at the lower end of the spectrum of skills, our expatriates have largely been replaced by cheaper or more efficient labour from countries like India, Bangladesh, Sri Lanka, the Philippines and Afghanistan. If Pakistan still claims exclusive status in the Saudi strategic calculus, the credit must be given to some good work done in the past.

Personal relations do matter, especially in tribal societies like the Arab. Both Zulfiqar Ali Bhutto and Zia-ul-Haq were remembered fondly in important Saudi circles. Nawaz Sharif too had developed contacts that helped him after General Musharraf toppled his government. Prince Fahad-bin-Sultan, the then Governor of Tabuk, told me that he was on his treadmill when he got a call on his cell phone from Sharif to tell him a coup was underway. (The Prince must have been pretty high on Mian Sahib's SOS list.) Some other factors were indeed more important: our investment in the training of the Saudi Armed Forces, the triangular relationship between the US, Saudi Arabia and Pakistan—lately on the decline but one that had once served us well—and most importantly, the Saudi belief that the Pakistanis (due to their devotion to the holy places) could be counted upon to remain loyal to the Kingdom, even if it lost its oily glitter.

I started my assignment in September 2000 with all the aforementioned advantages, plus one more. My Saudi counterpart when I was heading the ISI, Prince Turki-al-Faisal, was still in the office that he had held for over two decades. In the Saudi system, before an Ambassador is accredited, he pays an introductory call on the Foreign Minister. (The presentation of credentials to the King may take months or more.) When I was first presented to the late Prince Saud-al-Faisal—his father, King Faisal, and he had kept this portfolio in the family ever since the Kingdom was founded—he made it very clear that our bilateral relationship was in a class of its own. Their Foreign Secretary would often teasingly dare me to improve upon it, "if it was at all possible". I think, in a subtle way, he was conveying the message that the ties had passed their peak and needed some serious attention and probably a bit of good luck to restore them to their once high pedestal.

With the enormity of 9/11, the stroke of good luck took precisely one year in coming. Before that there were plenty of ups and downs—mostly downs. Nawaz Sharif and his family were given asylum soon after my arrival. I am not sure if the Saudis were grateful that their offer to host them was accepted, or were unhappy with the treatment meted out to him. When in office, Sharif and his tribe used to overtax the Saudi hospitality with their all too frequent visits to the Holy Land, but then he had also learnt the art of doing business (pun intended) with the Royal Family. Instead of pestering anyone for an audience with the Crown Prince, he would wait patiently in the Royal Guest House till called. [3]

Since I was completely out of the loop during the entire back-and-forth leading to Mian Sahib's extended stay in the Holy Land, the Saudi government rightly concluded that the important business of state would be conducted by special emissaries and through back channels. The new Ambassador could therefore get on with more mundane affairs. It did me a world of good.

An almost million-strong Pakistani community is spread all over the Kingdom. Our missions, especially the blue-blooded diplomats in them, are not known for patience with the endless complaints of the working classes. And if that required leaving the comforts of one's office and traversing long stretches of sun-scorched landscape, some of them would rather rough it out indoors. An old soldier had no problem with either. The monthly Durbar that lets the troops tell their commander, as gently as possible, what they thought of him, had taught me that a sympathetic hearing was more important than redress of the grievance. If, in the process, one could tour the length and breadth of the Arabian Peninsula (all expenses paid), for someone smitten by wanderlust, it was the optimum combination of duty and pleasure. Having camped in the Himalayas, the Alps, and on the Arctic Circle, one was now looking forward to spending some time under a Bedouin tent.

I never made it to the Empty Quarters even though the Saudi Minister for Petroleum and Natural Resources, Ali Al-Naimi, an outdoor man himself, promised that he would try to make it possible. But I did find out that the Desert Kingdom had much more than sandy dunes. The highlands running south from Taif all the way to the Yemeni border could provide as much solace to a secular soul as the faithful would find praying in the holiest of places in the north. One was lucky to have made the best of both worlds on many an occasion. Interface with the humblest of our compatriots who tough it out in harsh conditions to provide some relief to their families back home was a very fulfilling experience.

Expatriates, especially from countries like Pakistan, certainly suffer from some grave handicaps when working in the Gulf countries. They are virtually at the mercy of their local sponsor and must pay him, or an occasional her, a share of their earnings. The *Kafeel* legally owns even an enterprise wholly financed and operated by foreign workers. Of course it works out pretty well most of the time but the fear that it might not is like a hanging sword. Then there are handicaps that are Pakistan-specific. Our labour force is outclassed and undercut by those from other developing countries who are more educated, better skilled or willing to work for lower wages. Moreover, our recruiting agents are amongst the least principled. They lure the wannabe workers with promises of better pay and job packages than those that really await them in the Holy Land.

Nevertheless, given a chance to air their grievances, for example to the Ambassador, our ordinary workers showed remarkable understanding. They may have recounted all their woes and more, but also understood the limits of both the systems, the Saudi and the Pakistani. Another of their good traits was that even when desperately looking for work, it did not prevent them from standing up for a few principles that were important to them. They refused to accept jobs that paid less than their rightful due, and it made me very proud of our countrymen to see that most of them took no nonsense, even from their employers. Many a Saudi referred to the Pakistanis as "tough cookies".

One episode was particularly revealing. A father and son team from our Pashtun belt was assigned to manually haul a heavy consignment of bricks to the third or the fourth storey of a building. When the job was done they were offered lower payment than was originally agreed upon. They refused, went right up, brought all the bricks back to the ground, and walked away. They did twice the labour, only for the principle of it.

Of course, not all our compatriots were known to have left behind fond memories. King Faisal's family has traditionally had a soft spot for

Pakistan and its people. One of his grandsons started a dairy business—which grew in the meantime into one of the world's largest—employing mostly Pakistanis. They were all fired after their ringleader instigated a strike in order to get more money. The ability to lead, other than from behind, is a positive trait. Very few from the expatriate communities have the courage to voice their gripes with the local authorities. Many more lead processions to their embassies or consulates, often more in pursuit of a recognition of their leadership, than for commitment to a cause. Those of them who can mobilise political support at home, even blackmail their diplomatic missions.

Pakistan must be one of the few countries that create chapters or franchises for domestic political parties in foreign lands. In the Kingdom it was illegal to do so but their activities were tolerated as long as these remained within four walls. Post 9/11, the Saudis became extra sensitive to any show of public unrest and extradited some of our higher profile political figures. Paradoxically though, as a special gesture to President Musharraf after he had become an ally of the US in its "war on terror", the Kingdom permitted us to conduct the referendum that legitimised his office. The use of postal ballots as well as of polling stations in cities with large Pakistani populations was facilitated. Electioneering was, of course, forbidden. Some claiming to be the aides of Ajmal Khattak and Tahir-ul-Qadri still dropped in to canvass for the General. When told this could mean expulsion from their host country, they disappeared in no time.

The Hajj is a high-profile event in Saudi Arabia and a major engagement for the missions from countries with a large number of believers. The maximum number that a country could send to perform the annual ritual depended upon its Muslim population: one for every thousand of them in my time. Pakistan's quota thus came to about a hundred and twenty thousand at the turn of the century. The total number hosted by the Kingdom every year was about two million. For the aspirant Hajjis, it is a religious obligation and an opportunity for spiritual resurgence, but for the organisers of this mammoth congregation it is a logistic exercise of heavenly dimensions. Assembling millions of people coming from all over the world and putting them through an elaborate drill requires superhuman efforts. A tent-city comes alive just for a couple of weeks and the world's largest butchery operates merely for a day and a half. The overall supervision rests with the ministry of interior—ostensibly the most powerful in their system—and is headed by "a first category prince", a direct descendant of King Abdul Aziz, the founder of the country. But a technocrat heads the ministry of Hajj and plans and executes the operation. In the early 2000s, it was Dr Iyad bin Amin Madani, later the Secretary-General of the OIC.

Though our own Ministry of Religious Affairs lays down the policy and has a permanent staff based in Jeddah, the Ambassador oversees the work at the Saudi end. As a former military man, I was struck by the constant *movement* of pilgrims. Thousands of flights bring them from all over the globe. Once on the holy soil, they are transported to Mecca and Medina in seemingly endless convoys. During their stay, they move on wheels or on foot to the two holy mosques. Except throughout the five prayers, circling around the Kaba (*twaaf*) never ceases, and all two million of them (more in the meantime) move on the same day to Mount Arafat and thereafter go en masse within the prescribed spaces fixed for performing the actual Hajj over the next few days.

Having learnt something about moving troops and convoys, I once thought of teaching the Saudi movement control office the science of making graphs. I learnt something more valuable instead. I was told, though not in as many words, that man can only plan so much—after that Allah takes over. I did not have to recall Napoleon, who believed that one-third of an operation should be left to chance, to be convinced of the wisdom of the Saudi traffic controllers. Just when we started suspecting that one might not get in or out of Arafat, things started moving.

It is true that the overall ambiance is serene and spiritually unique, but the occasion also has its worldly rewards. The perspective that one gets on the state of the *Ummah* in only a few days may otherwise only be obtained over a lifetime. The effect of being amongst a conglomeration professing the same faith impelled by matching fervour and performing similar rites, can be overpowering. The wearing of *Ihram* adds to the feeling of oneness. Beyond that, the faithful display the diversity of their stock rather starkly. The variety of physical features, conspicuous as it is, provides, as in a bouquet, a heart-warming mix. Some other differences are more revealing.

The best organised and briefed were the Malaysians. Uniformly dressed and steady paced, they stalked the place so much at peace with themselves. The Iranians too were tightly regimented and distinctly attired. Unlike the Malaysians though, they recited their prayers with audible gusto. The Indonesians were the most numerous, almost two hundred thousand of them. Many must have been there to fulfil a marital pre-requisite. Though distinguishably dressed, they were noticeably invisible, as if dispersed over a thousand islands. The Hajjis from the Far East on the other hand were conspicuous because of their small number. Koreans always cleaned the washrooms before and after use. The most elegantly, but still modestly, attired was a group of Filipino women. They also formed the largest ethnic group among the nursing staff in the Kingdom.

Africans when out of *Ihram* looked the most relaxed and uninhibited in their colourful costumes. They did, however, become sombre when the going got tough, during the rush hours of Twaaf and Rumi (pebbling the 'Satan'), for example. One was then well advised to get out of their way. They were the only ones who risked taking on the *Shurta* (the Saudi police), at times physically. The Turks, who once ruled over this area, kept a remarkably low profile, though some of them did appear in group-uniforms bearing Turkish flags.

Forming groups and wearing signs of distinction not only help the Hajjis hold together but also provide protection against a stampede, critical factors in view of the growing number. If that has any parallel with the regionalisation that in this great game of globalisation assists individual countries from being trampled over, I would not know. Coincidentally, though, the area farthest behind in this process, namely the subcontinent, was also the slowest to catch up with the latest Hajj practices.

Most Hajjis from India and Pakistan were averse to the rigours and discipline of moving around in groups. The unit of their activity was the family or a group of friends. But here the similarity ended. Nearly half of the Indians working in the Kingdom, the largest expatriate class, were Muslims. They were an industrious and a competent lot, and in certain skills superior to their counterparts from elsewhere. Most of their Hajjis, however, arrived directly from India and clearly showed the inhibitions of an oppressed community. Coming from a country where to prove loyalty and secular credentials, one had to at times marry into other religions, the Indian Hajji, unlike his Pakistani co-religionist, tended to remain within himself while performing his rituals.

Hajjis from Pakistan, on the other hand, were all over the place. Over a hundred thousand of them evenly dotted the landscape. In their shalwar-qameez and the prototypic 'Scissor-Hawaii' slippers, with which they alone could walk kilometres every day, they were easily spotted. They were also very audible, except when reciting prayers, which they liked to share only with the Almighty. Over time, they came to be regarded as the most ill-briefed and unprepared of pilgrims, a reputation that they did not quite deserve.

I concede that our Hajjis arrive a bit 'extemporaneously', as they are not particularly fond of briefing sessions at the Hajji camps. Also, not many would or could read what might pass for 'joining instructions'. All these worldly details, they believe, would be taken care of in good time. On spiritual matters though, the pilgrims from no other country were so widely tutored as ours. Before departing for the Holy Land, they were exhaustively counselled by the local veterans and the 'muftis'. Upon arrival, consequently, they became very suspicious when told that the rituals of Hajj were actually quite simple, and its spirit was essentially communion with the Creator and His creation.

Pakistanis perhaps belong to the oldest age group of pilgrims. Not all of them could make up for the frailties of years through devotion. But it was not the older Hajjis who made our medical missions work overtime. Many men and women, sick or unfit for the rigour, duped the system to fulfil their wish, the last one in some cases. An insane man was sane enough to kill himself when he learnt that he was about to be deported. Of course, not all deaths during the pilgrimage were intentional, but I presume that all births must be. It was illegal to go for Hajj carrying certain diseases and in advanced pregnancy. A fake medical certificate was then the key to be able to die or be born in the most sacred of places at the holiest of times.

If there was any Fatwa that decrees over the legitimacy of this sacrament in violation of rules, I do not know. But I do know that there were thousands of such devotees, mostly locals, who did so. Since they were not registered they had no prescribed quarters. The Saudi solution was pragmatic. If they could not be prevented from performing Hajj, one might as well prevent them from spoiling the holy soil. Sanitary facilities were also built for these gatecrashers.

I am sure Allah's reward is not dictated by any earthly laws. Many of our compatriots stayed on after their visas expired merely to sneak into

Arafat and seek atonement. Some of them turned themselves over to our missions or to the Saudi authorities to be repatriated or jailed. Considering the hardships they suffered and the risks they took, it is quite possible that their Hajj was adjudged superior, and they were better rewarded than the freeloaders who, as official delegates, had all their expenses paid by the government, and (some of whom) did not even clear their bills.

My best worldly reward was the opportunity I got to observe the events of 9/11 from the Saudi vantage point. The day after the twin towers collapsed, I asked to call on the Foreign Minister. I was summoned to Jeddah on the following day. Before leaving Riyadh, I had a word with the Foreign Secretary, Inam-ul-Haq, who told me that the US was pestering us to join their war against the Taliban regime in Afghanistan. It was accused of harbouring the Al Qaeda leadership suspected to have masterminded this enormity, but indeed we had reservations and also some problems meeting the American demands. I could imagine the dilemma we were faced with, collaborating with a distant power hell-bent on attacking our neighbour, but I had no idea that the Saudis had other worries till I met Price Saud-al-Faisal. Since fifteen of the nineteen allegedly involved in the attack were Saudi nationals, the Kingdom was under immense pressure to explain. I was advised that Pakistan had no choice but to play ball with the Americans.

On my way out, I was trying to fathom the gravity of the matter when I was informed that Musharraf had submitted to Washington's demands. I must admit that I felt relieved for a variety of reasons. Firstly, since Delhi had already offered to stand in for Islamabad, one did not quite savour the thought of American planes flying over our territory from Indian bases. Secondly, the decision was in line with the wishes of my Saudi hosts. And, lastly, defying the world community was not a very comforting idea. How Pakistan followed up on this decision is another matter and discussed in the chapter that follows, but right then I had to observe the Saudi handling of the aftermath, and, indeed, bask in the limelight thrown on my country for the further year that I was to spend in the Kingdom.

I cannot recount all the factors that mean Saudi Arabia should not hold together. That the very name suggests a family fiefdom is bad enough. The nexus between the Al-Sauds and the Sheikhs of Nejd that provided the raison d'être for this dynasty is not very popular in the other parts of the Kingdom that were annexed by force of arms. Then, there is the oil that has made the country what it is today. It all comes from a region that has a large Shiite population—a not insignificant factor in a society that professes puritanical Sunni beliefs. But indeed, oil wealth alone could not have kept a disparate country under one roof, especially when so many forces in the region and beyond were looking for internal fissures that could be exploited for political or financial gain. Maybe it is the desert itself that teaches the art of surviving in adversity!

After America invaded Afghanistan on 7 October, I sought a meeting with Crown Prince Abdullah, the country's de facto ruler. He looked worried but kept reciting *Allah Khair* (all will be well) to console me. He also agreed that the invasion was essentially to assuage domestic frenzy in the US, and then he shared a few pearls of desert wisdom, "If there is a storm, the Bedouin ducks his head till it blows over". Of course, this makes more sense than facing it headlong as our urban bravado would have us believe. The other sounded more Machiavellian but Kautilya also would have approved of it, "If you cannot twist a hand, shake it". With so sound a grooming, no wonder the Saudi leadership had mastered the balancing game.

During the next weeks and months, Prince Naif, the Interior Minister, went round the country assuring its people that as the guardian of Islam's holiest places the Kingdom would not let any harm come to the *Ummah* or allow its soil to be used against a Muslim country. Probably, the reference was to the use of the Prince Sultan Air Base for the US war on Afghanistan. The Saudis might have suggested quietly that, if undertaken, such missions should be listed as training flights. The confidential message to Washington was that no efforts would be spared to undo the damage done to their invaluable relationship. Giving a decent pause, Riyadh played its master card. Crown Prince Abdullah, virtually the regent (though often designated the "vice-regent"), announced a peace proposal for the Middle East. He offered to recognise Israel, provided the latter vacated all the lands it occupied during or after the 1967 war. Indeed, there was no chance that this plan would see the light of the day, but for a considerable period this earth-shaking initiative upstaged the attack on the Twin Towers in the regional headlines. To demonstrate that he seriously wished to address the root causes of 9/11, on his subsequent visit to the US, the Crown Prince made it very clear that he only wished to discuss Palestine.

This was just one example of how the Saudis survived, in fact thrived, by deftly combining the art of keeping many balls in the air with the patience and the realism born of living in the desert. None of that would have worked if on the internal front; a delicate balance was not kept there either. The rest of us may not approve of the extravagant and corrupt practices of the Royal Family, or the wasteful culture and ostentatious display of wealth by its elite, but then enough benefit trickles down to the masses to keep them calm. Even the religious commissars, the Al-Sheikhs of Nejd, get ample worldly reward and choose to look the other way when the Kingdom violates heavenly edicts. But if they did not, and Saudi core interests were to be threatened, the same regime could be quite firm. When after the Kuwait war of 1991, a *Shurta* objected to an American female soldier moving about without an *abaya*, Prince Sultan, the then Defence Minister, suspended grants to the religious police. Indeed, the system is not in line with modern and efficient practices, but the Saudi argument was that the social order had evolved—in their case, slowly and painfully. In the desert, one was well advised not to force the pace.

Before the enormity of 9/11 forced the Saudis to change their external outlook, they were gradually mending fences in the neighbourhood. A longstanding dispute with Yemen regarding the interstate boundary was settled, generously accommodating some of the poor neighbour's claims. Some Yemenis were also permitted to sneak across the borders and seek work. Relations with Iran had improved remarkably. Gone were the days when the revolutionary fervour of the Iranian pilgrims led to their banning from Mecca, or when the Saudis financed Saddam to keep the Mullah regime at bay. I was told that efforts were also afoot for a reconciliation with the battered Iraqi dictator. The realisation that the conflicts in the region resulted in foreign intervention had motivated these initiatives. The Saudis were hoping that if and when they struck peace with their neighbours, the Americans could be asked to wind up their military bases on the sacred soil. The US had justified this presence on the pretext that, even though his forces had largely been depleted after Iraq was thrown out of Kuwait in 1991,

Saddam continued to be a threat to regional resources and the world order. In due course, one would come to learn more about the American rationalisation of protracted military involvement.

This entire strategic design or desire fell apart after the Gulf War of 2003. Soon after, when Obama visited Saudi Arabia, expecting a long lecture on how America's pro-Israeli policy was the root cause of anti-Americanism in the Muslim world, the same Prince (now the King) asked only that the US chop off the head of the snake: Iran. Initially, I suspected that this reversal in Saudi outlook was because, after the ouster of Saddam, most of the oil resources were controlled by the Shiite regimes or, as in the Kingdom, were in areas where there were large Shiite populations. After it attacked Yemen in 2015, it appeared that the Kingdom lost its ability to keep the balance that had once made a deep impression on me. Possibly, its inherent fragility was now coming to the fore.

As Ambassador to the Kingdom, I was also Pakistan's Permanent Representative to the OIC (the Organisation of Islamic Cooperation, once called the Organisation of Islamic Conference). Such multinational bodies suffer from many handicaps. Consensus, desirable and often mandatory, is almost impossible, especially when critical decisions have to be made. Members may agree when the matter is of common interest, usually economic. On an odd occasion, a predominant power may arm-twist some and pay off the others to clinch support for the required resolution. Twice in recent times, the US pulled off this feat at the UN. The world body sanctioned military action in 1991 against the Iraqi occupation of Kuwait and in Afghanistan after 9/11. Otherwise, the "common minimum denominator", the principle in practice, rarely goes beyond the condemnation of an atrocity or the expression of a hope. The OIC, since it has never done anything beyond the minimum, collectively or selectively, is often mockingly called "Oh, I See!".

The expert from the Foreign Office who came over to assist whenever the OIC had its debating sessions, used to advise us merely to reiterate our known positions and ensure that the domestic press adequately covered it. But, of course, the OIC had its benefits. It paid its establishment well and Pakistan being in the Saudi good books frequently got loans from the Islamic Bank in Jeddah. India, with nearly as many Muslims as Pakistan, once tried to secure a foothold. Pakistan only had to threaten a walkout to shut the door on its ambitions. Like all such organisations, the OIC can also help its member states to avoid taking difficult decisions. If you merely referred the matter to Jeddah, that would be the last time you would ever hear about it.

When it came to getting Saudi investments for Pakistan, it was more or less a repeat of my German experience, if anything more starkly. We were, after all, the Saudis' all-time favourites. Our Finance Minister, Shaukat Aziz, might have left a name behind after a stint as a banker, but still could not get me a sound feasibility report which, like the Germans, the Saudis kept asking for, as the basis of economic cooperation. And I kept wondering if Mr Aziz was actually an "economic hit man".

Before returning from Saudi Arabia in September 2002, I got an opportunity to take part in organising one more visit by Musharraf, the first after 9/11 and that too as the President. The Crown Prince received him with a guard of honour at Jeddah Airport. He was no longer merely a military ruler of a Third World country. His decision to join the US-lead "global war on terror" (GWOT) had catapulted Pakistan onto the international centre stage and himself to that of a leader "who had the courage to turn his country's core policies around". For this visit, I had prepared a special brief, suggesting that this time the issues and priorities would be different, and sent it as a "for your eyes only" document to his Military Secretary, following up to ensure that it was put up to the President. Of course, he did not read it, nor did he believe that he needed to. Full of himself, he embarked upon the beaten track and was taken aback when the Crown Prince cut him short. "What is the problem in Kashmir?" was the royal way to tell Musharraf that it was time to discuss some other, more urgent, matters.

I had known Musharraf ever since he was commissioned in our formation in 1964. On this occasion, I did not recognise him. Back home, I would learn some more about the transformation.

7

# POST 9/11

## PARTNERS OR PAWNS IN THE "GLOBAL WAR ON TERROR"?

Pakistan's decision to band with the US-led coalition that invaded Afghanistan on 7 October 2001 was understandable. The UN Security Council had authorised the mission, America was raging mad, and our country, under military rule, was desperate to shed its pariah status. For some of us, another factor was perhaps more important. Though it was Pakistan whose help was sought, India offered to stand in, with the plea that since Pakistan was part of the problem, it was unlikely to be a helpful partner. The very thought that a mighty war machine would have its air armada fly over Pakistani territory—and from Indian bases at that—to bomb our western neighbour and jettison some lethal cargo every now and then, was not very comforting. Pakistan, when it agreed to come on board (even though with a gun to its head), got the role, as it was better placed geographically and because of its involvement in the Afghan wars since 1980. India was obviously not amused. One of the precious memories from my Riyadh days is the distraught look on the Indian Ambassador's face when Musharraf was roundly being applauded for his courage to execute the famous U-turn on Pakistan's Afghan Policy. A message I received from a retired Indian Deputy Chief of Army Staff aptly reflects the psyche of our eastern neighbour: "Pakistan may bask in the limelight for now, but wait till the

Afghan tradition of revenge [for our part in the war against them] brings it to grief". If it sounded like the curse of an old woman, it still came true, though not because of any Afghan venom.

Taking a decision, especially an expedient or a popular one, is no big deal. Striking the right deal after some nifty bargaining is the hallmark of statecraft. In diplomatic lingo, this is called "playing hardball". We might have consoled ourselves that as an ally we had a better chance to influence American decisions (and indeed we tried to get Osama bin Laden out by non-military means), but Islamabad's original sin was that it did not negotiate any red lines which, if violated by the US-led coalition, would harm our national interest. Instead, it settled for monetary returns for its services. Of course, no payoff could have compensated for the disaffection of its own people with the policy. In due course, some of them took up arms against the state. Since the invading forces, even after the regime in Kabul was toppled, continued to hunt for Al-Qaeda and the Taliban with B52s, causing extensive damage to lives and property in mainly Pashtun areas, the groundswell of popular feeling in Pakistan was once again hostile to the US. The resurgence of the Taliban was therefore quietly greeted by a good number of people and the government started losing favour for its "unstinted support" (in Musharraf's words) for the "Great Satan". To make matters worse, hundreds of suspects, including Pakistani nationals, were rounded up and handed over to the US for onward dispatch to Guantanamo Bay. That we did it without due process of law, in order to get millions of dollars—as conceded by Musharraf in his book, *In the Line of Fire*—became evident when most of them returned without being charged.

Other developments were not very helpful. The Pakistani province of Balochistan has often been restless due to a certain sense of alienation from the country's mainstream politics. Bordering both Iran and Afghanistan, and because of its long coastline on the Indian Ocean, Balochistan attracted moles from every country interested in the New Great Game (more on the NGG in Chapter 13). Some of these countries provided substantial support to the dissenting Balochis to wage an armed insurgency. Islamabad blamed the US and the Kabul regime for ignoring, even abetting, Indian intelligence operations launched from the Afghan soil. Pakistan's relations with Kabul and Washington were now on a downward spiral. The Taliban were, in the meantime, gaining ground on both sides of the border, and the insurgency they led soon became a war of liberation engulfing Pakistani tribal areas where the people have close ties with the Afghans across the Durand Line.

The invasion of Afghanistan also led to a few hundred extra-regional allies of the Taliban, who had nowhere else to escape the coalition forces, seeking shelter in Pakistan's border regions. Islamabad was now coerced to crack down against them. Musharraf's decision to send the Army into South Waziristan in 2003 turned out to be cataclysmic. Anyone familiar with the history of that place would have known that posses in khaki were not sent into the tribal areas before exhausting all other options, especially those that had been worked out and agreed upon between the state and the tribesmen precisely to resolve such issues. Musharraf, however, had convinced himself that he was infallible. He had after all survived his own sacking by an incumbent Prime Minister, risen from the status of a military dictator to that of the "Saviour of Pakistan" (a title bestowed upon him by the Saudi leadership), and been exalted by the West as the "Man of the Moment". He was, therefore, unlikely to be impressed by the ways of the tribesmen or the romance of their history.

Many of us who had dealt with this region and had studied its past protested, at times publicly, against employing the Army too soon. As a President in uniform, Musharraf was understandably upset with his former colleagues, even though they were no longer in uniform themselves. We, after all, were part of the fraternity. The problem was that this action had all the potential of leading to a widespread insurgency. One of our most experienced civil servants, Mr Roedad Khan, predicted that it would set the frontier regions on fire. The consequences turned out to be worse than our worst fears.

Much that has gone wrong in Pakistan is best explained by social scientists or those who understand our collective psyche. On one account hardly anyone differs: the leadership at various tiers has failed to address the sense of deprivation amongst the depressed segments of our society. This sentiment has been exploited by all kinds of fortune seekers, political forces, secessionist movements and religious ideologies. And there is plenty of room to do that. Unrest in Sindh and Balochistan has simmered for decades. The unsettled dispute of Kashmir often led to conflicts with India and anxiety at home. Even in areas not affected by such major issues, the common man is hardly enamoured of the privileged elite. Against this backdrop, the military operation in South Waziristan provided the spark that set in motion a chain of tumultuous events that in a short while spread to the other tribal areas and, in due course, engulfed the entire country. Moreover, when we unwisely labelled all the estranged elements as "anti-state", many of them ganged up to improve their chances of success and survival.

The state responded in panic, without adequate preparation, or belatedly, which also extracts its own cost, but almost always with the wrong military means and without the requisite civilian support. After a few false starts, we got the hang of tempering force with persuasion, and also learnt the art of keeping the less belligerent or the more reconcilable militants out of battle. Of course, both the functions—synchronising battle with manoeuvre, and separating insurgents according to their degree of hostility—are complex. In our case, the task was further complicated by the US, whose aims and designs were different from ours. We failed to draw a line beyond which we would not obey the Americans' bidding—the operation in South Waziristan merely adding to the list of meek submissions such as giving free access to the CIA, the Pentagon, and a hoard of undercover US agencies. It was no surprise that our so-called ally subverted all our attempts to deal with the militants who were not in sync with American objectives. It was not clear if Pakistan's peace deal with a militant commander from North Waziristan, Nek Mohammad Wazir, known as the Shakai Agreement of April 2004, was for real or was merely a tactical move. When he was killed by an American drone shortly thereafter, it was certainly a warning shot.

As the insurgency grew and expanded, it became obvious that we could not put out all the fires raging in the border areas by military means, and therefore some serious dialogue was needed to placate the rising anger amongst the tribesmen, who, after all, had been our loyal citizens for six decades. In October 2006, a few hours before such efforts were to begin with a tribal Jirga in Bajaur (one of the seven agencies that constitute FATA), American missiles struck a madrassa killing over 80 students. Musharraf, who was under fire for surrendering the country's sovereignty to the US, claimed responsibility, in the belief that murdering our own children was a lesser crime than letting a foreign power violate our borders. No one believed him, nor did anyone take him to task for confessing to a bigger crime, that is, executing our own people without proof and formal investigation. The insurgents responded by killing nearly forty recruits under training in Malakand, the closest military facility they could lay their hands on.

The Lal Masjid (a mosque-cum-madrassa complex in Islamabad) episode of July 2007 was another landmark in our so-called War on Terror.

The controversy over this operation usually dealt with the evolution of the crisis. Why was it allowed to function as a madrassa in the heart of the capital? While the state was looking the other way, the mullahs were drilling militant ideology into the students' heads, weapons were being stored in a compound only a stone's throw away from the ISI headquarters, and it took the state six months to launch the military operation in the first week of July 2007. Like in South Waziristan four years previously, the means used were hardly discussed.

Some militants had indeed planted themselves inside the compound, but their number and disposition was not too difficult to ascertain, since the public and the press were freely moving in and out of the complex. Since hundreds of students, male and female, were also within its boundaries, any action against the armed infiltrators had to be designed so that the maximum number of non-combatants could be rescued. Special Forces are trained for such missions. The Rangers who formed the vanguard for this operation knew nothing better than burning down the entire structure.

After the operation, a police inspector remarked that it was actually the task for an SHO (the head of a police station). Having learnt in the Army that certain errands were only assigned to those who rose from the ranks, I could only agree. Policemen who keep contact with the masses have a certain ability to deal with situations like these. They would have used a combination of threats, bribes, even a bit of blackmail. When I later asked one of the Generals in the decision-making loop if the police option was considered, he said, "Yes, the Inspector-General of Police was consulted". I am not sure if the IGP sought permission to first talk to his SHO. As to why the operation could not be designed to save innocent lives, the rationale was pathetic: that it would have cost casualties amongst the troops. The cost paid by the security forces and the civilian population in the aftermath far exceeded the number of soldiers who might have been martyred if the thinking was less colonial.

The tribesmen who lost their children had to take revenge, which is one of the pillars of *Pashtunwali*, the code they abide by. Like after Bajaur, their response was swift and effective. Using suicide bombing, the technique that in the meantime had arrived from the Middle East via Afghanistan, they killed scores of soldiers in a Special Forces camp in Tarbela (about 50 Kilometers north of Islamabad). An audacious attack on the Army Headquarters accounted for a three-star General among others. Musharraf, already in trouble after a tiff with the country's higher judiciary, was now fast losing support even within the military ranks.

Sometime in early October, I heard it being whispered that the General-President was all set to impose E+. The term, "Emergency Plus", was invented to soft-peddle the "Martial Law Minus" that Musharraf had declared on 3 November 2007. This, he believed, would help him get the legal cover for his re-election as President while still in uniform. It turned out to be yet another straw being clutched by a drowning man. The overall environment had become so adverse that even some high profile ex-servicemen came out into the streets. Ultimately, he could retain neither his military gear nor the high civil office. He shed the uniform a couple of weeks later and was ousted from the presidency in August 2008. Ashfaq Pervez Kayani replaced him as the Army Chief, and Benazir Bhutto's husband, Asif Ali Zardari, who took over the party after her assassination in December 2007 and led it to victory in February 2008 elections, succeeded him as the President.

Not many tears were shed when Musharraf left, even though his period was marked by some positive developments, especially on the economic front. It was not a comfortable decision for people like me to join the movement for his removal. I had known him for a long time. For old times' sake, he offered me a prize post like the Ambassadorship to Saudi Arabia. And though he was aware of my views on some of his decisions while in power, he and his wife still attended the weddings of my children. The problem was that he was so full of himself that he actually believed that he could get away with murder. When he was in trouble with the country's higher judiciary, he (reportedly) said, "I will get away with it, like I did with Nawab Bugti's murder". (Bugti was a powerful Baloch leader, who fell out with Musharraf and died during an Army operation.) This *hubris* was also the hallmark of his autobiography, *In the Line of Fire*.

BB's murder shocked the world and the people of Pakistan genuinely mourned the tragedy. Considering that there was hardly anything to mitigate her two terms in power, and that she had returned after a dubious deal with a military ruler who was now at the nadir of his standing in the country, this phenomenon is difficult for me to explain, as is the motive and identity of her murderers. I will therefore only describe such aspects of her legacy as I witnessed from close quarters.

Indeed, she had reasons to be upset about my part in the dismissal of her first Government in August 1990, but then she was also grateful for the support that I gave to Asif Nawaz who, as the Army Chief, wanted to bring her back to power. Aware of the fact that she had contributed a great deal to my premature retirement, when back in the saddle she got me the coveted assignment of Ambassadorship.

Her second stint was marred by grave acts of corruption, not only by her husband but this time, as disclosed to me by one of her close aides, also by herself. In an envoys' conference in Madrid, to which all of us accredited to European countries were invited, the Prime Minister's special assistant, Shahid Hassan, briefed us on the government's ingenious formula to attract private investors to build power plants. However, when he told us that the policy was so attractive that foreign companies were queuing up to get a share of the pie, and the PM had decided to accept bids on "first-come" basis, anyone could have seen through the scam. Normally, if there was a healthy number of competitors one could select the best amongst them, and then negotiate to get the best possible deal. The misgivings that a selected few had been forewarned, in order to prepare their bids and thus get a head start over the others, were now vindicated.

Fired by an inept missionary zeal, I, then the Ambassador to Germany, went to meet the Prime Minister when she was visiting the UK in 1995. I intended to talk to her about the worsening situation in Sindh but almost on impulse blurted out that the state of corruption was not doing her government any good. That evening, I was invited for dinner with a select group. Besides Ms. Bhutto and her spouse, the federal minister Ghulam Mustafa Khar, the High Commissioner to the

UK, Wajid Shamsul Hassan, and a well-known academic working on Kashmir, Victoria Schofield, were also present. I was quite embarrassed by the Prime Minister's opening salvo, "General Durrani says my government is seen to be corrupt". Both Mr. and Mrs. Zardari tried to convince me that the charges were highly exaggerated. That was the inner voice of guilt. A few months later, Transparency International was founded in Berlin as a corruption-rating agency, and gave Pakistan the dubious distinction of being the Vice-Champion. Zardari rang me up to ascertain if I had contributed to this assessment.

BB was paranoid about losing power and had convinced herself that only two countries, where she had spent a good part of her life in exile, the UK and the US, could provide her succour. On the aforementioned visit, the British Defence Secretary had to wait for five minutes because I had overstayed my allotted time. She apologised to him more than once and the man must have been wondering why he had to call on a Prime Minister who could have been summoned to his office. The fact that, when out of power, she used to beseech the US State Department to allow her to call even on low ranking officers, was well-known in Washington, and also that she was often rebuffed. Jamshed Marker was one of our illustrious Ambassadors. As the Country's Permanent Representative in the UN during BB's second stint in power, he had to brief her whenever she was in New York. In his latest book, he writes of how embarrassed he would be because the Prime Minister was always accompanied by Mark Siegel (the lobbyist) and her old friend, Peter Galbraith. No surprise to those who had to take emergency measures when she came to the GHQ for an exclusive briefing and brought along the American Ambassador (see Chapter 2).

My last encounter with her was in 2006 in Doha on the sidelines of a US-Islam conference sponsored by the Brookings Institute, a Washington-based think-tank. During the meeting, it became quite clear that she was anxious to get back home with the help of America and the Army. As she said, these were the only two "A"s that counted. I do not know if the other two revered in Pakistani folklore, Allah and Aawam (the people), ever figured in her calculations, but I am sure she had no idea that her death would be most mourned by the masses she so ignored. Of course, she came back for power and not for the love of democracy as some of her collaborators in plunder would have us believe. All the same, considering the grand send-off she got after her death, she must have done some good, which I myself cannot fathom.

After both BB and Musharraf left the scene, the next hotspot that invited a major military operation was Swat, a former princely state in the Northwest and one of our most prized tourist resorts. Before it was incorporated into the country's mainstream political and administrative structure in 1969, it was ruled by a benign dynasty. The corrupt and inefficient bureaucratic structure that replaced a people-friendly system created a favourable setting for anyone promising a return to the good old days. A cleric, Sufi Mohammad, twice tried to exploit this sentiment to impose his version of Sharia but failed. Post 9/11, the movement now headed by his son-in-law, Fazlullah (also known as the Radio Mullah for his deft use of an FM radio network), with the help of a US-returned zealot Muslim Khan, found the right opportunity to resume Sufi's mission.

As the Army was then deeply embroiled along the borders with Afghanistan and the provincial (ANP) government in Peshawar was singularly inept, the timing was good. However, due to their brutal methods, they soon lost the support of the people. Nonetheless, since the battle between the militants and the security forces was taking too heavy a toll on civilian lives and property, the government in Peshawar concluded a peace deal, *Nizam-e-Adal*, with Fazlullah. Soon thereafter, a few vehicles of this group, now called the *Swati Taliban*, moved into the neighbouring district of Buner. The panic in Islamabad was endemic. On a small-scale map, the hundred-kilometre distant militant bridgehead looked uncomfortably close, and the hills and the mighty Indus in between not very formidable. Goethe once famously said, "No one ever deceives you, you deceive yourself". We could say the same about "terrorism". Having terrorised ourselves, we rushed the Army in without adequate ground work, civil or military. Under pressure to save the capital, the military deployed the Air Force and artillery. The use of area weapons, normally to be shunned in population centres, and inadequate time available to gain intelligence, so vital in counter-insurgency operations, resulted in avoidable harm to the population and casualties amongst own troops. The consequences for people in remote areas mean nothing to our elite as long as they can be spared the same fate.

The inevitable outcome of employing conventional tactics against the insurgents was that most of them, along with their leadership, escaped to Afghanistan, where, at a later date, Fazlullah was chosen to lead the TTP (Tehreek-e-Taliban Pakistan), the umbrella organisation of assorted groups that had taken up arms against the state and the system.

The Swat operation was still a success in the sense that the insurgents' stranglehold over the valley was broken, people got back to their business, and the infrastructure was restored. The Army, however, had to stay on to provide physical and psychological security, since the population had lost faith in the capacity of the civilian agencies to prevent the insurgents from bouncing back. When Kayani wanted to hand over a large number of prisoners to be tried or rehabilitated by the civil administration, both the federal and provincial governments refused. Having had to bear the non-military burden of the counterinsurgency as well, the Army Chief must have concluded that never again would he start another operation unless the political leadership agreed to play its part. Far more important than the military operation, which merely buys time, is the political settlement. This experience made the military very reluctant to undertake another major operation unless the civilian authorities claimed the so-called *ownership* and provided enough space for the military to conduct its part by more effective means, namely, acquiring reliable and actionable intelligence, followed by deliberate operations, mostly by small groups or through covert means.

Compelled by circumstances, the Army continued to operate where necessary. For example, it had to once again go into South Waziristan to check the menacing power of a Mehsud faction, but this time it could prevail upon two powerful commanders from the area, Maulvi Nazir and Hafiz Gul Bahadar, to stay out of battle. When the TTP created a sanctuary in the hilly areas of the Orakzai Agency, the military made extensive use of the air arm to bomb the militants out of that area. We were compelled to pursue these groups in our tribal areas, but since the source of the trouble lay on the other side of the Durand Line, the evolution of a grand strategy was becoming increasingly essential. And that was where the federal government finally started playing its proper role.[4]

Many of us have often wondered how Zardari's regime, which provided probably the worst governance in our history, survived to complete its full tenure. I do not have a good answer, but it probably had plenty to do with his penchant to let everyone do whatever they wished, good or bad. So, while his partners in crime were going full steam ahead with plunder, those responsible for the country's security policy were laying the foundations of a sound regional policy, indeed with a focus on Afghanistan. By a rare stroke of good luck, all three relevant departments—the Foreign Office, the Army and the ISI—were headed by competent professionals. During a visit to Afghanistan in 2011, I was gratified to learn that our missions had a good rapport with all the major Afghan factions. The idea was that at some opportune moment, Pakistan would be able to persuade them to work for a grand reconciliation—the only way the Afghan Humpty Dumpty could be put back together.

Almost in tandem, an exterior manoeuvre was launched to secure help from the regional countries for the Afghan peace process (see the details in Chapter 13). The initial indicators that these efforts were bearing fruit appeared in the second round of the Istanbul Process, which is an Afghanistan-specific initiative. In November 2011, a "new gang of four"—Russia, China, Iran and Pakistan—were seen to be closing ranks. India, too, could participate in this round because, unlike in the first, Pakistan did not veto participation by its arch-rival.

In 2011, Pak-US relations, already on a slippery slope due to conflicting interests in Afghanistan, plummeted to an all-time low. In March, an American agent Raymond Davis gunned down two Pakistanis in Lahore who were reportedly tracking him on behalf of the ISI. He was kept in custody for a few weeks and then released after blood money was paid to the victims' relatives. While people were still fuming at the pathetic handling of the case by the Army and the ISI, the two institutions to whom the government had outsourced all such matters, the US carried out one of its deadliest drone strikes, killing forty members of a tribal Jirga to convey its displeasure at our having had the nerve to jail their man. The use of drones to target "militants" in the tribal areas was always a bone of contention between the two countries, essentially because the Pakistanis saw it as a means to humiliate them for not cooperating with the US in its war in Afghanistan. I do not know what deal was made when Davis was whisked away in the dark of the night, but the nature and timing of the drone strike made it obvious that the US did not keep its part of the bargain.[5]

Kayani's fulminating statement the next day confirmed that the Army leadership felt it had been hoodwinked. Mariana Babar, a respected journalist on defence affairs, who herself came from an illustrious military clan, sought my opinion on the Army Chief's exceptionally harsh tone. My reply, that he was shedding crocodile tears, reflected my anger with the hands at the helm of our national affairs that had let themselves be repeatedly short-changed. It made headlines in *The News*, a local daily. True to military norms, my former colleagues appreciated the statement and those from the younger generation thought it was blasphemous.

After this strike, the situation resembled more of a low-intensity war between the two countries. A few weeks later, the malevolence acquired global dimensions.

I arrived in Abu Dhabi on the morning of 2 May 2011 to participate in an Af-Pak conference hosted by the government of UAE. As I walked into the Officers' Mess where it was to take place, I learnt that on the night before American "Seals" (naval commando troops) had killed Osama bin Laden in Abbottabad, a town about a hundred kilometres north of Islamabad. With all that had been building up in the previous months, one obviously had a bad gut feeling. A few hours later, a lady from the BBC who had tracked me down, persuaded me to take part in a special addition of *Hard Talk*, one of the channel's flagship programmes. I did tell her that, being out of the country, I had no access to details, but two of her arguments were disarming. First, that since I had often stated that OBL was likely to be in a big city and not, as generally believed, in the Tribal Areas, wouldn't I like to bask in the limelight now that I had been proven right? Then she threw down the gauntlet. Exceptionally, there would be two other guests, General Michael Jackson, a former British army chief, and David Miliband, once their foreign minister (subsequently substituted by a former deputy national security advisor in the Bush administration). The onus of defending Pakistan was now all on me.

A studio in Abu Dhabi was arranged and the episode was telecast on 4 May. In my assessment, Pakistan was in on the strike, which otherwise would have been too risky, and the cost of failure politically unbearable. As to why Pakistan was denying any part in the operation, my response was again in terms of political cost. For the people in

Pakistan, our complicity with the US against someone whom they considered a heroic figure was a greater culpability than our inability to intercept the American raiders. Obama's initial message thanking Pakistan for the "cooperation" reinforced my argument. Still, Pakistan was roundly blamed for incompetence or deceit for protecting the world's most wanted terrorist, with all its adverse effects on a relationship already at its ebb. All subsequent analyses of this event had two points in common: Pakistan cooperated in some form, and the US let us down once again. How we acquitted ourselves in the next showdown showed that we had finally learnt our lesson.

At the end of November 2011, US airstrikes killed 24 of our soldiers, including an officer manning a post close to the Afghan border. By all accounts, it was yet another action to force us to yield to their diktat. Our response must have shocked them. Boycotting the Bonn Conference that was held to conduct a major review of the West's Afghan Policy in early December did not overly impress the others— even though some on our side deluded themselves that without our participation the conference would be like staging Hamlet without the Prince of Denmark. But when we decided to block all ground lines of communication (GLOC) that provided logistic support through Pakistan to NATO forces in Afghanistan, and sustained the embargo for seven long months, the US agreed to review the bilateral arrangement. Whatever else may have been agreed upon, the two countries did vow to do their best to avoid another big crisis in their relations. Irritants, however, were bound to remain, because American and Pakistani interests, objectives and approaches remained irreconcilable.

In early 2006, the Afghan embassy in Islamabad contacted me to convey an invitation from President Karzai to visit Kabul as his guest. Earlier, he had conveyed the same message through the VCOAS when the latter called on him during a visit to Afghanistan. But by that time, I had fallen out of favour with Musharraf, and since for him the standard of loyalty to the state was unflinching personal obedience (a trait that he shared with his bête-noire, Nawaz Sharif), there was no further action. In May, I spent a week in Kabul and was deeply impressed by the Afghan trait of never forgetting an old relationship. Even those like the former President Mujadadi, now clearly at odds with Pakistan and the ISI, met me as in the olden times. "The ISI was bad but General Sahib is OK", was the ruling by the Chair of the Upper House. Yunus Qanuni, now the Speaker of the Lower House, was in the team of Massoud's I had met in September 1990. When I called on him, his welcome was indeed disarming, "General Sahib, *aap to abhi jawan hain*—you are still youthful". The message that he conveyed was of course the right one: "What did I ever say that Pakistan holds against me?". Actually, he never did, but the problem is that too many of our people speak out of turn. Professor Sayyaf, probably the sharpest mind in Afghanistan (the most "evil" according to some), meaningfully attributed the bad blood between Kabul and Islamabad to a "misunderstanding", and suggested the formation of a small standing body to service the bilateral relations, advice accepted a year later but never implemented.

Meeting Karzai was indeed the high point of my visit. Before our meeting, he asked his Foreign Minister, Rangeen Dadfar Spanta, who had just arrived after over two decades in Germany, to spend an hour with me. By mutual consent, we conversed in German. Mr Spanta and the Afghan Ambassador in Islamabad, Mr Tarzi, were part of the group that included their Deputy Head of Intelligence when I met the President. Despite the turbulent times he had been through all these years, Karzai could recall even our last, chance meeting at an airport. When he mentioned that he had kept track of my writing, I could not but help thinking of his Pakistani counterpart. Musharraf would not even look at a brief, especially prepared for him by someone whom he used to call, even if hypocritically, his mentor. I volunteered to convey his message when I was back in Pakistan.

After my return, I requested to call on the President and the Foreign Minister. That I got no response from the former was no surprise, but the latter, Khursheed Mehmood Kasuri, bowled me over. He said, "No need for any appointment, whenever you are in Islamabad and I am in my office, walk right in". I may have been a lateral-entrant Ambassador, a class that the blue-blooded diplomats never particularly liked, but I was never refused entry into the Foreign Office. Kasuri's offer was still a bit unusual. During our meeting, the Foreign Minister asked me to write a brief for his next call on Musharraf, which I gladly prepared, but with no illusion that the penny would drop this time.

The May visit led to many more and it renewed my interest in the Afghan affairs; the result is reflected in Chapter 13. One episode, in particular, seems worth narrating, not because it pumped my ego, but more because it left the Indian brass hats present—usually delighting in the blitz of Paki-bashing done by the Kabul elite—shell-shocked.

During a Track Two conference in Kabul, in which delegates from India, Pakistan and Afghanistan participated, we were invited by Karzai for an exchange of views. There were former ministers, Foreign Secretaries and a retired four-star General, all of them taking precedence over me and therefore seated closer to the Presidential chair. Karzai went round shaking hands with everyone except me, whom he embraced as "my brother". The best was still to come. He started his address with "General Durrani, ladies and gentlemen". Later, two of the Indian participants wanted to know how well we had treated members of the Mujahedeen hierarchy when they were our guests! Karzai was indeed a close associate of Pir Mujadadi at that time, but those who have dealt with the Afghans know that for the tribesmen it was the relationship forged in difficult times that actually counted.

From within or without the corridors of power, the most rewarding and also probably the most lasting of my impressions came from my engagement with our western neighbour, also the home of my ancestors.

8

# IN THE SUPREME COURT


In September 1990, a few weeks after I had taken over as the DGISI, the COAS, General Aslam Beg, told me that some businessmen from Karachi who were at the receiving end of PPP's recently dismissed government, would like to contribute to the Opposition's election campaign. However, since the time was short (the elections were due in October) and they had no means to ensure that the money would reach the right hands, could I help? It was also conveyed to me that the funds would be distributed according to directions received from the election cell in the President's office. Whether I could have refused for any number of reasons has been argued in many circles and, eventually, in due course, even in the country's highest court. The fact is that I accepted the task because it was given to me by my former boss from when I was the DGMI, who was also the one who had helped me to acquire the current post, and perhaps, more importantly, since I had been witness to the events that led to the dismissal, and was therefore not averse to the idea that BB must be denied another stint in power. That the President, also our Supreme Commander, had taken charge of the entire operation was also a significant factor.

As I was reluctant to involve my new organisation in an operation that required trust, I decided to get it implemented through my previous outfit, the MI, with which I had spent two years, and through which I knew some people I could rely upon. The operation had the sanction of the Army Chief, and the acting DGMI, my deputy till recently, was taken on board. With the help of a few selected individuals, I collected Rs 140 million from one Mr Younas Habib, a banker by profession and presumably acting as the middleman of the donors. Nearly half the amount was distributed from accounts opened in Karachi, Quetta, and Rawalpindi, to the individuals or the parties as indicated by the Presidency, directly to me, or at times through General Beg. The rest was deposited in a special fund in the ISI, with which I was told the donors had agreed.

By a strange coincidence, at that time unrelated with this operation, but later of great relevance, I was given another mission.

Air Marshal Asghar Khan, a former chief of our Air Force, now heading a political party, had joined in an election alliance with the PPP. Since the official hierarchy had thrown its weight behind the opposition, someone suggested that we should at least apprise the Air Marshal of the grounds for our bias. I therefore called upon him and suggested that he might like to review his position. Asghar Khan exercised his right to decline and said that his mind was already made up. A couple of days later I received a call from him informing me that some elements encouraged by the bureaucracy in Punjab were harassing his party workers in Lahore, and since I was the only one in the "establishment" he knew (having met him recently), would I please provide some relief? Whether my intervention helped or not, a few years down the line, when information about my fund distribution operation became public, it was the Air Marshal who filed the case with the Supreme Court.

In March 1994, a CD was recovered from the possession of Mr Younus Habib who was probably being investigated on some other account. The data on the CD also referred to Rs 140 Million that were given to Aslam Beg. Now retired, the General was approached by the media and his response was that this money had been passed on to the ISI for "political intelligence". When I read that in the paper, I met him to ask if that statement was necessary. Beg's explanation was that it was given "under pressure" as the press had pestered him. A few weeks later, I proceeded to Germany to take up my ambassadorial assignment. In July, Mr Rehman Malik, a former police officer, later the country's interior minister, arrived in Bonn on a special assignment from the Federal Government. According to him, the Prime Minister had decided to set up a judicial commission to enquire into General

Beg's statement that the money, probably embezzled from a bank, was given to the ISI.

I contacted Naseerullah Babar, a highly respected and decorated retired General who was now the country's Interior Minister, to confirm Mr Malik's version. I was told that the matter had already been discussed with the Prime Minister and the Army Chief (General Waheed Kakar at that time), and asked if I could please provide any information that would help. Since the Army's name was involved, I expressed some reservations, but he assured me that the investigations would be highly confidential. In a hand written account, I provided the details that I could recall, some of them from a few notes that I had, and also wrote a "for your eyes only" memo to the Prime Minister to handle the case with care. Soon Mr Malik was back with my statement, now typed as an 'affidavit' to be used before the Commission.

The next I heard about this case was when, some time in 1996, General Babar produced my affidavit in the Parliament to argue that the opposition alliance led by Nawaz Sharif had unfairly benefited in the 1990 National Elections. Soon thereafter, Air Marshal Asghar Khan, based on the Interior Minister's statement, filed a petition in the Supreme Court that this operation had violated his human rights. The first hearing of this case was in June 1997 soon after my return from Germany.

Two successive chief justices, Sajjad Ali Shah, and Saeed-uz-Zaman Siddiqui heard the case. After a number of hearings, the latter declared that the judgment was reserved. Why it was not announced, I learnt from Justice Siddiqui a few years later. It was because "General Babar pleaded in his chamber that he had additional evidence". (I have some idea what his decision was, but, of course, it would be improper to talk about it.) In the meantime, Siddiqui retired and the case was not taken up by the Supreme Court till early 2012, when the then Chief Justice Iftikhar Chaudhry reopened it. This time, the Supreme Court did give a verdict in October the same year. Thereafter, the Federal Government, General Beg and myself, filed review petitions that the Supreme Court started hearing in early 2015, and that is where the case rests as of now.

Since the matter is still subjudice, I should not state more than what is already in public knowledge, except that I have chosen to comment upon my decision to give the affidavit in 1994. I think it was perhaps the most imprudent of my career. The details are in Chapter 17, where I have indulged in some introspection.

PART TWO

IN HINDSIGHT

9

# THE KHAKI CAMOUFLAGE

After my retirement from the Army, I was twice the country's Ambassador. In some circles this post is rated higher than that of a General. I have, consequently, at times been addressed with the diplomatic title and not with my last military rank. Given a choice though, I prefer my soldierly tag. One reason is obvious: it was achieved after decades of hard work (and a bit of luck). The ambassadorial licence, too, was granted because I had attained a fairly rich epaulet. More importantly, the army is my identity and the only fraternity with any binding affinity. After I was prematurely retired, my most emotional moment was when I took my uniform out of the wardrobe and tucked it away in a trunk. All the same, the Pakistan Army is not the divine institution that most of us from within, or some even from without, believe it to be.

Militaries are a mirror image of the social environment in which they exist, with all its good and bad attributes. The institutional restraint and the nature of the job do make a mark, and therefore all of us, though coming from the same stock, develop distinctive traits in practical life. Civil bureaucrats must be worldly wise; a policeman deals with the underworld and hence learns to survive against great odds; politicians might travel from the death cell to the throne and therefore merely have to be able to survive; a diplomat having measured their words all of their working career is likely to become hawkish when free; and a military man trained to make the ultimate sacrifice assumes a hallowed existence. Nevertheless, they are all subsumed by the overarching ambiance around them. It is no surprise, therefore, that the decline of values in our society has also infested the military. The syndrome may have affected all walks of life, but the consequences for the military are graver because of its unique character.

No other profession demands that its followers risk their lives to kill complete strangers, and use stealth and deceit while still believing in the sublime human traits of honour, fair play, and gentlemanly conduct. It would perhaps be more befitting to regard the military as a way of living, often with its own way of dying. Over time it has developed a certain culture that may not be universally uniform (since it depends upon a nation's historical experience and social values), but still has the same core values. Because these *grundnormen* are more about the human than the material side of war, which despite all its complexity essentially remains the art of handling men in combat and the clash of will amongst adversaries, they have withstood the test of time. Their fundamentals—character, trust in leadership, and a spartan way of life—are in principle sacrosanct in all armies. Keeping allegiance to this code in face of an indifferent social climate, and that too over prolonged periods, has, however, never been easy. Sustaining the military culture during peace is thus a bigger challenge than training for war.

After doing away with British rule and breaking away from the old India, in our desire to transform the army that had served a colonial agenda into a national institution, we unwittingly tampered with some of these *grundnormen*. As cadets at the Military Academy, we were drilled in the code of honour. While still under training, some of us went to a restaurant in the nearby town of Abbottabad. Unhappy with the service we received, we complained to the owner. Without any argument, the man accepted our version because according to him, "a *gentleman cadet never lies*". A few years later, I was back as an instructor at the academy and during that tenure took the entrance test for the staff course, probably the most important milestone in an officer's career. Some organised exchange of notes took place amongst those who must have lectured their pupils on honesty and integrity only the day before. The slide in the Army may not have kept pace with the rot outside due to service discipline, but it was nearly in tandem.

A time-tested refrain in the military was on involvement in business. The mere thought that one had to raise money for as worthy a cause as welfare of troops would raise eyebrows. We used to wonder why a Brigade Commander of the old school refused permission to start a vegetable garden to spice up food for the men. In due course we found out. The practice snowballs. Before one realised, the units and formations were building bakeries, welfare shops, CNG stations, and shopping plazas. It not only distracted us from our professional pursuits but it also commercialised the military's character.

The welfare of the officers, according to the old dictum, was to be the last priority. Provided a slight opening—access to real estate, for example—it created a corporate culture in a class that has to lead troops in combat. *An eye for the ground* was once the ability to select the right terrain for battle. Some amongst us were mocked for using this faculty to choose the right land for construction. The Army Housing Scheme was started to provide all officers with a modest home after retirement. With the passage of time, the original concept was left on the wayside. Residential compounds now reflect rank. The imposing sights—for instance, if you were to drive from Lahore Airport to the Cantonment—did no good to the image of an institution that has often been charged with repeatedly occupying its own country.

The Army's takeover of political power, whatever else it may have done to the country, never did any good to the service. It is irrelevant what ratio of its rank and file was involved in civil affairs. The mere fact that, under these regimes, loyalty to the Chief in the senior ranks counted more than merit, caused colossal damage. The slide could be judged by the plight of two of its once highly regarded organisations. The Frontier Works Organisation (FWO) helped create history when working on the Karakoram Highway (KKH), and the National Logistics Cell (NLC) cleared seemingly an impossible logjam in Karachi's harbour. Under Musharraf's military rule, any work that they subcontracted, (against hefty commission, of course), was a blot on the Army's name.

An old soldiers' favourite tip, "if one could be comfortable, it would be foolish not to be", became a pretext to avoid the hard part of soldiering. After the 1971 War, as the Brigade Major (the principle staff officer with the Brigade Commander) in Bhimber, a district headquarter in Azad Kashmir, I had to deal with the UN mission in charge of monitoring ceasefire violations in Kashmir (UNMOGIP). A Canadian officer who was often driven around hairpin bends in our mountains, and was convinced that the Pakistanis were the world's best drivers, whispered in my ear that whereas the young Indian officers stayed at the forward posts, ours did not. Many years later, I also learnt that a few of our youngsters with the Frontier Corps were reluctant to do the mandatory *gasht* (peacetime patrolling). Since our junior officers generally have done well in combat, these may have been rare cases, but were still symptomatic of an unhealthy trend.

"There are no good or bad armies, only good or bad officers", so runs one of the numerous maxims on the primacy of leadership. That places the onus to stem the rot squarely on the senior officers. But what if that class too was infested by the declining values, and infatuation with all things ostentatious? If Prado was now a service vehicle, Lexus could not be far behind; landscaping and waterfalls in a general's office, mega projects to win recognition, and much more followed. In one of the promotion boards, more officers got rewarded for their part in anti-dacoit operations than the number of dacoits killed, all because their superiors believed it would make their commands happy. On another occasion, similar considerations led to a few lukewarm cases getting flag ranks. Such propensity did not bode well for the future of a force that for all the right, and some wrong reasons, is regarded as a distressed nation's last hope.

It is also a very misunderstood institution.

Indeed, the Army, which for all practical purposes symbolises the military and determines its standing in the society, has enjoyed a special status in the country's polity. The reasons are largely historical. The territory that constitutes Pakistan today has so often been trampled by invading or transiting armies that the people here have developed a healthy respect for the force of arms. In 1947, when the subcontinent was divided into the twin states of India and Pakistan, the Army acquitted itself reasonably well with the task of helping with the transition. Born in conflict with its larger eastern neighbour, the armed forces of Pakistan understandably came to be regarded as the guarantor of its existence. When the country aligned itself with the US to achieve some semblance of balance in its equation with India, the new arrangement, essentially a military relationship, provided the Army with a powerful external prop. Despite so much going for the Army, as an institution, it did not cherish political power.

# THE KHAKI CAMOUFLAGE

I joined the Army a year after the military coup of 1958. Though at the lowest rung of the military hierarchy, one could still sense that the people were not overawed by the Army, nor for that matter was the latter throwing its weight around. In 1962, when Ayub Khan took the Army out of civil affairs, there was an audible sigh of relief right through the ranks. His reign saw the highest rate of economic growth in the country's history, but, in a fair fight, he still would have lost the 1965 elections—conducted under his own 'basic democracy' rules—to the Qaid's sister. My unit was deployed in one of the sub-districts of Cambellpore (now Attock), ostensibly to ensure law and order, but in fact to help the civil administration convey the desired message, "the electoral college better vote for Ayub Khan". How we hated being used as a tool of politics!

In principle, the Army does not relish non-military tasks. (A few indeed might enjoy the attending authority and relief from soldierly rigour.) During the few months in which some of our formations were called out in aid of civil power by Bhutto in 1977, I was commanding an artillery regiment in the field. A captain was posted in the neighbouring unit from Lahore. When asked if he missed the glamour of his last station, his response reflected a soldierly soul. He said he would rather be training with his men than waiting hours on end for his company to be called to disperse a crowd.

The High Command did not acquit itself well in the 1965 War against India (nor for that matter in 1971). At the tactical level, though, the Army was so well trained that it saved the day for us. However, since the strategic objective—presumably the liberation of Kashmir—was not achieved and the political direction of the war was poor, Ayub Khan, the President and the Supreme Commander, came out a much-diminished man. I am not sure if he was unnerved by the countrywide protests in 1969 and voluntarily handed over the baton to Yahya Khan, his army chief, or the latter forced him to step down, but I do remember that the perpetuation of military rule was resented in the Armed Forces. Under the successor regime, we lost the 1971 war against India and also the eastern wing of our country. (Once again, the performance of troops was beyond reproach, as so generously acknowledged by Field Marshal Manekshaw, the architect of India's victory.) The Army leadership was clearly responsible for the disaster, but then again it was mainly the revolt within its ranks that forced Yahya Khan to abdicate in favour of Zulfiqar Ali Bhutto, who had won the 1970 elections from the western half, later the rump Pakistan.

Bhutto's role in the country's breakup was suspect but the demoralised Army still saw in him a saviour. His rhetoric, even antics, gave us heart. An attempted coup against him in 1973—though masterminded by highly respected and professionally competent military officers—was roundly denounced by the rank and file. Ironically, the General who tried and sentenced the conspirators and thus won Bhutto's favour, Zia-ul-Haq, succeeded in 1977 in doing what the Young Turks had failed to achieve a few years earlier. Even though by then Bhutto's standing in the Armed Forces had fallen, Zia's was the most unpopular putsch in the Army's history. I was an instructor at the Command and Staff College, Quetta when Bhutto was hanged. Indeed, one did not expect any applause from the uniformed community. Even then, the overt dismay of the faculty members who considered themselves the crème-de-la-crème of the Army, and were therefore very career-conscious, was palpable. A year later, Zia, fully aware of this sentiment in the College (rightly regarded as Pakistan's best known military institution), changed the theme of his annual talk from the country's politics to the profession of arms. The secret grade that he got from this snooty club of Lieutenant-Colonels would have him apply for early retirement.

Mercifully, he did not. I have no idea how Zulfiqar Ali Bhutto would have handled the crisis that erupted in the wake of the Soviet invasion of Afghanistan, but having closely worked with his political successors I am happy it was Zia who was at the helm of affairs when it happened. For nearly a decade, he ran circles around many important powers till the Soviets vacated Afghanistan and in the process *Marde Momin Marde Haq, Zia-ul-Haq Zia-ul-Haq* (Zia, the faithful and the righteous) became the rallying cry not only amongst the Afghan Mujahedeen, but also with the Kashmiri freedom fighters when unrest erupted in the disputed territory in 1990. Ironically, that too did not endear him to the military's core. His 'double handshake and triple embrace' might have charmed many, both within and outside the country, but in his home constituency it was considered unbecoming of a soldier. He practically dispensed with superior officers' evaluation reports for his favourites. But perhaps his unkindest kick to the military's self-image was the 1984 Referendum that forced the rank and file to give him, literally, the stamp of approval. I do not recall if any tears were shed when his plane fell from the sky. His military successors from Beg to Karamat worked hard to undo the damage that Zia did to our military skills.

General Beg is better remembered for his intrusion in the country's political affairs (he considered it his divine mission to put them back on track), but during his three years as the COAS his main focus was to take the Army back to its professional roots. Fairly early in his stint, he held the largest exercise with troops in our history, *the Zarb-e-momin*. To ensure that the message was widely driven both at home and abroad, he invited foreign observers and the local press in droves. I am not sure who implemented Glasnost first, Gorbachev or Beg, but under the latter the Pakistan Army learnt the art of public diplomacy.

Asif Nawaz too was obsessed with restoring the Army's image. He may have overreacted to the Sharif family's overtures to woo him in their power struggle with President Ghulam Ishaq Khan (Chapter 3), but the impulse came essentially from his resolve to keep the Army out of palace intrigues. When an Army officer had some civilians murdered in Hyderabad, he ensured that the culprit was court-martialled and hanged, and dismissed the divisional commander from service. Kakar and his successor Karamat were quintessentially non-interventionist. Both got involved in the belief that the Army could help stabilise the system. Both ended up on the wrong side of Nawaz Sharif's camp for making unwelcome suggestions. Whoever said the road to hell was paved with good intentions had no idea that this would be so completely applicable to the Pakistani Generals. Much too late, a wise civilian bureaucrat counselled me never to offer advice to politicians in power.

Musharraf had convinced himself that after going overtly nuclear, Pakistan had effectively neutralised the Indian military threat. Before crashing into Kargil for reasons that had much to do with his notions of nuclear immunity, he was always primed to offer the Army's help for any task from reading electricity meters to uncovering ghost schools that his political bosses desired. He did that in the belief that under his command the Army would make short shrift of any external aggression and he could therefore focus on strengthening the country's internal defence. After the putsch of 1999, he had all the country's resources at his disposal, but since he mainly trusted the military, he planted members of the Armed Forces in many important civil institutions, and thus undid most of the good work done in the previous years to cleanse the armed forces of the unmilitary traits. During the earlier military regimes too, some from the Army were smitten by the civilian model of conducting business, but under Musharraf the exposure was endemic. When serving Generals started falling for prime land offered at bargain prices and their palatial houses were built by government contractors, one knew that the fish was now rotting from its head. No surprise therefore that the operations in South Waziristan (2004) and Lal Masjid (2007) were short on military skills.

Musharraf was succeeded by Ashfaq Pervez Kayani, professionally sound, and a General who was genuinely given to deep reflection. One of the few things that Zardari as president and the de facto chief executive did right, even if by default, was to give a free hand to the Foreign Office, the Army and the ISI—all three then in competent hands—to formulate regional policy. Vali Nasr in his book *America- The Dispensable Nation*, has acknowledged that Kayani was the sole defender of Pakistan's interests in Afghanistan. Under his watch, the Army conducted a fairly successful operation to free Swat from the Taliban's stranglehold, but at the cost of casualties both to the civilians and the military that could have been avoided with better training and preparation.

Our Armed Forces have been fighting insurgencies ever since the country's creation. A serious study of it, however, was undertaken as late as 1973, after yet another phase of the Baloch uprising. Having lost the 1971 War—essentially a consequence of the failed counterinsurgency (COIN) operation in our eastern wing—we finally wanted to learn this art. I was at that time a Brigade-Major in Kashmir and even though there was no likelihood of our formation being employed in Balochistan, we were tasked to brush up our practice for this type of warfare. Three decades later, when it was seriously challenged to conduct COIN on our western borders, the Army found itself unprepared. The manuals on Frontier Warfare that used to be part of our training syllabi, had been consigned to the archives by the time they were actually needed, after Musharraf's fateful decision to rush the military in South Waziristan in 2004. Over 200 men along with their commanding officer walked into the trap laid by the insurgents since they had ignored, or had never heard of, one of the basic principles of fighting in that area: mounting piquets to protect the flanks of the main column.

Though no longer in service, I was told that there was a big sigh of relief down the ranks when India mobilised its forces in 2002. They could now move to their battle locations and make up for the time lost in collecting cooked-up tax refunds. Similarly, the debacle in South Waziristan and the lessons learnt from operations in Swat also provided the Army with the much-needed pretext to start training for, and fighting, what was now called "fourth-generation warfare".

It has been tough going ever since, with an increasing number of troops getting sucked into the war against the internal enemy. The upside is that the Army not only learnt on the job, but its image too was restored in the eyes of a grateful nation. In the process, Kayani's successor, Raheel Sharif, was applauded as the saviour of the nation. And I have reasons to believe that organisations like the Frontier Works Organisation (FWO) and the National Logistics Cell (NLC) that had fallen on bad times too have been rejuvenated. The former may well be in the forefront to make the CPEC (China-Pakistan Economic Corridor, an ambitious development project) a dream come true.

Perhaps the most intriguing aspect of the Military's role in Pakistan is that every time it assumed political power, even though it administered better, delivered on the economic front and made the right impact abroad, it soon started losing traction and on its exit was replaced precisely by the forces that it had tried to keep out. After lording over the country for 13 years, the Ayub/Yahya combine had to cede the reins to Zulfiqar Ali Bhutto, who had fallen out with his military godfather (Ayub Khan). Zia's exit made way for the triumphal return of the Bhutto clan, whose head he had hanged. And Musharraf's departure promptly brought back the two political forces that he considered to be the most evil.

It is for some political or social scientists to explain this enigma in its entirety. I can only think of a few tendencies common to our military rulers, though each was of a different make and took over in different circumstances, that might have helped their antagonists to bounce back with vengeance.

Like Napoleon, our Bonapartes were obsessed with legitimacy. One of the first to be consulted after a putsch would be a legal wizard who could recommend a prescription to make the Supreme Court endorse the military takeover. That made Sharif-ud-Din Pirzada, the magician, and the Doctrine of Necessity, the mantra, household names in our political lexicon. The same quest for legitimacy led our men on horseback to create a political base. Since mainstream parties or individuals with grassroots support were often reluctant to soil their democratic credentials (some of them in any case being ousted by the coup), those who jumped on the military's bandwagon were usually the ones who needed a prop to get elected.

It did work in the beginning. The new environment, generally favourable to the military regime, and some arm-twisting, helped this miscellany of fortune seekers to power. The problem arose when their military patrons, now more or less fitting in the traditional political mould, failed to sustain the momentum and lost their sheen. The King's Party on the other hand still needed their support to remain in power. The rulers in khaki too did not need much persuasion to be convinced that their mission, which in the meantime had acquired a life of its own, was not yet fulfilled. So they recycled some of the old ruses, like coercing the higher judiciary to extend its cover, and invented new ruses, like referenda, to legitimise the perpetuation of their power.

All our military rulers and their camp followers thus kept digging themselves deeper into a hole and obviously did not come out looking good. Ayub Khan may have led the country to a phenomenal rate of growth, but was replaced by his deputy. Yahya Khan presided over a lost war and is therefore destined to be condemned by history. Zia might have been saved an ignominious end by the hand of God, but he did not receive credit for having rolled back a superpower from the country's borders. Musharraf was, for a while, one of our most acclaimed heads of state, but is now disowned by his own constituency, the Military, and is reviled by the media he unchained.

The Pakistan Army and its leadership, to be more precise, faces a serious predicament. It enjoys a special status in the country's polity but is also aware of its limitations, be it in direct political control or performing its assumed role from the sidelines. In both cases, it cannot act except like a military—inadequately in other words. The problem is that it does not believe that any other institution could do better. The impasse gets compounded because people expect more from the Army regardless of its role or its limitations. I recall meeting a worldly wise man during my stewardship of the ISI. He said he was happy that the country was under civilian rule but, if something happened to Pakistan, he would hold the Army responsible. 'Damned if you do and damned if you don't,' may adequately explain this quandary, but I find an Old Persian saying نا جائے رفتن نا پائے ماند ن (*nowhere to go and no place to stay*) more apt.

At the time of my writing this, at the end of 2017, the Army seems to be at its popular best. But not everyone is applauding—not, for example, the mainstream political parties.

# 10

## MY BRUSH WITH INTELLIGENCE

The first line of defence—that is what the foreign services believe they are. This claim is seldom contested by the Intelligence agencies, even though they operate much ahead of the diplomats and work towards the same end: expanding the country's security parameter. Identifying and evaluating live and potential threats, providing early warnings to the right quarters, and denying sensitive information to unfriendly forces, all take the role of the Intelligence beyond the defensive to the preventive, and if they are really competent, even the pre-emptive. But what actually makes the agencies different, powerful, and even feared, is their modus operandi. They can use covert means, are at times beyond the confines of law, and have the ear of the decision makers. Since power not only corrupts but can also be misused, those in this business are generally viewed with caution. Overall, the secret services evoke mixed sentiments: respect for the role, fear of their clout, and suspicion. For a mainstream military officer, however, service with the Intelligence means no uniform, and therefore not strictly soldiering.

As Defence Attaché in Germany, though never asked to do any prying, I was under the ISI's administrative control. Some other countries have a different arrangement—placing military attachés under service headquarters for example—but our system helped me understand a bit about this mysterious business. Moreover, my host department in Germany was the Intelligence branch of the Defence Ministry. I consequently had shed some of my misgivings about the nature of this vocation and no longer considered it a "cloak and dagger" job. All the same, when I was posted as the DGMI, though aware of the fact that, in many militaries, an outsider headed the Intelligence at the service and inter-services level, I was not quite sure what to expect. But it did not take me long to start liking my new assignment. Dealing with threats was exciting enough, and the perspective it provided was not usually available to a Major-General.

## The Stint with the MI

I had, for example, the privilege of watching the transition to civilian rule after Zia's demise, and also, at times, had to share its cost. On her first visit to GHQ as Prime Minister, Benazir Bhutto wanted to know why "M-One" was shadowing her. (She had probably seen a report on MI and mixed up 'I' and '1'.) When I asked her if she was sure it was the MI, she said, "Yes, because the person said he was from your setup". All I could do was suggest that in this business people could blur their identities. Maybe I should have been more truthful, as there are moments when all those in the "spook" business have to be around. The military top brass, too, was upset when the IB in Peshawar was hovering around a Corps Commanders' conference.

On another occasion, our conversation was more meaningful. She had asked Air Chief Marshal Zulfiqar Khan, a retired service chief whom she later appointed as Ambassador to the US, to recommend reforms in the country's Intelligence structure. We had received his report and, when asked for my view, I said all such exercises had reached more or less the same conclusions, but on one there was unanimity—that we must create a JIC (Joint Intelligence Committee) to work under the Prime Minister, headed by his or her nominee. Would she be willing to implement it? "Oh no, that would make the head of this body too powerful", was her reflexive response.

Power per se, and not necessarily as a means to achieve worthwhile ends, remained an obsession with our politicians, perhaps because they had not tasted it often enough. Mostly, however, it was the illusion of power, and we all suffered from it, as I have tried to highlight in this book. But now I speak of the paranoia surrounding the power of Intelligence.

The failure at Jalalabad (Chapter 2) was seen as a god sent opportunity by BB's team to snatch control of the "almighty ISI" from the Military. Zia's Eighth Amendment to the Constitution had left the authority of appointing its head with the Prime Minister (though God knows why). According to the rules of business, the DGISI could be a civilian, a politician, or even a woman. GHQ's claim on this post was anchored on the ISI's focus on military threats, and also because nearly eighty per cent of its personnel came from the armed forces. The Army's standing in the country's power hierarchy might, however, have been the decisive factor. Benazir came up with a solution she believed to be a reasonable via media. After Jalalabad, she installed a retired General as the ISI's chief. General Kallue was indeed an upright and competent man. The problem was that the entire second tier consisted of serving military officers (all from the Army except for one) who were likely to return to the active list. So, if the COAS was not comfortable with the Prime Minister's choice, the new head of the ISI could be turned into a lame duck. Military institutions are not like labour unions though, and Kallue was given all cooperation on professional matters. However, if the time came for a bit of political wheeling and dealing, the rank and file would obviously look towards the GHQ. So if the purpose of getting "her man" to head the ISI was to keep an eye on the Army, it was not likely to work. And it did not, neither in September 1989, at the time of the 'no-confidence motion' against her government, nor in August 1990 when she was dismissed by GIK. MNS too had similar designs when he asked me to continue after Beg's retirement. As I observe in Chapter 3, there was no chance that I would snoop over my mother institution on his behalf.

Fairly early in my new vocation, I was convinced that even if Intelligence was the second oldest profession, it was unfair to compare it to the first. So I tried to revive the old concept of creating a separate branch which, in our terminology, would be called "the Corps of Military Intelligence" (CMI). It existed in many other services including in the American Army and, since in those days we were still allies in Jihad, the antecedents were helpful. Reservations amongst the military ranks were, nonetheless, serious. A good number of individuals in Intelligence posts were misusing their authority and the immunity that came with the job. Then there were those who pulled strings to land such assignments precisely for those very reasons, and for a career that was unburdened by the rigours of military life and the compulsions of the uniform. Moreover, during the just concluded decade of Zia's rule, the job had become less taxing. Identifying threats to national security and tracking their sources and carriers required application and patience. Under military rule, many in this business could win their spurs merely by chasing political activists and learning how best to spice up their account.

Despite these misgivings, I still went ahead and had the project approved by General Beg and others who mattered. The environment was favourable and the military brass in a benevolent frame of mind. Some provisions did indeed have to be made to guard against the existing ailments and to prevent fresh ones that were likely to creep in if the new corps did become a brotherhood. What also had to be ensured was that all intelligence-related activities were not monopolised by the nascent outfit. Since the assessment of threats essentially depends on the study of information collected, the best option seemed to be that the analysts—some of them in any case not likely to be available within the CMI ranks—were borrowed from other branches of the Army, and if necessary even from the open market. The heads at the service level, as per good prevailing practice, were preferably to continue to be from outside the new corps. How this all eventually worked can only be judged by those who had to work with its product.

The primary duties of the DGMI are related to the army's operational role. The vantage point, however, provides an invaluable perspective on the country's core issues, with the added advantage that he is not directly responsible for dealing with them, unless of course specially tasked to do so. During my two years on that post (October 1988 to August 1990), I had the good fortune to be part of a committee constituted to review the country's Afghanistan Policy after the Soviet exit, to watch the initial phases of Kashmiri uprising that started in January 1990 and, due to MI's special role in Sindh and Baluchistan, to get a better understanding of what were, and still remain, two of our more complex internal issues. My personal involvement in all of them has been covered in Part One, and my assessment of these issues is included in this Part under the relevant chapters. Since I was reasonably familiar with these subjects when BB's first government was dismissed in August 1990, I was made head of the ISI.

# MY BRUSH WITH INTELLIGENCE

*The World's Best*

A few years after 9/11, ISI was sometimes declared the best of its kind in the world. Though gratified, it took me back to the period when it had started causing alarm precisely for being too good for its own good.

Indeed, it was not always that famous or that feared. When tasked to provide covert aid to the Mujahedeen soon after the Soviet invasion, it did so on a modest scale and by keeping a low profile. (I learnt about it merely by chance from an old colleague during my briefing as Defence Attaché designate in early 1980.) However, two years later, the involvement of the US and other Western countries in the region cata-pulted the ISI from a small-time player that undertook to punch above its weight into the big leagues, rubbing shoulders with the best in the game. Unsurprisingly, the ISI became a source of great concern, not only for its foes.

One may assume that the Intelligence agencies within a country and those from friendly nations cooperate as a matter of course, but in real life it is rare. BB had only one rationale for not creating a coordinating mechanism, and it was certainly not a very common concern. Spy agencies are possessive about their turf and their sources are reluctant to part with potentially valuable leads, and quite often it is doubt about the quality or veracity of information that prevents them from sharing it, lest they be embarrassed. It took a 9/11 for the US to create a halfway-coordinating house. Between the CIA and the ISI, however, communication and coordination worked well as long as the Soviets were in Afghanistan. The shared objective, the defeat of the occupation, was one reason; respect for each other's turf was the other more important one. The CIA hardly ever questioned how its Pakistani coun-terpart dispensed with the resources provided for the Jihad, or for that matter how it was conducted. And the ISI never asked if the American providers were overpricing the ordnance or undermining the Saudi contribution. It did not mean that they trusted each other.

Differences surfaced as soon as the Soviets withdrew. When I joined the ISI in August 1990, they were coming to the fore. Some of the key ISI operatives were vilified, allegedly for having favoured the more radical of the Afghan groups. The charges that the Agency was infested with rogue elements have continued ever since. Twice, under the

American pressure, there were major purges in the ISI's rank and file. If these ever led to a change in the policy is another matter. In the early 1990s, we in the ISI understood this shift in the American attitude as its desire to establish hegemony and, more crucially, now that the Soviet Union after its exit from Afghanistan had ceased to exist, to cut this upstart service to size.

The CIA was clearly at odds with our declared objective to help the Mujahedeen lead the new dispensation in Kabul, especially if individuals like Hikmatyar were to play any role in it. And the US was indeed unhappy with Pakistan's efforts to seek Iran's cooperation after the Islamic Republic had made peace with Iraq. But what seemed to have caused the most anguish amongst our American friends was the prospect of an increasingly confident ISI, vain enough to throw a spanner in the works of the sole surviving superpower.

These apprehensions were not entirely ill-founded, as the Iraq-Kuwait crisis of 1990–91 was soon to show. Some time in 1992, General Brent Scowcroft, a former national security advisor to US Presidents Ford and George H.W. Bush, reportedly conceded that the ISI's assessment of Saddam's forces was closer to the mark than their own, and that they themselves had highly exaggerated Saddam's capacity. The real danger that another intelligence agency could broadcast its account every time the CIA "sexed up" a threat to suit American objectives (the next time on Iraq's WMD holding, for example), meant the US were poised to pre-empt such judgments. Robert Oakley, the US Ambassador to Pakistan, often complained to me about some of my operatives, ostensibly because of their infatuation with the "Jihadists" in Afghanistan and Kashmir. In 1993, the ISI was subjected to a major reshuffle, described by an old colleague as the demolition of its memory bank. The purge may have helped a few careers, but when it came to taking decisions and making policies, the new guard had no choice but to support the Taliban that had emerged as the only group with a chance to reunify the war-torn country. This was the inviolable and, in principle, the condition for Pakistan's support for the "endgame", with no ideological or geo-political caveats.

Creating leverage can be useful in many other ways as well. Post 9/11 for instance, the Taliban did agree to our request to extradite Osama bin Laden, albeit to a third country. This was rejected by the

US, for reasons I discuss in Chapter 15. The ISI was thereafter subjected to another purge in the hope that the refurbished setup would put its heart and soul behind the new decree: "chase anyone resisting the American military operations in Afghanistan all the way to hell". That amounted to millions on both sides of the Pak-Afghan border, who were likely to be around long after the US troops had gone home, with some of them turning their guns inwards if pushed to the wrong side of the state. Under the circumstances, neither the ISI nor any other organ of the establishment had any intentions of clamping down against those groups that were chiefly primed to liberate Afghanistan from foreign occupation. If they had the right to do so, or how this external military presence was to be described any differently, can be discussed ad nauseam.

So this time as well, it was not any "rogue elements" in the ISI but the complexity of the crisis that necessitated the selective use of force, essentially against the rogue groups, some of them undoubtedly planted or supported by forces inimical to our past and present policies. If our political and military leadership also had the gumption to support the war against the NATO forces—in the belief that some of the turmoil in the area would not recede as long as the world's most powerful alliance was still around—that would be a very heartening assumption.

The ISI does, however, suffer from many ailments, most of them a corollary of its being essentially a military organization and of the Army's exceptional role in the country's politics. Whether the Army was in power or not, the military secret services fell short when tasked to pursue its political agenda. All their projects failed or provided only temporary relief. The creation of the MQM to offset PPP's domination of the Sindh Province in the 1980s may have given the estranged migrants from India a platform, but did not erode the PPP's vote bank. More importantly, the schism between the two communities, the Urdu and the Sindhi speakers, though not instigated by the ISI or the MI, became more acute.

The ISI underwrote the formation of an anti-PPP alliance (IJI) before the 1988 elections. It did not win that bout. But when it did in 1990, though again helped by the civil and the military establishment, the victory was largely because of the PPP's lacklustre performance. Soon after coming to power, the IJI embarked upon cutting both its civilian and military godfathers down to size. Still, nothing demonstrates the ineptness of the military in politics better than the spontaneous collapse of the entities it sponsors as soon as the khaki umbrella is removed. And if the idea was to keep the Army's nemeses at bay, they all bounced back with vengeance, as argued in the previous chapter.

The ISI also suffered when used as the military's political instrument. As mentioned earlier in this chapter, it attracted the wrong persons, more suited to throwing their weight around than for the grind of the Intelligence world. In return, they could not as much forecast the outcome of a poll with any reasonable accuracy, neither in 1988 or 1990, nor in 1970 when Yahya Khan risked elections only when assured that the likely "hung-mandate" would let the GHQ retain real power. Mujib's Awami League and the Bhutto-led People's Party won decisively in East and West Pakistan respectively.

Mercifully, the core that had to carry out the primary functions of the Intelligence remained more or less unaffected. It may not seem to be an extraordinary feat since both the MI and the ISI have been doing it for decades, but the fact that they kept track of the Indian formations and gave sufficient strategic warning to those who needed it, must count for something. The quality of its assessment of the Iraqi forces during the Gulf War of 1991 has already been mentioned, but that it did so without any assets on ground also speaks for its professionalism. As the icing on the cake, the agency had the confidence to warn of the impending war and to present its appraisal of the outcome even though it knew that some powerful figures in the hierarchy, like the Army Chief, would not be too pleased.

That is where I think the ISI can claim to be better than the rest. The CIA and the others in the West may have more resources and superior technology, but quite often they succumbed to political pressure and adjusted their assessment accordingly. Even without any tentacles on the ground or, for that matter, access to the reports by the IAEA, merely by following the events of the previous decade anyone could have determined that the possession of WMDs by Iraq in 2003 was not very likely. But since the US and the UK had already decided that Iraq had to be invaded—for oil, to create chaos in the Middle East, and to benefit the likes of Halliburton, or whatever other reason—the CIA and its affiliates counterfeited the required evidence.

# MY BRUSH WITH INTELLIGENCE

In April 1993, I led an NDC delegation to a NATO country where we were told that though the Cold War had ended, the Trans-Atlantic Alliance must continue, because it was essentially to keep peace in Europe which could otherwise again be at war within itself, as it had been for centuries. (What our hosts did not say was that the organizations always find new work to survive and expand, but in the spirit of Parkinson's Law would never dissolve themselves.) However, when we asked them whether, in keeping with their new self-assumed role, they were not supposed to do something to end the war in Bosnia, the response was that according to NATO's assessment it would take half a million soldiers to do that, and that it did not seem feasible to mobilise that number. Obviously, the decision not to intervene had already been taken and the Intelligence estimates were merely rationalising inaction. A genuine analysis would come up with a number of options, including what could be done with the available resources. Ultimately, when President Clinton decided to act, the mission was accomplished by a few aircraft.

Keeping track of the developments after Iraq invaded and occupied Kuwait was my first assignment in the ISI. If Saddam was "trapped" by April Glaspie, the US Ambassador (as some people suspected), or he had any historical grounds or economic incentives to annex Kuwait, one thing was quite clear: the US was raring to respond by force. When the UN intervened and gave Saddam the deadline of 16 January 1991 to vacate the occupation, the worst-case scenario for the Americans was Saddam meeting that deadline. Their aim of securing a military foothold in the region could only be accomplished by war. The policy to achieve that aim was to convince the Saudis that the Republican Guards had the potential to threaten the Kingdom's oil fields, an assessment with which we disagreed and General Scowcroft did too, perhaps two years too late.

Indeed, the second oldest profession can be half as honorable than the first, if practiced by people whose souls are for sale.

The ISI coped with multiple threats despite its limited resources. At times, paucity of resources may be a blessing; we relied on human intelligence. Those with satellites saw nuclear-tipped missiles where construction cranes were operating (witness the Indo-Pak faceoff of May 1990), and were looking the other way when the nuclear bombs actually exploded, as in the Indian tests precisely eight years later.

I have argued earlier that though all of us practicing different professions come from the same (national) stock, the nature of the job does affect how we go about our calling. That may explain why the ISI has acquitted itself differently than the other national institutions, including the armed forces. Firstly, since its mission requires it to remain constantly on a war footing, it cannot afford to lose focus. Peacetime slack is not an option for such institutions. Mercifully, the nature of its job also spares it undue interference, provided some key conditions are met. The head must not only be carefully selected, but should also have the trust of, in our case, both the political and military leadership, and he (or if ever there was to be a she) should have the backbone to protect the institution from external meddling and influence. I could only meet the PDPA's Intelligence Chief on my own initiative if I was sure that it would be understood by my bosses in the right spirit.

Lastly, for the character of any organization, its formative years are important. The ISI was very fortunate to have been founded by some very wise men who knew that the work culture introduced by them would shape its future course. When I landed in the ISI and was briefed on the system created and developed by my predecessors to support the Afghan Jihad, my first reaction was that even with the benefit of looking at that successful model, I could not have replicated it. The problem only arises when some people, in their desire to put down their own imprint, or with the belief that those that came before them have to be run down, try to reinvent the wheel. In this respect, the Agency has been mostly lucky, or had the resilience to withstand some rough handling. One of the aforementioned purges was so drastic that an old hand expressed the fear that the ISI could lose its memory. Institutional memory is always important. In Intelligence agencies it is critical.

The ISI may have resisted, mostly successfully, outside influences and internal subversion, but there is not much it could do about some structural flaws in the larger system. The Armed Forces, for example, provide the bulk of its personnel. Getting the right type is, of course, up to the ISI, but what it cannot do is to keep them for longer than permitted by the parent service, at times because of the career needs of the individual. During my MI days, I was told that in a particular sector our Indian counterpart had spent fifteen years in the post and knew our side better than we did. The contrast was amply highlighted in an excellent account written by Amarjeet Singh Dulat, a former RAW Chief and now a good friend, in his book, *Kashmir: The Vajpayee Years* (published in 2015). As a senior IB officer, he had served for ten years in Kashmir. After the unrest that started in the Valley in the 1990s, he was asked to head RAW and be the key man to handle the uprising. After retirement, he continued to contribute when assigned to the PMO, and later as an informal advisor to the governments in Delhi or Srinagar. After the uprising, while we were drifting under different dispensations, the other side was patiently pursuing a coherent counter strategy. If the movement is still alive it is because of the people's alienation from anything Indian, and Delhi's denial of this ultimate truth.

Strategy cannot compensate for the flaws of policy, and indeed it can never be a substitute for policy. Meeting with my Afghan counterpart in March 1991 was of no use unless followed up by a deliberate government policy. Even my meeting with the RAW Chief a few months later, which was undertaken with the consent of the Government, proved a non-event, since it was merely a one-off affair.

All the same, my stint at the ISI was not only a fruitful experience that continues to bear bounty, but also having been part of this world-class organization was, for me, a privilege. Mr Dulat, my "comrade in arms" (as he describes our new, and old, relationship), though quite an icon in his own country, has often jocularly expressed the desire to be, just for once, the DGISI.

11

# PAKISTAN'S TROUBLED SOUTH

*Sindh: the "Soft Underbelly of Pakistan"*

On 30 September 1988, an ethnic clash in Hyderabad, a city in the province of Sindh, took about 90 lives. In those days, Sindh was the most burning issue on our domestic front and it also turned out to be my first assignment as the DGMI. I was tasked to undertake a study tour of the troubled areas and brief the brass on the situation that was likely to play an important role in the general elections a few weeks later. Benazir Bhutto was the favourite, and was expected to do exceptionally well in Sindh due to her ethnicity. Sindhis indeed form the majority in the Province, even though a good number of them are Balochis (like Zardaris and Jatois), with a sprinkling of Punjabis. Most of them had settled there a long time ago and were now accepted as the sons and daughters of the soil.

After the partition of the subcontinent, most of the refugees from India, called *Muhajirs* in Urdu (which is their mother tongue), made their way to some major cities of Sindh. Better educated, flag bearers of a well-developed culture from the heart of India, and fired by the settler spirit, they transformed the medium-sized port town of Karachi into the biggest, the most dynamic and the richest city of Pakistan. That attracted two other groups from up-country in large numbers, the Punjabis and the Pashtuns. The Muhajirs, at times also called "the new or the urban Sindhis", dominated business, academia, and in due course also politics, not only in Karachi but also in two other cities, Hyderabad and Sukkar. When Zulfiqar Ali Bhutto became the Prime Minister of Pakistan and the party he founded, the PPP, was also elected to rule Sindh, the older natives, who were nervous because of rising Muhajir power, were compensated through some administrative provisions. That caused unrest amongst the Muhajirs, a sentiment that was exploited by Zia-ul- Haq, who, having toppled and then hanged Bhutto, was understandably apprehensive of the 'old Sindhis'. His antidote implemented vintage military tactics: using the ISI to persuade the Muhajirs to organise themselves under a political banner. The outcome was the MQM. All these machinations frustrated the original inhabitants to the extent that GM Syed, a prominent Sindhi leader once at the forefront of the Pakistan movement, was now opposed to its very existence. By the late 1980s, the tension between the two communities had brought the province to the brink of a civil war. "Sindhi Grievances" was one of the main themes of our studies at the NDC.

I do not think I understood enough about the complexities of the situation after my first trip to make any meaningful proposal. Since the two parties, the MQM and the PPP, were well anchored in their respective constituencies, urban and rural, a grand coalition between the two seemed the best way to restore peace and stability. When it did happen after the October elections, we were vain enough to believe that Sindh was now "over the hump". If only the politics in Pakistan were to follow the military's linear thinking! Though Ms Bhutto entered into an alliance with the MQM in 1988, it was merely to strengthen her claim to form a government at the centre—which she did. Once in the chair, though, she was not willing to concede even some of the reasonable demands of her coalition partners (the entire list of more than fifty posts was indeed mostly unreasonable). The honeymoon barely lasted the proverbial hundred days and by March 1991, the two communities were on the warpath again. All efforts by the President and the Army Chief to bring about reconciliation between them were to no avail and the alliance broke up in September 1989.

The tension between the two communities continued for nearly a year, dotted at times by bloody clashes, till BB's government was dismissed in August 1990. The successor provincial government was led (with all-out support from the establishment, civil and military) by Jam Sadiq Ali who had broken away from the PPP. Jam had fulfilled the nearly impossible mission of denying the PPP power in a province that was considered the party's invincible fortress, and thus justified the judgment of the President (who had chosen him against all advice, because of his grubby past). Once in office, he lived up to his reputation of being grossly corrupt and ruthlessly eliminating anyone who got on the wrong side of him. He once publicly praised a judge who was known for his integrity and uprightness, had him killed a few weeks later, and then mourned his death for three days.

The national Census was overdue, but when the Federal Government decided to conduct it at the beginning of 1991, Jam threatened to bloat the figures for the Sindhis on the pretext that the MQM would do the same for the Muhajirs. The exercise was postponed. He next plotted to pitch the Army against the MQM but luckily General Arif Bangash, the Corps Commander in Karachi, warned the GHQ in time. In June 1992, the Army did carry out a crackdown against the MQM but only after Jam had died of liver disease. Though the MQM was a partner in the ruling coalition, both at the centre and in Sindh, neither of its allies, Prime Minister Nawaz Sharif or Chief Minister Muzaffar Ali Shah, was comfortable with the Party's relentless pestering. Asif Nawaz, the Army Chief, had some bitter memories from the time he was commanding the Karachi corps and was probably looking for an opportunity to break the MQM's stranglehold. With the political climate already favourable, when some dissidents left the MQM, Asif Nawaz found the time was just right for action. Whether Altaf Hussain, the party leader, had an inkling about the impending operation and that was why he left the country, or if it was because he was sure that it was risky for him to stay with Asif Nawaz as the Army Chief, is not clear. However, President Ghulam Ishaq Khan, who wanted to deny the PPP any space to return to power, halted the operation in its tracks.

The collateral damage in this cycle of manipulation was that, first, the Sindhis, and in time the Muhajirs too, became receptive to Indian overtures. Ironically, the first time I heard Sindh described as Pakistan's "soft underbelly" was from Benazir Bhutto, who herself was not immune to enticement from the East or the West.

The next serious effort to defang the MQM was made in 1995–96 during BB's second term in power. It was well planned, with all the intelligence agencies on board and Major-General (retired) Naseerullah Babar, the Federal Interior Minister, steering the operation. It also failed because that vital element, a political strategy to reconcile the estranged Muhajir community, was not in place. As always, the elected leadership had a ready excuse for this failure: that the Government was dismissed before it could complete the task. (At times one got the feeling that our civilian governments were relieved to be removed.) Indeed, BB's second regime was sent packing in November 1996, but there were no signs that it had any plans to bring the angry Muhajirs back into the mainstream.

Musharraf's rule for the MQM was a GHQ-sent blessing. It acted with immunity and killed with impunity. When Syed Athar Ali, the Karachi Corps Commander, went to Musharraf with a folder full of the crimes committed by the MQM, he was sacked. I was reminded of my experience when I had taken a similar dossier to Prime Minister Nawaz Sharif. Always unwilling to tread on hot territory, he asked me to bell the cat and to take it to the President. GIK, still loyal to Zia's legacy, did not like it either, but at least he let me retain my job. Musharraf rationalised his tolerance of the MQM's highhandedness by referring to its stranglehold on the jugular vein of the Pakistan economy. That was what he told me after he had accepted Altaf Hussain's nominee, Ishratul-Ibad (who had a criminal record) to be the Governor of Sindh. I, alas, could never tell him what Karzai said when *advised* by Musharraf to induct more Pashtuns in his cabinet, "The President of a country where all the four-stars in the armed forces were from two per cent of the population [Urdu speakers] is not going to lecture me on ethnic balance". The free hand he gave to the MQM turned out to be the long rope with which the mafia may have hung itself. It might be nowhere near dead, but it is unlikely to regain its uncontested status in Karachi. Unsurprisingly, the forces that seriously challenge MQM's primacy are from within the community, vindicating Asif Nawaz' prognosis that the MQM was best cut to size from within.

Both the Muhajirs and the Sindhis might still be stuck with, respectively, the MQM and the PPP—not because these parties have done very much for their followers, but because the two communities have no viable political alternatives. The MQM cadres are organised and their methods are brutal. The PPP relies on its feudal hierarchy. In neither case is any clear political alternative on the horizon, but both communities would be happy if there was a change of guard or a collapse of the existing order. Five years of Zardari-led rule at the Centre all but wiped out the PPP from the rest of the country—but only because other options were available. In rural Sindh there are none, and, as of now, the old Sindhis are stuck with the Bhuttos. In Muhajir areas, the inroads by parties like Jamaat-e-Islami and various factions of the Muslim League are of dubious potential, but the military led operations against the militants have certainly weakened the hold of the existing gangs, some of them affiliated with the MQM. This has provided space to those in the party's hierarchy who were wary of Altaf Hussain's messianic hold. The hesitation on the part of the dissenters among the rank and file of the party primarily stems from their past experience. The MQM dealt ruthlessly with those who collaborated with the Army or the Intelligence agencies in previous crackdowns once the action was called off.

It is not clear if our establishment has finally learnt that when operations like those in the former East Pakistan, Kashmir, or Karachi do not achieve their objectives, groups or individuals who had helped us pay for their loyalty with their lives, and often also with the lives of their kith and kin. But one thing should be beyond any doubt: the price that we have to pay as a result of these reprisals; when help is next needed, we may not find many willing to cooperate with us.

## Balochistan: No Place for the Fainthearted

Balochistan is a fascinating place. Its vast and empty spaces, rugged landscape, fresh and crisp air, and its hardy people provide much solace to a restless soul.

My infatuation with our 'Wild West' started with an accidental journey through its Pashtun areas, once called "British Baluchistan". In the summer of 1964, three of us, all Captains, decided to take the land route to Quetta to attend a course of instruction. Since the main road over Sukkhar and Sibi was flooded due to heavy monsoon rain, we took a detour via Dera Ghazi Khan, Loralai and Ziarat. Most of the way, the road was just shingle or a dirt track. At times, we had to drive through watercourses that usually remained dry but during the rainy season were often closed for hours because of flash floods. On a couple of occasions, the villagers had to literally lift our car to take it across. Accepting money in return for their services was for them against their tradition of hospitality. Similarly in Ziarat, which gained fame as Jinnah's favourite resort and hosts the world's largest juniper forest, preserving its reputation as a tourist-friendly place, we learnt that no one there ever stole or cheated. The staff at the Loralai Frontier Corps mess, where we arrived unannounced, seemed shell-shocked. They probably had never hosted three dishevelled army officers riding a rickety Austin. Indeed, they gave us three of their best rooms and asked some notables from the city to join us for a delicious feast. We arrived two days late for the course, but in the meantime, the news of our cross-country safari had spread across town.

Quetta was a young officers' paradise. Most of them were on a training course, and after the rigours of the day, were to be found in the city in the evening. Since the messes in our schools of instruction were notorious for their limited cuisine, the good number of outstanding food outlets in the town was an added attraction. That, combined with the smugglers' market, had many of us seeking bank loans.

I returned many times thereafter, especially because it is the home of the famous Command and Staff College. For those of us who became involved with Afghan affairs, Quetta was almost as important as Peshawar. If it was because of Balochistan that I was smitten by wanderlust, I cannot say, but I did travel the length and breadth of the province, mostly in my free time and often with my family. In the process, I learnt to respect the solemn Baloch and admire the vibrant Hazara. The latter, though a miniscule Shiite community in Pakistan and Afghanistan, still stood out in education and in sports. Even the diminutive Makranis from the southern coastal areas produced some world-class wrestlers, boxers and footballers. All of them are very mobile communities. There are many times more Balochis in the rest of the country than there are in Balochistan. The Pashtuns are indeed the most enterprising and, like the Sikhs from India, are found everywhere at home and abroad. In those days, most of our army units got their canteen contractors from Pishin, a small town north of Quetta and one of the few green patches in this arid and parched landscape. So scarce is water in most parts of the province that in drier years we went riding on the bed of the Hanna Lake, not far from the Staff

College. As if this ethnic and sectarian potpourri in a town of barely an odd million (before the influx of Afghan refugees) was not amply impressive, Quetta also claimed a significant religious diversity. The Parsis ran a profitable pharmaceutical concern, the Marker Alkaloids, and our favourite general store was Hindu-owned. Of course, no place in Pakistan is free of a significant Punjabi presence. Still called "settlers" after over a century of existence in Balochistan, they monopolised many businesses. In the meat market, one was better served if one spoke Punjabi.

I must admit that it took me a long time to realise that there was plenty of unrest simmering under the surface.

Present-day Pakistani Balochistan is an artificial construct and yet another victim of the unwise policies of our officialdom. To tame a diverse country by what it fatuously calls "mainstreaming", it imposed its chaotic order on well-run and benign states like Swat and Bahawalpur—and FATA may well be next on its hit list to bring about uniformity. The lumping together of the three *Baluchistans* from British times into the present-day hybrid proved disastrous, both politically and administratively.

The founder of Pakistan and its first ruler, Mohammad Ali Jinnah, cognisant of its peculiar history and having often pleaded the cause of Balochis during the British period, adopted the area as "his own charge", and promised fundamental reforms to address its problems. However, he died soon after the Partition and when the area was formally granted the status of a province in 1970, the ethnic and tribal mix spread over a large area with poor infrastructure presented some daunting challenges. An elected assembly in Balochistan, even if some of its members have formal political affiliations, consists of individuals representing distinct clans. To prevent them from creating trouble, almost all of them have to be included in the provincial government. Such top-heavy regimes obviously cannot deliver on the developmental needs of the people.

It may be a ruler's nightmare but Balochistan is a geo-strategist's dream. It is a vast area, demographically diverse, with topography varying from high arid mountains to deserts and coastal areas, sparsely populated, rich in mineral resources, and located on the southern fringes of a region which has witnessed many versions of the Great

Game. Understandably, it has attracted foreign interest and intervention. With Afghanistan in the north having become the centre of world attention, the province has clearly acquired more importance.

The proximity of its coastal areas to the Strait of Hormuz provides special linkages with the south-eastern regions of the Arabian Peninsula. Oman, in particular, has a sizable Baloch population. Oman once owned the port of Gwadar and surrounding areas till they were acquired by Pakistan in 1958. Iran has, adjacent to Pakistani Balochistan, its own Baloch province with which it has ethnic and sectarian issues. That has at times led to acrimony between the two countries.

Its subsoil holds a substantial portion of Pakistan's energy resources, accounting for 36 per cent of its total gas production. It also has large quantities of coal, gold, copper, silver, platinum, aluminium, and uranium, and is a potential transit zone for pipelines that may one day transport natural gas from Iran and Turkmenistan to India. The coastline provides Pakistan with an exclusive economic zone potentially rich in oil and gas. Two of Pakistan's three naval bases, Ormara and Gwadar, are situated on this coast. The exploitation of these assets, especially in an under-developed region, needs investment of both financial and human capital from the more developed parts of the country, and from abroad. Nowhere are these anomalies simple to reconcile. In Balochistan, they have resulted in a power play between external powers and created an unusual predicament for the locals. They want development but suspect that the outsiders would benefit more from their natural resources and, over time, the small Balochi population would become a minority on its own territory.

The foreign interest in Balochistan is not only because of its minerals. In fact, the real significance of this area lies in its geo-strategic location. In conjunction with Afghanistan, a landlocked country, Balochistan with its multiple port facilities on the Indian Ocean provides an ideal foothold for the US and its western allies to position themselves for the so-called "New Great Game", originally a battle for the Central Asian hydrocarbon resources but now increasingly about the global balance of power.

The rise of China most certainly is an important factor. To meet its galloping energy needs China has been investing in the Central Asian oil and gas fields for nearly two decades. It therefore views the

American presence in the area post-9/11 with considerable concern. The US and India on the other hand have always been wary of China's close relations with Pakistan. Now that China has helped develop a deep-sea port at Gwadar, with its potential to be linked with the Chinese Xingjian province through an ambitious road and railway project, the CPEC, the game is entering a more serious phase. Gwadar, before one forgets, is rather conveniently located to receive oil shipments from the Gulf States and Iran. Chinese have also been working on some mega mining projects in places like Saindak and Reko Dic (both located at the tri-junction with Iran and Afghanistan) that have large reserves of gold and copper. Understandably, attempts against the Chinese working in Balochistan are often regarded as sponsored by America or India.

Iran is another important factor in the power games in this area, inter alia because of its uneasy relationship with the US. Jundullah, a Balochi militant group with its roots in Pakistan, initially came into being due to Iran's conflict with its Sunni Balochis in the Siestan Region. As US-Iran relations soured, and especially when Iran and Pakistan contemplated working together on a gas pipeline, the militia started receiving support from the US. After 9/11, the two neighbours have worked together to reduce its operational effectiveness. Iran, like Pakistan, has serious apprehensions about the Western military presence in Afghanistan. Together with the American influence in the Arab countries, it presents a two-flanked threat to the Islamic Republic.

India, never very enthusiastic about the (IPI) pipeline project that provided Pakistan with a certain leverage on the flow of gas, has now under American pressure and because of its developing ties with the US, practically lost interest. The idea, once acclaimed as a milestone confidence-building measure (CBM) in the South Asian region, if and when realised would probably exclude India. The long-standing animus between our two countries motivates India to support some dissident Baloch individuals and movements. It operates a wide and well-established intelligence network in the province.

Till 2011, the American presence in Balochistan was quite visible. Most of the U.S. military operations in Afghanistan were launched from Pasni and Dalbandin bases located on Baloch territory. A substantial portion of logistical supplies for the American troops that arrived at the Karachi port were transported over Quetta and Chaman. In fact, the US had an extensive security and intelligence network because of the Taliban sanctuaries in the province, mostly in the Pashtun areas. In the foreseeable future, relations between America, China and Iran are likely to remain uneasy, and therefore the US has been trying to create some local assets with the help of its Indian and Afghan collaborators.

Due to the significance of Balochistan, besides the US, Iran, India and Afghanistan, countries like Russia, Israel, the UK and a few from the Gulf, have also deployed their intelligence tentacles here. Some of them are known to have exploited the unrest in the troubled province to help it break away from the rest of the country.

The state of Pakistan has failed to address some of the legitimate grievances of the Balochis and fallen woefully short of meeting the challenging task of governance. In fact, this task was not easy. The polity is too ethnically splintered, and there are long-standing rivalries amongst the tribes. The area is vast and the scarce infrastructure, physical as well as human, makes the distribution of goods and services a formidable undertaking. That was the logic of why—even though politically imprudent—a commodity produced within the Province, namely gas, came to the people of Balochistan long after the rest of the country had started benefiting from it. The Sardari (fiefdom) system in the Baloch tribes has been a great impediment. The Sardars (chieftains) have no interest in any development and use their sway over their tribes to extort money from the Central Government.

Under such circumstances, a deprived people, especially a proud community like the Baloch would have revolted, even without foreign support. During the last six decades, the Baloch areas have experienced serious uprisings five times. Since the number who took up arms and the affected area were limited, all the uprisings were contained. This inherent inability of the people to wage an effective insurgency has been, perhaps, the main reason that successive Governments found the use of force more practicable than the harder task of providing development across the board. Even in present times, despite powerful foreign forces trying to create dissent and divisions, the number of activists in the breakaway movements may not be more than a few thousand.

All the same, the main reason preventing separation from Pakistan is "no better alternative". Joining Iran or Afghanistan is not an attractive choice, and of course these countries do not desire to annex any part of this area. An independent Balochistan, especially because of its rich potential, is a feasible proposition for some people in the area. Considering, however, that this 'free' country would be a hotbed of international intrigues and therefore dependent on some foreign (read American) protection, remaining part of Pakistan is the preferred option of all but a few.

Balochistan had overwhelmingly supported the creation of Pakistan. Despite the raw deal they have got ever since, that spirit is not completely lost. All the surveys and studies conducted in the area indicate that granting them the autonomy promised under the 1973 constitution would be an acceptable starting point to bring them back in the mainstream.

12

# TERRORISM

## A POLITICAL TOOL OR A TECHNIQUE OF WAR?

Even though the term "terrorism" was first used during the 'reign of terror' unleashed during the French Revolution in 1792, the phenomenon has existed in all ages. One of its earliest practitioners is believed to be Hassan bin Sabah, who in 11<sup>th</sup> century Iran used to get his followers high on hashish to go on a killing spree. All of us were thus familiar with the "T" word but the first time I seriously thought about it was in the wake of the Kashmiri uprising in the early 1990s. With the Soviet Union in its death throes, the sole surviving superpower was toying with the idea of resuming its love affair with India. To prove its sincerity, the US was asked to get rid of its Cold War infatuation with Pakistan. We were warned to stop hobnobbing with the Kashmiri insurgents or else we might be declared a "state sponsoring terrorism". I was the DGISI at that time and our own lobbyist in Washington was sent to convey the message.

Luckily, the civil and military leadership at that time had more spine, and the messenger was told that it was he who was being paid to take care of such irritants. Six months later, we were sounded out that if we rolled back our nuclear programme Pakistan might be taken off the 'terrorism watch list'. We knew how the US played these cat and mouse games and how to respond. That was also my first lesson about the use of the "T card" to achieve a political objective, defanging our nuclear programme in this case.

In 1997, I was invited to Germany to take part in a conference on the "new forms of terrorism". These, I learnt, included money laundering, organised crime, and cyber terrorism. To justify my presence, I had to talk about 'Sectarian Terrorism in Pakistan'. There was a strong contingent from Israel and the US, which included one Yossef Bodansky, an Israeli-American who was the director of an organization that called itself the Congressional Task Force on Terrorism and Unconventional Warfare of the US House of Representatives. "Terrorism" as a tool of business was to become very profitable in the course of time.

An Israeli Major-General, probably an intelligence hand, said something quite interesting during one of the sessions. He claimed that the Shiite suicide bombers were so effective that the Jewish state was seeking a *fatwa* from Sunni religious scholars against this practice. This should have alerted me to the use of this "tactic" in asymmetric warfare. The most useful information that I carried home from this conference was an affirmation by an Austrian scholar that the state committed more terror than the non-state actors (NSAs).

Despite all the clamour about the T factor over the last many decades, ask anyone to explain it and the chances are that you will draw a blank. We all believe we know what it is but still struggle to define it. This reminds me of an American judge who, when asked to describe "pornography", admitted that he could not, but "would recognise it when he saw it". Nevertheless, there were times when attempts at decoding this marvel were seriously pursued, along with finding a generally acceptable definition. I vaguely recall that it was the US State Department that once wrote of "deliberately targeting non-combatants to achieve a political objective". It was a sound and succinct way of describing terrorism, and more or less "the minimum common denominator" in most such efforts.

No wonder that the quest had to be abandoned. States have also been targeting non-combatants, in fact more than the non-state actors have. It would have made America the leading terrorist entity for nuking Hiroshima and Nagasaki, bombing civilians in Iraq and Afghanistan, and endless other acts. Britain's bombardment of Dresden in World War II was a quintessential act of terror. Uri Avnery, an Israeli peace activist, makes the same points on this subject and gives some of the same examples in *The Reign of Absurdiocy*.[6]

Unlike the search for a consensus on the definition, discourse on state terrorism was not abandoned till 9/11. Then the US took charge and got the *state* immunity from the tag. Hereafter, only NSAs could be called "terrorist", although states on the "wrong side", Pakistan and Iran, for example, but never India or Israel, could still be hauled up for "sponsoring terrorism". In fact, a state may now declare any dissident group, even if it is fighting an oppressive regime or resisting occupation, "terrorist", and all its actions against this nuisance become kosher. Consequently, terrorism as a label is now an invaluable instrument of state policy.

I have argued elsewhere in this book that India prefers to maintain the status quo in its relations with Pakistan. Confident in the knowledge that there are no concrete criteria on which to prove that cross-border terrorism has been purged (and even if there were, a terrorist act could always be stage-managed to refute the claim), India uses the "elimination of terrorism" as a political ploy, a pre-condition to improve relations, and thus to keep bilateral ties frozen.

Sir Hillary Synott was a former British High Commissioner in Pakistan. He later resigned from an assignment in Iraq in protest against his Government's policy. In 2004, speaking at a conference in the UK he called terrorism a technique. As a soldier, I was gratified that a civilian, too, understood this aspect of warfare. Years later, I learnt that a military man, the American General William Odom, had also stated, on C-Span, that "terrorism was a tactic and we [were] not going to win the war against it". I recall that after 9/11 when we decided to wage a "war on terrorism", with GWOT as its unsexy acronym, some people were wondering how we were going to fight an abstract noun. Since then, the challenge has become more daunting: how does one fight "a technique of war"? Normally, when fighting social ills like ignorance, bigotry, even terrorism, we should be declaring a crusade or Jihad—of course in their exalted sense of a virtuous struggle. But since both these terms provoke religious sensitivities, courtesy of the Clash of Civilisations, their usage is now politically incorrect. Perforce, we have to continue to wage a "war on terror". So there is no harm in looking at this phenomenon in the context of war.

Even in wars between conventional armies, as in the examples quoted above, of Hiroshima, Nagasaki and Dresden, non-combatants have been deliberately targeted. (The Indo-Pak wars of 1965 and 1971 were amongst the honourable exceptions.) But in asymmetric wars, waged between the state and the non-state actors (now defined as 4th or 5th generation warfare), this technique is nearly unavoidable. In fact, the NSAs who lack the ability to hurt the state security forces have no choice but to go for soft targets. In this contest, the dice are heavily loaded in their favour.

Anti-terrorist operations are the most complex forms of sub-conventional warfare.[7] Compared to fighting insurgents, partisans, and resistance movements, we have far less experience in combating those who were once called "urban guerillas" and now "terrorists". Counter-terrorism therefore remains a largely unexplored discipline. While we have developed fairly workable doctrines to fight other forms of small wars, against the terrorists we only have some broad principles: good intelligence, the ability to act with speed, and trying to win over "hearts and minds". A cursory look at the advantages that the terrorists enjoy over the state explains the problematic of developing effective counter-terrorism techniques.

To believe that the main objective of terrorists is "to terrorise people" is at best an over-simplification—actually a disingenuous argument. The welfare of the general population may not be uppermost in a terrorist's mind, but a hostile environment is not exactly in his interest. But then it is also true that if creating chaos best serves their purpose—that may range from targeting a section of the society to discrediting a state or the supra-state order—the terrorists have no qualms about disturbing public life. That gives them their first big advantage, which is access to almost unlimited number of soft targets. Since they operate clandestinely in small groups, at times even individually, they are hard to detect and be dealt with. Even when an odd person or a group is compromised, the network survives.

The terrorists also have no time and often no space constraints. They know that their goals cannot be achieved in a short time. Not infrequently, as in our sectarian strifes, their wars are eternal. They can therefore pick at will their targets, locations, and timings. Such freedom of action is not enjoyed by any of the other sub-conventional warriors, and it also explains the terrorists' higher success and lower detection rate as compared with the militants of other categories.

Terrorism in some form may have existed in earlier times too, but at present, it has achieved extraordinary dimensions. Grievances also led the oppressed or the weak in the past to perform militant acts, but recent developments have provided them more effective means to commit them. Better and more lethal weapons are now available to almost everyone, so are improved methods to transport personnel, goods, and messages. More importantly, the state no longer has a monopoly or handle over these means. That makes the terrorists of today at least as mobile, and often more flexible, than the security forces.

Being more often the perpetrator or the initiator of an action, the NSAs remain a step ahead of their adversaries. All of us can now move across international borders more easily, including terrorists, often interacting with others of their ilk or with their sympathizers. That has added a new dimension to this spectacle, aptly called "international terrorism", inevitably leading the states under threat to improve mutual cooperation and coordination. Such actions became all the more desirable after the Second World War when the two blocks, the Communist East and the Capitalist West, encouraged terrorism in countries on the other side and organised counter measures in client states. Once again, it was the terrorist groups that networked better than the states.

In theory, globalisation helps both officialdom and the citizenry to transcend state frontiers. In practice, individuals can do it better. A fugitive can, even without permission from the recipient country, cross inter-state borders. Security forces cannot. Even when permitted to do so, they will not have full freedom to pursue their target, a prerogative that no host country was likely to abdicate, not willingly at least. Monies can always be moved easier than human beings. Money laundering thus became an effective tool to help terrorists all over the globe. States can try to keep track of such movement but other than freezing suspect accounts there is little they can do.

These are the odds, and the list is by no means exhaustive, against which the state and its security apparatus must work to fight the terrorists. To add to their discomfiture, the main tool available to the state for this messy task, Intelligence, has some genuine limitations.

Intelligence is an inexact science and often an abstract art. Under optimum conditions it can give a fairly accurate big picture. But even against a more visible conventional target all that it promises is "no strategic surprise". Once the battle is joined, the real picture is only possible through technical means, which are, in turn, susceptible to jamming, deception, and misinterpretation. Obviously, the prospects of tracking down nebulous terrorists are even less promising. Sustained good work will help us gain plenty of useful information regarding their network. Preempting, even preventing, a terrorist act would often be a matter of luck.

The effectiveness of the other tool, the one used to strike against the terrorist—*kinetic action*, to use a postmodern term—is also limited. Faced with an evasive enemy, possessing skimpy and rarely real-time information, and pushed for time and success, the state tends to make up for these deficiencies by using massive force. The objective may or may not be achieved but some unintended destruction of life and property is almost unavoidable. This is called "collateral damage", and has in the meantime become a cover for all honest and culpable lapses of the security apparatus. The real damage that it does is much more than what can be seen on ground, or, for that matter, measured in the aftermath. It provides the opposition additional ammunition to alienate masses from the government and recruit volunteers.

Over time, the NSAs have discovered the "ultimate weapon". The human being embraces most of the attributes desired in a perfect weapon system. He can carry a warhead and manoeuvre his way around obstacles, is hard to detect and intercept, can identify the target, choose the time to release his lethal cargo, and, if needed, abort the mission even at the last moment. There still remains the matter of motivating him to make the ultimate sacrifice. Depending upon the individual, money, a worthwhile cause, and indoctrination, are some of the tools available. In military terms too, it is cost-effective: the loss of many foes in exchange for just one of their own, with terror as the collateral or, in fact, the real benefit.

Looking at terrorism as a war-fighting technique may also explain its ever-expanding practice, especially from the time we declared "war" on it. However, in view of the high stakes, and considering how heavily the cards are stacked against us, we can no longer remain stuck with a debate on how to fight a *tactic of war*, but have to get on with how best to fight those who practice it. The following are a few thoughts that might help to do that.

# TERRORISM

The wisdom behind the Geneva Convention is the recognition of a reality. Since mankind is not likely to give up war, it might as well fight according to some decent norms. There are also some mundane reasons to have clearly defined rules of engagement.

The combatants now know what rights and obligations they are entitled to if taken prisoner. In desperate situations, they might therefore be more willing to give up hopeless resistance and save unnecessary loss of life. Once in the enemy's custody, enabling them to communicate with their friends and relatives serves a humanitarian purpose. When permitted to receive provisions from specified sources, it provides relief both to the captor and the captive. Another factor is perhaps even more important.

The ultimate aim of war is lasting peace. But that can only happen when those at war today become friends tomorrow. Towards that end, it helps to observe civilised norms when fighting wars. Peace and tranquility are also the objectives when a state conducts unconventional operations. Putting down insurgencies, fighting partisans, and rooting out terrorism differ in many respects. Insurgents are largely our own countrymen. Partisans usually resist a foreign occupation. And terrorists of today are not inhibited by national boundaries and local aspirations. It has therefore been difficult to evolve clearly defined rules of engagement for any of them, besides uniform rules for all.

When the adversaries—insurgents, dissidents, even terrorists—are our own nationals and enjoy support or sympathy from a faction of population, the state should not, and often does not, give up the option of a negotiated solution. That confers on the other side the status of a "worthy opponent" who, when the time is right, might have an incentive to reach a political settlement. The insurgents of Northern Ireland were accused of acts of terrorism for over three decades but the doors of negotiations were not closed on Sinn Fein. The results were a truce and prospects for peace.

Then there are other examples where the state resisted or refused to talk to the resistance groups because they were "terrorists". Ultimately, when the cost of repression clearly exceeded its returns, the state had to relent. In principle, finding peaceful ways to resolve conflicts is preferable, but humans do not work on the basis of logic alone: emotions play a leading role. One would expect a state to be less emotive, but the complicated state system usually comes up with a halfway solution at best. That perhaps explains why decades are required to defeat insurgencies.

The matter becomes even more complicated when more than one state is involved with the same terrorist organisation or network. If one of the states, presumably the worst affected or more benign one, wished to open a dialogue with the terrorists, the other(s) would accuse it of capitulation or appeasement. Many of our initiatives to talk to our "terrorists" were subverted by the US, our so-called ally in GWOT (some instances given in Chapter 15). All the same, no wise enemies ever close the back channels.

Assuming that, in the present environment, the conventional counterterrorism tactics were to continue, that these were to fail in combating terrorism or even result instead in its proliferation, our last option, if we were still interested in eliminating this menace, may well be a semantic one. But before that, let me explain what I mean by "semantic terrorism". The astute use of terminology can influence perceptions, which are always more important than reality.

To explain, one may start with "Fundamentalism". The Christian Fundamentalists of the early twentieth century, stressed a literal interpretation of the Bible. "Islamic Fundamentalism", on the other hand, as described by scholars like Olivier Roy and John Esposito, is more about the "opposition to the perceived corrupting influence of the Western culture" and about "Islamic revivalism". Even Bernard Lewis, hardly ever accused of sympathy for anything Islamic, considers the use of this term ("Fundamentalism") "unfortunate and misleading" in the Islamic context. In one German think-tank, the use of this term was once taboo.

However, the "terminology tyrants" not only use it, they also associate it with "political activism, extremism, fanaticism, terrorism, and anti-Americanism" (Esposito again). Any Islamic movement that makes them uncomfortable can thus be conveniently reviled as "fundamentalist". Aping them, we in Pakistan have followed suit. Anyone even remotely suggesting that the religion might provide an answer or two to some of our recurring confusion is now labelled a "Fundo".

Jihad, like a "crusade", was a concept that described having the fortitude to fight social ills, like ignorance, illiteracy, and bigotry. The use of arms indeed had its place, especially—some would say, exclusively—in self-defence. But not beyond that. The mere mention of the J word can now send chills up many a spine. No one even dare suggest that Jihad might also be waged without arms, and this is its most sublime form. The UN may sanction armed resistance against foreign occupation, but if waged in the name of Jihad, it must be condemned, and a Jihadi prosecuted as a terrorist.

Indeed, "terrorism" is the latest and the deadliest phase in this game of "give the dog a bad name and hang him". There were times one could sensibly discuss this phenomenon to distinguish it from a fight for freedom, but not any more. After 9/11, Chechens, Uyghur, Hamas, Hezbollah, Kashmiris, and indeed militants of all hues, once they get labelled "terrorist", have become fair game. The injunction, "strike terror into the hearts of your enemies and those who are the enemies of Allah", was once merely the religious equivalent of deterrence. Now many people in the West actually believe that the Islamic concept of Jihad was based on terrorism. Madrassas may have contributed only 17 per cent of all Muslim terrorists according to Professor Pape of the US, but many of our pseudo-liberals continue to call them "nurseries of terrorism". When asked to suggest reforms, most can think of nothing better than equipping them with computers. I am sure, in due course, Madrassas will come to be blamed for the increase in "cyber terrorism".

According to Phil Rees, a film maker who has made documentaries on terrorists, or as he calls them, "militants", "If we don't want to describe Britain and America as terrorist nations, then the only principled alternative is to purge the word from the lexicon". Let no one be called a "terrorist". One would be surprised at the positive effect there would be if the name-calling were to stop.

Since terrorism has survived through the ages, is it possible that it is part of human nature? As children, we were afraid of the "bully on the block". When the local *badmash*, a strongman, terrifies the neighbourhood, we want someone to do the same to him. Deep inside, we relish the thought that the others live in fear of us. Maybe terrorism is merely a more radical version of this desire. But that is a subject for social scientists and psychologists to examine. It is difficult to discuss it under the present environment in which, more than anyone else, we have terrorised ourselves.

# 13

# AFGHANISTAN

## THE BERMUDA TRIANGLE OF THE EAST

Arnold Toynbee, the famous historian, described Afghanistan as the *"eastern crossroads of history"*. Located at the meeting point of the Middle East, Central Asia, and the South Asian subcontinent, the territory has been frequently trampled and violated by raiders and migrants who came to plunder, conquer, or inhabit India. But that was before the birth of Afghanistan. After 1747, the year Ahmed Shah Durrani united tribes and communities to create this country, this former highway became a quagmire for the invaders. Toynbee might as well have called it the Eastern Bermuda Triangle, as this is the land that consumes empires, and many of those who happen to be in the neighbourhood. The reasons for this are not too difficult to figure out.

All possible fault lines—geographic, demographic, tribal, even sectarian and cultural—run through this country. It became a political entity through a grand bargain amongst its components and it is that alone which holds it together. More important, it cannot be dominated unless all its major centres of resistance are overpowered. That explains the pattern that is so familiar to us by now. An aggressor faces little resistance from a conventional Afghan army but fails to subdue the tribesmen who have mastered the art of unconventional warfare. When the first British-Indian expeditionary force reached Kabul in 1842, the

Khan of Kalat famously quipped, "And how will they get out of there?" They could not get out, in fact, not because of any mighty army, but because the local militias inflicted upon the force death by a thousand cuts. Of course, Britain, the sole superpower of that time, had to save face. It took revenge by undertaking another incursion and bribed its way to Kabul and back.

At the turn of the twentieth century, the Russian and British Empires were poised for an epic battle for influence in the region, famously called the Great Game. The clash was averted, not least because of the sagacity of the Afghan Emirs. Afghanistan got the role of a buffer between the Empires, but had to cede some areas to British India. In 1893, the Indo-Afghan border was redefined and named the Durand Line. Slightly modified by the Anglo-Afghan Treaty of 1919, it was inherited by Pakistan in 1947.

## The Af-Pak Era Kicks in

Pak-Afghan relations had an inauspicious start. Kabul was reluctant to accept the border imposed by an imperial power as the interstate boundary. Nevertheless, it found a modus vivendi. The Durand Line had legitimacy under international law and the population on both sides was comfortable with the status quo. Moreover, Afghanistan's land access to the outside world was almost exclusively through Pakistan, making it heavily dependent on the latter's goodwill for foreign trade and, being an arid country with few natural resources, for most of its worldly needs. Afghanistan thus had legitimate interest in the well-being of the country that provided it with strategic depth, Pakistan. This was amply demonstrated during the 1965 and 1971 wars that we fought against India. King Zahir Shah offered to ensure all remained quiet on the western front while Pakistan moved its forces to the eastern.

## The Soviet Invasion

When the Soviet Union invaded and occupied Afghanistan in December 1979, Pakistan lost the buffer in the west, and with India aligned with the Soviet Union to the east, was now, so to speak, caught in the jaws of a nutcracker. The decision by Zia-ul-Haq, the military ruler, to provide covert help to the Afghan resistance was prompt but risky. There was no assurance of any substantial support from outside. Inaction, however, would have let the Soviets consolidate on the Durand Line (as the Russians had done, nearly a century ago, along the Oxus) and, at an opportune moment, resume their advance southwards. However, the traditional Afghan penchant for waging protracted wars against foreign aggressors afforded some hope that, in due course, the occupation could be rolled back. Two years later, when the US and its camp followers joined the Jihad, the chances improved.

As Pakistan was already involved with the Mujahedeen, the ISI was the most appropriate agency to coordinate all logistic support to the resistance. The US sanctions imposed on Pakistan because of our nuclear programme were, therefore, circumvented through a legislative provision, the Pressler Amendment. Besides receiving substantial military and economic aid, Pakistan was now also a frontline ally of the powerful Western alliance. The Afghan resistance became more effective, and, when Gorbachev assumed power in the Soviet Union, Moscow decided to vacate the Soviet occupation by mid-February 1989.

The Afghan resistance could rightly claim credit, as could some others like Pakistan and the US, who provided crucial support. However, those like Brzezinski who claim to have *lured* the Soviets into the Afghan quagmire were being disingenuous at best. The confusion that prevailed in the Western corridors of power (including Brzezinski's flip-flop), have been brilliantly documented by the Greek historian, Panagiotis Dimitrakis, in his book, *The Secret War in Afghanistan*. The Americans dragged their feet over the provision of critical weapon systems like the Stingers, which suggests they had not really prepared any sort of trap. If there was one indeed, considering that the Soviets had a good chance of securing a firm foothold in this key region, it could well have backfired. But, of course, success has many fathers.

The events that followed the Soviet withdrawal amply reflect the complexity of the Afghan state, as well as the character of its people. The ensuing turmoil in Afghanistan was proof enough that Zia's proposal to form an interim setup before the Soviets withdrew was eminently sensible. The formula he offered—equal shares for the resistance, for the Soviet legatees in Kabul (the PDPA regime), and for the

Afghan diaspora—was fair, even generous. Prospects for its implementation were, however, bleak. The Mujahedeen did not support it because, as the victors, they wanted a larger cut. The Soviets could not wait long enough for this arrangement to take shape and the US was not interested, while the new regime in Islamabad, installed by Zia himself, was eager to prove that it could defy its military godfather. Prime Minister Junejo called an All Parties Conference in 1987, and won its endorsement for the Geneva Accord sans any agreement on the transfer of power in Kabul or the supply of weapons to the PDPA and the Mujahedeen. There was now a good chance that the withdrawal of the occupation forces would be followed by a civil war with the throne of Kabul as the prize. It would look more like the Afghan game of Buzkushi—in which the trophy is a dead goat.

## Post-Soviet Afghanistan

To pre-empt this worst-case scenario, or at least to minimise the damage if it were inevitable, the ISI persuaded the Seven-Party Alliance that had spearheaded the resistance to coalesce as the Afghan Interim Government (AIG). It was expected that Pakistan would recognise it, and, with some others following suit, this disparate group would eventually become the legitimate regime in Kabul. However, the Ministry of Foreign Affairs was of the view that to claim recognition, the AIG had to have a foothold in Afghanistan. This led to a pitched battle around Jalalabad, for which the Mujahedeen were ill-organised and untrained.

After the debacle, Prime Minister Benazir Bhutto ordered a review of the country's Afghan Policy. Some from the old guard argued that a policy that had seen off the mighty Soviet Union needed to be continued till the PDPA regime too was defeated. But then it is a fundamental principle of military teaching that when the situation has substantially changed, the existing plans must be re-evaluated. A team was constituted, with Ashraf Jahangir Qazi, the then Additional Secretary for Afghanistan in the MFA (later an illustrious Ambassador and the UN's special envoy for Iraq); Jahangir Karamat, the DGMO and in due course our Army Chief; and myself as the DGMI, to carry out the review. The findings were pretty sobering and the effort was, therefore, well worth its while. Ironically, for want of an agreement on an alternative, it could only recommend the continuation of the current strategy, if anything with more vigour. "AIG to get its act together, the military operations to be better coordinated, and the ISI to be more innovative in pursuit of a political solution", were its salient recommendations. The consensus that the AIG did not enjoy sufficient support in Afghanistan and therefore needed to become more inclusive was perhaps the most useful outcome of this exercise. To follow-up on the commission's advice, over the next two years the ISI undertook a number of initiatives.

In September 1990, I, now head of the ISI, flew to Garam Chasma (the famous hot springs about a hundred kilometres north of Chitral), where Ahmed Shah Massoud, the legendary resistance commander had his base camp. I persuaded him to come to Peshawar and meet some other prominent field commanders. The idea was to form a high-level council to more effectively coordinate military operations. Besides Massoud, the other prominent members were Ismael Khan, an illustrious Jihadi leader and the unchallenged warlord of Herat, Jalal-ud-din Haqqani, whose faction was to acquire worldwide fame (or notoriety, depending on your point of view) a decade later, and Abdul Haq, reportedly America's first choice to head the interim regime after it reclaimed Afghanistan in 2001. The rivalry between the Jamaat-e-Islami led by Burhan-ud-Rabbani (Massoud's party leader) and Gulbudin Hekmatyar's Hezb-e-Islami was always a serious matter. In Massoud's presence, the two bigwigs agreed to mend fences. Indeed, none of these smart measures had any real chance of succeeding with the Afghans, who follow their own logic.

To broaden the AIG's base, as was most emphatically recommended by the review, the ISI reached out to some eminent Afghan factions that were not part of the Jihadi coalition.

An envoy was sent to King Zahir Shah in Rome with a concrete proposal (Hamid Karzai, later the President of Afghanistan, had a significant part in this initiative). We believed that the exiled King could play a role in restoring peace and stability in Afghanistan and hence offered to help him establish a foothold in Quetta, a city close to Kandahar (his traditional constituency) and within the Durrani territory of Balochistan. It would then be up to him to mobilise his followers and present himself as the unifying figure that he once was. There was no real assurance of the success of this plan, as some powerful figures among the Mujahedeen were opposed to the monarchy. The king's refusal had less to do with his advanced years than with the prospect of likely failure and the ensuing embarrassment the former Royal was not prepared to face. For once, I wished he had the thick skin of a Pakistani politician.

In April 1991, I went to Geneva to meet Colonel General Ghulam Faruq Yaqubi, a police general and, as head of Ministry of State Security, something like my counterpart in Kabul. The idea was to make an assessment of how tenaciously the PDPA regime wished to hang on to what obviously looked like an untenable position. Though the Mujahedeen had largely failed to dislodge Najeebullah's forces from their fortified positions, the latter remained confined to a few big cities while the resistance controlled the countryside. As any military expert knows, the side that enjoys the freedom of manoeuvre ultimately wins the war. This being our first meeting, no breakthrough was expected, more so since Yaqubi was escorted by a political commissar, in the Soviet style. When I learnt that he, like many Afghan police officers, had been trained in Germany, I suggested we have a bilateral meeting conducted in German. If he was uncomfortable with the offer, he did not show it. My plan did not work, because though the two of us went in a side room, all that the poor man was allowed to do was to write down what I said and was not allowed to respond. It was hard to judge if he was a cautious intelligence man or one constrained by the system. Years later, a learned erstwhile colleague, the late Colonel Yahyah Effendi (probably our best hand on the region, who had a long and productive stint with the ISI), told me that even this careful conduct did not find much favour with his patrons in Moscow.

We, on the other hand, had plenty of room to act freely. I had not informed any of my political or military bosses before this meeting. Kabul, however, leaked the information and, by the time I returned, many relevant quarters had learnt about it. The AIG leaders were pretty sanguine, the Foreign Office a little curious, and the Army Chief, in fact, quite appreciative. Our American partners though were deeply dismayed. Only a few months back, Ghulam Ishaq Khan had dismissed a government (that of Benazir Bhutto in her first incarnation) without informing them, let alone seeking their blessings. And now this: an ISI initiative they had only learnt about from the Afghans! Obviously, the Pakistanis had no idea that the US would soon be the sole surviving superpower. (Even if we did, in the vain belief that we had played a key role in vanquishing the other, outgoing superpower, I would not have sought America's permission for the Geneva mission.) In my briefing to Prime Minister Nawaz Sharif, also attended by Beg and a representative of the Foreign Office, I was asked what was to come next, after my encounter with Yaqubi. I suggested a meeting with Najeeb, except that as the Head of State, he was unlikely to meet me in a safe house. If non-recognition of his regime prevented an overt contact, I could do it covertly but only with the Government's permission. I never heard about it thereafter.

As part of the process to explore new avenues, some known members of the Afghan diaspora were consulted. I do not recall if any fresh ideas emerged from these rounds, except that they all offered their services if and when the situation in Kabul became conducive.

Khost, a small town next to North Waziristan, fell in April 1991. The story of its conquest graphically explains Afghan gamesmanship. Situated in a valley surrounded by the Haqqani militia (a decade later exalted to the status of a network), the township was tenuously held by the PDPA troops. For its capture, the ISI had provided money and weapons more than once, but indeed the elder Haqqani had no intentions of killing the goose that laid the golden eggs. When told that this was the last package he would get for Khost, he knew that the ploy had run its course. He bribed the garrison, staged a mock fight, and facilitated its escape. In the broader context of the post-Soviet standoff between the Mujahedeen and the army of the PDPA, the two sides had learnt to share guns and butter to ensure that the supplies both from Moscow and Islamabad kept coming.

In the meantime, it had become amply clear that the two countries that had provided substantial support during the Jihad, the US and Saudi Arabia, could no longer be counted upon to help resolve the Afghan imbroglio.

Much has been made of the US abandoning the region after the Soviet withdrawal, thus precipitating a civil war that provided space to Al-Qaeda and some others of its ilk. To be fair, the Americans had warned us in good time that they would leave (at the latest when the

Soviets pulled out); that their involvement in Afghanistan was not open-ended; and, of course, that they would be back to punish Pakistan for enriching uranium under the cover of being a 'frontline state'. American reluctance to remain stuck with a faraway country's travails was understandable. They also had no obligation to do so. Moreover, there was precious little that the US could do to restore stability in Afghanistan. In fact, it would have been yet another meddling power with an agenda, political or ideological, not in sync with regional interests. During the resistance, it may not have openly taken sides, but thereafter it was quite obvious that even a disengaging America continued to patronise certain groups and individuals. Massoud and Abdul Haq were but two of the familiar names. To help restore stability, we needed an honest broker and the US was not likely to be one.

The Saudis remained engaged and even though they too had the odd favourite and were quite upset when the AIG leaders did not endorse the Riyadh supported anti-Saddam coalition, they decided to go along with us, but mostly stayed in the background. On the other hand, when we found we were not making any headway with an "Afghan-led and Afghan-owned" formula, we sought relief from whatever passes for 'the international community'.

The OIC had never inspired the belief that it could reconcile disputes between Muslims, be they states or cliques. There was no point, then, in seeking its good offices. At best, if some initiative (such as by the UN) interested the Afghans, the OIC could provide a useful fig leaf. About the UN too, one was no longer sure if it had credibility. During the 1990 Middle East crisis, the world body had acted more like a handmaiden of the sole surviving superpower. All the same, Benon Sevon, the UN special representative for Afghanistan, persuaded Pakistan to give him a chance.

In May 1991, the AIG agreed to grant the UN the lead role, implying they would wait and see what it could come up with. The confidence that the Afghans had in their own ability to scuttle any arrangement they did not like afforded them remarkable flexibility. They could go back on any undertaking, even an oath in the holiest of Islamic shrines. Twice they were taken to Mecca to pledge unity. They abided by their vows only as long as they were on holy soil. Back home it was business as usual. Nevertheless, their endorsement cleared the way for Mr Sevon to start working on a UN sponsored peace plan for Afghanistan.

Pakistan was, in the meantime, gearing up to seek cooperation from another neighbour of Afghanistan. Iran, now free from its war with Iraq, responded positively. The first formal exchange took place in Islamabad with the two Foreign Ministers. The Afghan groups based in Tehran and Peshawar, and the ISI, were also represented. I only attended the evening reception, when Ali Akbar Velayati, the Iranian Foreign Minister, invited me for the second round of talks to be held in the last week of August 1991 in Tehran. By then, we had inducted a faction of the Hizb-e-Wahdat led by Ayatollah Mohseni into the AIG. A member from this party was also included in our delegation led by Mr Akram Zaki, the Secretary-General in the MFA.

The Tehran session had an awkward opening. Afghans who had sought refuge in Iran in the wake of the Soviet invasion were mostly Shias from the Hazara community. Some of their notables formed the *Hizbe Wahdat* ostensibly to wage a war of liberation but, since Iran did not permit any military operations from its soil, their activities were limited. In protest against this policy, Mohseni, a prominent member of the Hizb, relocated his group to Peshawar where the largely Sunni Mujahedeen received them warmly. The Iranian government was obviously upset with the Ayatollah and, when it refused permission for his deputy to take part in the conference, the Pakistani delegation had a problem. Some of the members of the delegation were looking at me accusingly for bringing along a *persona non grata*, and some were imploring me to rescue the situation, depending on their view of the ISI.

Mohsen Rezai was, in those days, the head of the Iranian Revolutionary Guard Corps (IRGC), arguably the most powerful institution created by Imam Khomeini. I had met him on his visits to Pakistan, and even though the Iranian Foreign Ministry had invited us, he asked me to be his guest and stay in a palace that was once the Shah's favourite. I sent him an SOS. He immediately despatched a Brigadier who escorted the unwelcome guest to the table and remained there, just in case. The Iranian faction of *Hizb* staged a token walkout but had the sense to return before the IRGC sent a posse to bring it back. The parleys made no headway, except that we learnt from our hosts how to play hardball. They had already persuaded us in the first round of talks to accept *their* Afghans as being on par with the Peshawar-based Mujahedeen, who, having done all the fighting, were a bit upset. More important, with hardly any ability to influence events in Afghanistan, Tehran insisted that the war-torn country be modelled after post-revolutionary Iran. The call on President Rafsanjani was, however, very rewarding. He advised all participants to make the best of the favourable environment, for which, he said, none of us could claim any credit. He was probably referring to the collapse of the Soviet Union, and telling both the Afghans and the Pakistanis not to exaggerate their contribution. Another round followed in Islamabad, but this really only served to give the trilateral track a decent burial.

Pakistan had not recognised the PDPA regime installed by the Soviets after their invasion in 1979, but still allowed the Afghan embassy in Islamabad to keep its staff and the premises. (I think these diplomatic norms are immensely sensible.) Some time during my MI stint, probably in late 1989, I got a call saying that the "dysfunctional" Defence Attaché of Afghanistan wanted to meet me. The message that he left behind was quite meaningful: "Pakistan wants Najeebullah to hand over power to the Mujahedeen, but who would take over on their behalf?"

By the time I met Yaqubi in Geneva in March 1991, who also said something along the same lines, it was becoming abundantly clear that the AIG had to find an answer to this question. On 6 September 1991, during the Defence Day reception at the JSHQ in Rawalpindi, Benon Sevon walked up to me and put it as clearly as possible: if the Mujahedeen could come up with a consensus formula to assume power in Kabul, Najeebullah was prepared to quit. My team in the ISI had often warned me that if Najeeb left without an arrangement in place to quickly fill the vacuum, the scramble for power would sink Afghanistan in a chaotic civil war. The unspoken operative clause in our Afghan policy, therefore, was that the PDPA regime must survive till the Jihadists agreed on how to replace it.

I left the ISI in the first week of March 1992 and heard a few days later that Najeeb had declared he would abdicate in favour of a Mujahedeen government. What made him state that publicly was his own best kept secret. We never found out, but what followed was its inevitable outcome. Rashid Dostum, head of the feared Jauzjani Militia, was the first to defect, and when some others also jumped from what obviously was a sinking ship, Najeebullah's regime collapsed. Benon Sevon, whose peace project too bowed out along with the fallen president, provided him asylum in the UN's Kabul compound.

# AFGHANISTAN

*A Pyrrhic Victory*

"Think before you make a wish; it may be fulfilled"

a Russian proverb.

In an emergency meeting in Peshawar, the AIG leaders accomplished in three days what had eluded them for three years. An interim coalition was quickly cobbled together. Sibghat Ullah Mujadadi was to head it for the first two months. High up in the religious hierarchy, Hazrat Mujadadi was always the first choice of the Illustrious Seven, probably because as the leader of the smallest party he could do no harm. He would be followed by Professor Burhan-ud-Din Rabbani, the leader of the largest Jihadi party, who was to ensure countrywide elections within two years. The agreement came to be known as the Peshawar Accord. Gulbuddin Hekmatyar left the deliberations halfway when he learnt that Ahmed Shah Massoud, his nemesis and Rabbani's ace commander, was marching on Kabul. Six months later, Hekmatyar was accommodated as Rabbani's Prime Minister through the Islamabad Accord. By that time, Massoud was too well entrenched to let his arch-rival enter the city. The two stalwarts of the resistance destroyed Kabul, which had remained largely unscathed during the Soviet occupation.

Ahmad Shah's dash to Kabul was reminiscent of the Soviets winning the race for Berlin at the end of the Second World War. The consequences for Afghanistan, as in the case of Europe, were equally critical. Whether Pakistan could or should have prevented Massoud from gate-crashing into Kabul will remain a moot point, but the implications of our failure to do so were not lost. Many years later, Pakistan pleaded with the US (in vain) not to let the Northern Alliance enter Kabul after the ouster of the Taliban.

The power struggle in Afghanistan was indeed a matter of great concern for Pakistan, and not only because the two accords it had underwritten had failed to restore peace. The Soviet Union had unravelled and the Central Asian countries were no longer its satellites. Continued turmoil across the Durand Line was now the only hurdle in the fulfilment of our newfound dream, which was access to the region beyond Amu Darya (the Oxus) in pursuit of cultural, historical, economic, and, as some suspected, ideological goals. With no signs of Afghanistan reverting to normalcy any time soon, the quest to find a safe route to the nascent states, who were also keen to find openings in the south, led to some novel ideas. Some time before I left in May 1994 to take up my ambassadorial mission in Germany, General Babar, the Interior Minister in BB's second government, asked me for my opinion. I am not sure if I was the only one who suggested exploring the approach over Kandahar to Herat and then northwards. Since the area was less affected by the civil war, this option seemed feasible. Later that year, when I heard that a trial convoy launched from Quetta was heading north, I was quite excited. A few days later, we learnt that it was stuck in Kandahar. The relief, however, came soon and a group that called itself the Taliban rescued the convoy, which resumed its journey westwards.

## Under the Taliban

Thereafter, the Taliban went places. Anyone who knows anything about entities created by patronage could tell that this was not one of them. It was an indigenous uprising that soon became a mass movement, since the masses were fed up with the infighting amongst the Mujahedeen and their sidekicks. The fact that some powerful warlords like Akhundzada of Helmand, Ismael Khan from Herat, and Hekmatyar in Logar, were all swept away by this tsunami was proof enough that the new militia had popular support.

It was no surprise that the ISI jumped on the Taliban bandwagon. Their ethnic affinity with some Pakistani tribes was less important than the fact that the Pashtuns were finally rallying around a platform. When the Durranis accepted a Ghilzai, Mullah Omar, as their leader, this promised to bridge a chronic intra-Pashtun divide. Indeed, the Kabul regime's failure to honour the Peshawar and Islamabad Accords had lost it Pakistan's goodwill, but it was the fear that a Tajik-led rule could trigger a lasting North-South divide, which probably forced Pakistan to support the Taliban. Though difficult to foresee, there was a faint hope that this fanatically focussed group might succeed in reunifying the country: one of Pakistan's core objectives.

For some time, the Taliban were also wooed by the US and Saudi Arabia, though for different reasons. The movement controlled areas through which UNOCAL, an American/ Saudi enterprise, planned to build a pipeline. In due course, both the countries had a change of heart, probably because Mullah Omar refused to expel Osama bin Laden even though Turki Al Faisal, the Saudi Intelligence Chief, came in person to seek this favour.

There were also reasons to believe that if and when the Taliban reunified the country, and they seemed to be the only ones in a position to do so, the Afghans would get rid of them subsequently. In that society, mullahs could lead prayers, or even wars, but could not dominate peacetime politics (examples to prove this abound on both sides of the Durand Line). Moreover, the Taliban ideology was an anathema to the Afghan society and their imposition of a centralised rule over the tribesmen could not be endured for too long.

The thesis could not be tested, since the Taliban were removed from power before they could reintegrate the North. The Government of Pakistan, probably including the ISI, had made some half-hearted efforts to convince the Taliban that political engagement with the non-Pashtun Northern Alliance would be the better option. Like most of our earlier efforts, this one also fell short. It is possible that persuading Mullah Omar to extradite Bin Laden after 9/11 would have had more success. The fact that he, not quite in keeping with tribal traditions, publicly appealed to his guest to leave the country, and later even showed some inclination to hand him over to a third country, were signs that Pakistan might have prevailed. Of course, it was not possible in the three weeks before the US invasion on 7 October 1999. It was also not what Washington desired. Only a spectacular response like a military invasion could appease American ire.

## Post 9/11

Afghanistan was invaded ostensibly to round up the leadership of Al-Qaeda. Toppling the Taliban regime was incidental to achieving that objective. However, since the means used were primarily air power, population centres, almost exclusively in Pashtun areas, suffered heavily. Even then, it was the Taliban that took the initiative for peace. In early 2002, they approached the Karzai regime—which had in the meantime been installed in Kabul as the protectorate of the occupying powers—hoping for reconciliation. Karzai was, of course, not free to take such a critical decision by himself, and the Pentagon, which was actually in charge, rejected the offer, presumably because the ousted militia no longer mattered. Thereafter, the Taliban had no choice but to start an insurgency that soon became a war of liberation, engulfing Pakistani tribal areas where the people have close ties with Afghans across the border. Supporting the Afghan Taliban, some Pakistanis even joining them, was the natural corollary.

By the time Barack Obama was elected President in 2008, it had become clear that the war against the Taliban was not making any headway. The occupiers, therefore, needed a fresh look at the policy, and the change of guard in Washington could make the transition less painful. The chances improved when, soon after he took change, Obama formed an Afghanistan-Pakistan (Af-Pak) team that had some of the best experts and old hands specialising in the region. When the President announced the new policy on 1 December 2009 at the Officers' Academy, it had all the elements of a good exit strategy. Some optimism seemed in order.

A couple of days before this speech was delivered, I was asked by the BBC to watch it, in order to comment on it soon after. When I was questioned as to why I considered this part of an exit strategy, my explanation was that the military surge, with thirty thousand additional troops, was intended to act as a reserve force, just in case the main thrust of the policy—talking to the Taliban—needed some backup support, or if it failed. I also shared these views with Barnett Rubin, a top hand on Afghanistan, who at that time was Obama's Af-Pak man. My hunch that the plan was likely to be scuttled by the US military was also conveyed to him.

Instead of keeping the reinforcements in reserve, these were immediately launched in battle to weaken the Taliban, so that the US could talk to them from a position of strength. It is a notion that may have become part of our strategic vocabulary and for the militaries an article of faith, but is in fact quite flawed. To start with, what if, in the process, the adversary who was meant to be weakened became stronger? And that is what actually happened. In the years that followed, the Taliban not only controlled more territory but also, having withstood the onslaught, exuded more confidence. Secondly, if the other side had more patience, which the insurgents usually have, even if it suffered losses, the likes of the Taliban would rather withdraw to recover their strength than negotiate with a weak hand. Most importantly, when in a strong position, hardly anyone engages in talks. The US did reject the Taliban's peace offer when the latter were down and nearly out. That the US wanted neither an exit nor a negotiated settlement dawned on me much later.

After failing to reduce the Taliban by military means, another option that the Pentagon tried to exhaust was to raise an Afghan National Army to ensure security in the country. This was one mission the ANA had no chance of accomplishing, mainly because security is not merely a military affair. Within the country, the armed forces can function effectively only under a generally acceptable political framework. This principle applies to Afghanistan perhaps more than anywhere else. Its configuration, physical and political, has helped the Afghans wage piecemeal resistance against the most powerful invaders. Just in case anyone believed that if the foreign forces had failed due to the Afghan penchant to defend their freedom then a national force with its indigenous credentials would be more successful, one only had to recall the post-Soviet plight of the PDPA Army (alluded to earlier in this chapter). Years later, a scholarly American General explained to me that the real purpose behind creating the ANA was to foster national cohesion. Since we in the Pakistan Army also believe in that role, I could empathise with the thought. Of course, ensuring security was another matter. One wondered, therefore, why the US was sinking billions of dollars in a project that had no chance to deliver.

In May 2006, I met a retired American general at Kabul Airport. He said he was the boss of a private company that was training the Afghan Army. To someone who once headed the Training Branch at the GHQ, it sounded a bit weird. Of course, one knew that when a new piece of equipment was inducted in the armed forces, some technical hands from the manufacturers would conduct introductory courses, but I had never heard of private enterprises coaching professionals for war. These soldiers of fortune are more interested in making money. They would rather have their recruits trained badly and get their contract extended, in order to make more money. Defence contractors training and equipping the Afghan military and also building barracks have a huge stake—billions of dollars—in the continued build-up of the ANA. Incidentally, this entrepreneur-general was on the next flight to Islamabad to sell helicopters.

Michael Semple is an Irishman who has spent nearly three decades in our region, mostly in Pakistan, and is the son-in-law of the late Major-General (Retd.) Abubakar Osman Mitha who raised Pakistani Special Forces in the 1950s. In 2007, he was declared *persona non grata* by the Karzai regime for "undesirable activities", and then worked with the odd American institution before taking up a teaching assignment in his home country. When I asked him about the US rationale for building up the ANA, he said (though not in quite these words), a billion-dollar proposal from the Defence Department had a better chance of approval than the millions demanded for schools and hospitals. That reminded me of the insatiable Arab princes who never touched a project that would not bring in a fat commission.

The next step to save Project Afghanistan was for the US to subtly convey that the total withdrawal of combat forces was not on the cards. In May 2012, President Obama descended on Kabul to clinch a "strategic treaty" with Afghanistan. Besides providing long-term assistance to the regime, it stipulated keeping a certain number of American troops on the Afghan soil beyond 2014, which was already an extension of an earlier deadline—and as it turned out a couple of years later, was not to be the last. President Karzai who understood the implications of the continued foreign military presence—an unending war—astutely got that part suspended for a year. Early 2013, he referred the issue to a Jirga that "welcomed" the American offer but imposed a caveat: this force could only stay if subjected to Afghan Laws. Knowing fully well that the American troops when stationed abroad do not abide by local edicts, at times not even by their own, this was the polite Afghan way of saying, "we've had enough of you". But, of course, great powers never give up so easily. Further financial assistance was made contingent on signing a Bilateral Security Agreement (BSA) that would permit this military presence up to 2016, to begin with.

The pressure worked, and understandably so. Against the total Afghan GDP of two billion dollars the expenditure on ANA alone was twice as much. This white elephant was now more like a millstone around Kabul's neck. It could not be maintained without foreign aid, and would not deliver in spite of it. Another Jirga was summoned later that year, handpicked (as conceded by Philip Hammond the then British

Defence Secretary in our conversation in Islamabad) to put its collective seal on the BSA. The Assembly did precisely that. Karzai, however, had made it clear even before the outcome that he would leave it to whoever was elected to be his successor in 2014 to take the final decision. There may be any number of reasons for Karzai's gamesmanship. If some of his preconditions to sign the treaty—no more violation of private homes, release of Afghan prisoners, and resumption of dialogue with the Taliban—were met, he could claim credit. If not, since the residual military presence would inevitably provoke the Taliban to target local forces (the foreign troops being in fortified bases), his refusal to sanction it would be vindicated.

Before going over to the post-Karzai developments, a brief account of how the Region reacted to the turmoil in Afghanistan.

## The Regional Response

Regional countries with their cross-border cultural, ethnic and religious affiliations have obviously been affected by the war in Afghanistan and consequently often toyed with the idea of joining hands to restore peace and stability in the troubled country. After the Soviet withdrawal, a number of combinations (like 2+5; US, Russia, and five of Afghanistan's neighbours) were explored to find a regional solution. However, where bilateral efforts—by Pakistan and Iran in 1991, for example—made no headway, there was no chance that the multilateral group could forge a consensus. Soon after 9/11, a group called "Shanghai Five" launched the SCO (Shanghai Cooperation Organisation). Though counter-terrorism was its declared aim, the new forum was expected to build upon its original mission—"to work towards a common security arrangement for Continental Asia"—and address the implications of an occupied Afghanistan for the Region. In the last thirteen years though, it has little to show. The Istanbul Process, a Turkish initiative, is Afghanistan specific and even though it includes almost every country that could help or disrupt, it did manage to crystallise certain national and regional positions. But, of course, it is too unwieldy to do much more.

Pakistan, being the most affected country, could not solely depend upon the outcome of these nebulous enterprises. Since the American commitment to peace in Afghanistan did not seem serious, Pakistan started positioning itself to play its key role to help restore stability in the war-torn country. It reached out to other countries in the neighbourhood and sought their cooperation, mending some fences in the process.

With Iran, it removed a longstanding irritant. Working in tandem, in 2010 the two countries defanged Jundullah, a militant group based in Pakistani Balochistan that was operating inside Iran with significant external support. Moreover, despite American pressure, both Tehran and Islamabad kept the Iran-Pakistan Pipeline (IPP) project alive. Iran on its part, unlike in the past, refrained from criticising Pakistan for the Shiite killings that in 2012 had assumed alarming proportions.

Pakistan's adversarial relations with Moscow during the Cold War turned around remarkably. I spent a week in Moscow in the fall of 2012 and was pleasantly surprised that the baggage of the past did not come in the way of how my Russian hosts treated me. In fact, they were quite keen to get my account of how we handled their legacy in Afghanistan. Russia seemed supportive of Pakistan's full membership of the SCO and offered to modernise the Karachi Steel Mills using the Soviet technology of the 1970s. That was followed by Moscow pledging financial aid to bring electricity from Tajikistan to Pakistan. Gazprom was at one time the only group willing to build the IPP. Putin was all set to visit Pakistan in October 2012, but when Islamabad got cold feet on signing the pipeline deal, he changed his mind. Thanks to the Ukraine crisis two years later, Russia resumed its engagement with Pakistan.

Islamabad also tried to win Delhi's cooperation. Initially, it had blocked Indian participation in the Istanbul Process, but for the second round that was held in November 2011, Pakistan did not use its veto. If India showed no enthusiasm to work with the regional countries on Afghanistan, it was essentially because conceding a lead role to Pakistan would not have gone down well with its domestic audience. Indeed, the burden of history makes it difficult for the two countries to cooperate even on matters that may benefit both.

China probably holds the best cards in the game. It has built energy infrastructure in Central Asia and invested in Afghan minerals. Eighty billion dollars in bilateral trade effectively took care of any illusion that India might one day be persuaded to "contain" China (but, of course,

Delhi would continue to use the China card to get the most from its relations with the US). China also kept shipping oil from Iran through the Straits of Hormuz, unmindful of the American armada or embargo. By early 2015, it had agreed to facilitate reconciliation amongst the warring Afghan factions.

Besides reaching out to important regional countries, Pakistan had retained leverage with the Taliban and established rapport with most of the major Afghan factions. It was now only waiting for the right time to play its preordained role to bring the key Afghan factions to the negotiating table.

*Post Karzai*

Initially, the 2014 Elections in Afghanistan looked like a real "game changer" for reasons that all depended on one's perspective. Pro-regime forces were ecstatic because of the good number that had voted and by implication 'rejected the Taliban'. Some keen observers however attributed the peaceful conduct of the electoral process largely to local deals. In a decentralised polity, it clearly works better than any arrangement imposed from the top. And then, for once the Taliban acted in support of the democratic process. In the runoff round, in areas where they wielded influence, the insurgents lined up men and women to vote for Ashraf Ghani, their fellow Pashtun, to offset the edge that the Tajik Abdullah enjoyed in the first phase.

Pakistan had its own reasons to be pleased with the outcome when the two frontrunners formed a grand coalition, the unity government. That brought the number of parties involved in the conflict practically down to two, the minimum and therefore the most manageable: the Kabul regime and the Taliban. When Ashraf Ghani, the elected leader in Kabul, made all the right noises including beseeching the GHQ to facilitate a negotiated settlement with the Taliban, the time Pakistan had been waiting for seemed to have arrived. With some prospects, however remote, of NATO forces departing and China indicating support for reconciliation, Pakistan started pushing the Taliban to the table.

If the fables have it right, a Pashtun cannot be pushed, even into heaven, but can be lured into hell. In early 2015, Pakistan still arm-twisted the Taliban—despite strong opposition from within their ranks that believed it was now only a matter of time that Afghanistan would

183

fall into their lap—to start a dialogue with Kabul. These efforts were making some progress when Ashraf Ghani undertook his US visit in March. There he implored the US to retain its military presence in Afghanistan beyond the 2016 deadline agreed under the BSA. This alone would have provided the Taliban, whose sole precondition to talk to Kabul was a firm commitment that all the foreign forces would leave, sufficient pretext to refuse negotiations. What must have stunned even the non-Taliban Afghans was Ghani's expression of gratitude for the sacrifices the American forces made for Afghanistan. Those who had lost millions fighting foreign aggression were not likely to applaud a President commemorating the four thousand dead of a military force that had been bombing their country for the last fourteen years.

The Taliban hardliners were now in full cry and even Mullah Omar, if alive, must have found it hard to veto their opposition to a peaceful settlement. Another spanner in Pakistan's efforts was cast by its own Prime Minister. On his visit to Kabul in May, Nawaz Sharif called the Taliban a terrorist outfit. This is what even the Americans had resisted, since at some stage they might have to negotiate with the insurgents. Despite all these unhelpful acts, those entrusted with the task had been working behind the scenes to ensure that eventually Pakistan would fulfil its role to bring the Taliban to the table. The first structured dialogue took place on 7 July in Murree, a hill resort close to Islamabad. Besides observers from the US, China and Pakistan, participation from the Kabul Regime and the Taliban was of a fairly high level.

The second round was to take place on 31 July. It had to be postponed because only a day before, the news of Mullah Omar's death (rumoured for some time) was confirmed. He had died in 2013, but both the ISI and the Taliban were keeping it under wraps to preserve his unifying aura until the peace process took roots. Since the news was leaked by some sources in Kabul and that too on the eve of the crucial second round, one had reasons to suspect that not everyone there was keen to accommodate the Taliban. Considering that for a sustainable settlement the Taliban could secure a major share in power, these fears in Kabul could be understood.

I made two subsequent visits to Afghanistan in September 2015 to take part in the Herat Security Dialogue and in January 2016 for a BBC-sponsored event. These made it quite clear to me that besides the

# AFGHANISTAN

traditional anti-Taliban forces, like their Intelligence apparatus, a legacy from the Soviet days, returning diaspora that landed in Kabul along with Ashraf Ghani, were strongly against any dialogue with the opposition. With some more facts about the 2014 elections finding their way to the people, the notion that the much-hyped democratic breakthrough was massively manipulated started festering just below the surface. Ghani, before one forgets, was fielded because the credentials of Zalmay Khalilzad, the real American favourite, who had served as Washington's envoy in Kabul, were highly suspect.

The hawks amongst the Taliban might have deluded themselves into believing that in due course Afghanistan would be all theirs, but judging by the Kissinger Criterion, "the guerrillas only have to survive to win", the militia had won the war soon after its revival. (A former US General, Daniel Blogger, had conceded victory to the Taliban a long time back.) No major development work could be started without the Taliban getting their cut. As the first decade of the US-led occupation was drawing to a close, even the NATO convoys had to pay the Taliban to move in comparative safety: 150 Million dollars alone in 2011. A similar amount per annum was their due in the drug trade. Every year, nearly 500 Million dollars flew into the Taliban kitty from the Western sources.

Militarily, the US could not have prevailed. Its political strategy failed due to internal conflicts. The CIA and the Pentagon were at odds with the State Department on both the policy and its execution. Obama, after his December 2009 framework was subverted by his own Army, let all three do whatever they deemed fit. That was an abdication of his role as the President and the Supreme Commander. And, of course, almost every institution in the American hierarchy got its pound of flesh from the Afghan enterprise. One only has to read reports prepared by the Pentagon watchdog to fathom the extent of this skim-off. But if the US still would not let go of Afghanistan and was bent upon maintaining the military presence that is a red rag to the Taliban, it reasonably supports the hypothesis that stability in certain regions was not in the American interest (see Chapter 15). Mullah Omar's successor was Akhtar Mansoor, who, as the de facto head of the Taliban had been sending his deputies to take part in various peace efforts, two rounds each at Doha and Murree, and a high profile conference sponsored by Pugwash in Qatar. He was eliminated by an

185

American Drone in May 2016, only a few days after the quartet—Afghanistan, Pakistan, China and the US—had agreed to revive the peace process, which made the American aversion to a negotiated settlement in Afghanistan quite clear.

The occupation forces, too, have a dilemma. In their desire to leave behind a politically acceptable dispensation—an anti Taliban one, to put it plainly—they have dug themselves deep into the Afghan hole. Like the proverbial blanket, the country swirls around anyone who takes a plunge to retrieve it. Distant powers when caught by the Afghan blanket may get mauled and battered but can still wriggle out. The British used a mix of money and diplomacy, and the Soviets sought Pakistan's help. The US dilemma is more complex. Even when convinced that its Afghan policy was unsustainable, it is reluctant to add Afghanistan to a long list of failures—Iraq, the broader Middle East, and Ukraine—to name but three. Then, the temptation to keep a foothold in the region to either play or spoil the New Great Game must be irresistible. It may therefore have decided that the cost of remaining stuck in this quagmire was lower than beating a retreat. If, at some stage, the the scales tilted to the other side, the US would have to swallow some more humble pie.

## The Afghan Enigma

To have checkmated three superpowers in succession may be a remarkable achievement for a small country like Afghanistan, but it can still be explained. I have attempted to do so in this chapter. However, the real challenge that Afghanistan presents is not to the mighty military powers but to the ever-expanding circle, especially post 9/11, of academics, analysts and area experts, who want to get this country right. Consider the plight of a collection of forty individuals, including some of the best from around the world, invited by a British foundation in November 2014. In its concluding session, "The Way Forward in Afghanistan", almost everyone agreed that where things clearly went wrong, "more of the same" must be avoided. The assembly could do no better than to recommend more of the same, only with greater resolve. It reminded me of our policy review after the Soviet withdrawal.

There is a common thread between these talking shops and the dissertations that have the Af-Pak archives spilling over the rims. Mostly, there is a long list of blunders made by the occupying powers: flawed political, developmental and military strategies, a lack of coordination between implementing agencies, American unilateralism, and so on. The conclusion, however, besides routinely mentioning Afghan failings is, "but for Pakistan, the venture could still have worked". It is now up to us, the Pakistanis, to either go on the defensive or to bask in the limelight. If the Taliban, a rag-tag militia helped by the failing, fumbling, stumbling state of Pakistan, could frustrate the designs of the world's mightiest alliance (NATO), I prefer to bask, having twice tabled a motion that the duo should be given a big hand, even if grudgingly. Though the land that prides itself with the spirit of Eton and Harrow was the host on both the occasions, no one applauded. That Afghanistan has affected us in many different ways, one knew, but that it has robbed us of all sporting spirit, I had no idea.

To be fair to the outsiders, there are serious paradoxes within Afghanistan and its society that make our assessments, especially our quest to find the right recipe for peace, so exasperating.

My first brush with Afghanistan was in November 1968 when I drove back after a language course in Germany. It was late evening when I was nearing Herat. Passing through a defile, I could see with my headlights that the road was blocked with a tree trunk and there were armed men standing on both sides. It was a perfect ambush site with no space to turn around. So I had to stop and discovered (to my great relief) that they were policemen who merely wanted their inspector to be given a lift to the next town. That was the first lesson I learnt about the Afghans—even when they sought a favour, it would be done at the gunpoint. The second observation turned out to be still more useful. Wide valleys separated by series of hills and mountains dot the Afghan landscape. While driving through I got the feeling that one was not ever likely to be over the hump. With every succeeding hurdle more daunting than the one behind, those who must deal with this country are faced with challenge after challenge.

The numerous fault lines in the country that exhaust a foreign intruder, are also the main impediments against restoring peace and unity once the aggression is vacated. God knows how Ahmed Shah Abdali could convince the disparate Afghan groupings to forge a grand consensus in 1747, but all efforts to do so after the Soviet withdrawal floundered on schisms between tribes, ethnic groups, political aspirants, ideologically diverse forces, factions under external patronage, culturally incongruous cliques, and indeed because of their historical experience in which some Afghans were betrayed by others who jumped on an invader's bandwagon. Most of us who romanticise the Afghans because of their heroic resistance against occupiers make a flawed assumption that all of them love their freedom and fight for it. For every Afghan who resists there is another who collaborates. As the tide turns, some amongst them switch sides. The changing loyalties of the Afghan Emirs exhausted the British. After the Soviet withdrawal many Khalaqis (members of a left-leaning party, mostly Pashtuns) grew beards and joined the Mujahedeen, and later the Taliban. This time around, the former Northern Alliance, the drug lords, and the imported whiz kids (the beneficiaries of the occupation), might have outnumbered the freedom fighters. Most of them do, indeed, have a stake in maintaining the status quo. It is not only power they risk losing, but if history is any guide, also their heads.

A lack of trust is the explanation we use when we cannot understand the real cause of conflict between belligerents. I am not aware of any two countries that trust each other. Many may still coexist peacefully because it is the better option. Essentially, the tribesmen too live by the same edict, except that, in their case, all they can afford to trust is their own ability to defend themselves. They live under harsh conditions, compete for meagre resources, and must, therefore, keep their powder dry. Being suspicious rather than trusting is their tactic for survival and it is also the bane of those who try to broker peace among them. They would rather rely on their own ability to endure adversity than fall for an attractive option over which they will not have control. The peacemakers, on the other hand, often make the fatal mistake of losing patience with the tribesmen.

Having long survived on the historic crossroads, another art that the Afghans have mastered is playing external actors—those getting involved in Afghanistan—off against each other. Since the goals of the meddling powers—occupation or influence—were best served through local collaborators, all of them find their own set of native clients. These proxy wars are fought mostly by the Afghans on their own territory. The country suffers, but in the process the Afghans have acquired a flair for getting the most out of their foreign patrons by doing the least for them. A war economy is the natural upshot, creating a vested interest in the continuance of conflict, both between the clients and among their external sponsors. Maybe that is the reason that a regional approach is one of our favourite methods to resolve the Afghan tangle. At the time of writing, our preferred option seems to be joining hands with Iran, Russia and China.

## The "Conjoined Twins"

That is how Hamid Karzai once defined the Af-Pak duo. The American equivalent, less elegant, of course, would be, "joined at the hip". That they could so easily be separated by some loose talk would have sounded absurd, if it was not so real. A wise Afghan, who had spent many years in Pakistan as a refugee, described the long diatribe between the two countries, as a consequence of "misunderstanding". He was being polite. The fact is that, despite having lived next to each other for centuries, there is a large number amongst the decision and opinion makers, even scholars, on both sides who have a problem understanding the other.

Post 9/11, many Pakistanis naively believed that with Afghanistan in dire straits and our friends the Americans exercising influence in Kabul, it was time to coerce the Afghans into recognising the DL as an international border. They were obviously unaware of King Abdul Rehman's thinking when he signed the agreement: he had ceded only the administrative control of some areas to the British, not the affiliation of the tribesmen. Pakistan did well to win over their loyalties and the Afghans thus know that they have no realistic chance of regaining this territory. They are also aware of the economic and other benefits of the status quo: seeking asylum or sanctuary when needed, for example. However, since they believe, rightly, that the areas were taken away through coercion, they will not give this arrangement official sanction. When Pakistan came under pressure to curb the movement of the militants to Afghanistan, it suggested fencing and mining the borders. That the terrain would have made these measures futile, if not impractical, was not that important. More damaging for the bilateral relation was the concern it caused on the Afghan side, who thought it was yet another Pakistani ploy to get the DL recognised by Afghanistan as the international boundary.

Afghans are usually generous in expressing their gratitude for Pakistan's support during their resistance against the Soviets and for hosting the millions who sought refuge. However, when the Pakistanis recall all these favours, the Afghans retort by reminding them that but for the Afghan resistance, the Soviets might have gobbled up at least Balochistan. What is certainly unhelpful for bilateral relations are the repeated Pakistani threats to send back the refugees. At present, Afghanistan is not in a position to bear that burden. More important, by hosting millions of them we have made a long-term investment in that country. Even in terms of Realpolitik the Afghan refugees have a significant stake in the well-being of Pakistan.

People in Pakistan are understandably upset when certain Afghan quarters blame our country for their troubles. Some of the criticism may be politically inspired, or rise out of the misplaced belief that Pakistan wants a pliant regime in its backyard. It was, indeed, imprudent for Afghan official circles to blame Pakistan for the current insurgency. The real reason for the re-emergence of the Taliban was the military strikes, ostensibly against the remnants of the Taliban and Al-Qaeda, in the Pashtun areas. Since it affected both countries, the two Governments would have found more support from the people if they had jointly resisted the American-led approach, instead of displaying mutual spite.

The Indian factor in Afghanistan has been highly exaggerated in Pakistan. Indeed they have consulates, only four, which existed in the earlier times as well, and they do indulge in espionage, as is the norm. But Pakistani assets and influence in the areas of its concern outweigh the Indian capabilities by a wide margin. One only has to look at the Afghan markets which are awash with Pakistani goods. India's advantage, on the other hand, as conceded by some of their own old hands on Afghanistan, lies in not having common borders with Afghanistan. That may be because it saves India from the debris of the Afghan wars, or due to the code described by Kautilya himself, that preaches hostility towards the neighbour but friendship with the neighbour's neighbour. The Afghan infatuation with Bollywood is, however, genuine.

# AFGHANISTAN

*Some Thoughts on the New Great Game*

The (old) Great Game, though long-drawn-out—Imperialist Russia and Britain fought for influence in Afghanistan for most of the 19th century—was largely played by spies and diplomats. It also ended quite well for Afghanistan, which won itself the status of a buffer state, and lasting peace. The New Great Game (NGG) that was kicked-off after the collapse of the Soviet Union, ostensibly to exploit the natural resources of Central Asia, seems far more complex. To start with, one is not even sure if it was merely about geo-economics.

Regardless of what led to the invasion of Afghanistan post 9/11, the invaders are still there more than a decade and half later, and at least their American component has hunkered down for the long haul. The sole superpower's perceived objectives—containing the new global rival China, keeping a watch over nuclear "rogues" like Pakistan and Iran, and maintaining a strong presence in an energy-rich region—make this the greatest game ever, with geo-economics, geo-strategy and geo-politics all rolled into one.

Actually, the NGG predates 9/11. Who would extract oil and gas, and how these would be delivered to the users, were the real issues. Russia might have lost its empire, but it still cracked down against the Chechen rebels to save a crucial pipeline. It kept its foreign neighbours on a leash by creating the CIS (Commonwealth of Independent States) and the CSTO (Collective Security Treaty Organisation), which might not be very effective, but still worked better than the absurd ruse of the PFP (Partnership for Peace) invented by NATO to weaken the Russian stranglehold on some of its former satellite states. The Saudi-American efforts to woo the Taliban to construct the TAPI and obstruct the IPI can also be understood in the same context. The arrival in force of the US and its allies post-9/11, threatened to tilt the balance against the regional players who responded by creating the SCO in the belief that, in due course, it would become a bulwark against the intruders.

Shortly after the Cold War ended, Strobe Talbot, an American academic, diplomat, and a specialist on Soviet affairs, wrote about the consequences for Central Asia. He concluded that "the New Great Game" could either be played by all parties or by no one at all. Like Afghanistan, the broader region cannot function without an overarching consensus. When there are too many actors who, irrespective of their size, can throw a spanner in the works, nothing will work until all or most of them are on board. Insurgents or saboteurs can only blow up pipelines, but cross-alignments amongst competing centres of state power might keep the region in turmoil for decades to come.

14

# THE INDO-PAK CONUNDRUM

I am a veteran of two wars against India, those of 1965 and 1971. I believe these were gentlemanly wars since neither country deliberately targeted non-combatants and treated the prisoners of war in a more or less civilised manner. In the 1965 war, our unit captured an Indian officer, Lieutenant Sharma, along with his runner, in the Chamb Sector (now part of Azad Kashmir). In violation of the standard operating procedures as laid down, both were given hot cups of tea right on the frontline. After the 1971 War, as the Brigade-Major in Kashmir, I took part in many flag meetings on the LOC and found each side's conduct, despite the tense environment, correct. As Defence Attaché in Germany, I had a good rapport with my Indian counterparts and once even pushed the Defence Attaché's car to help it jumpstart. I was, therefore, quite surprised when, soon after I took over Military Intelligence in October 1988, an Indian defence publication called me a "hawk". I have no idea how their Intelligence or any other Pakistan watcher in New Delhi came to that conclusion. I think that the verdict had more to do with the history of our relationship, as neither side expects any softness from the rival spymaster.

During my MI days, I met J N (Mani) Dixit, the Indian High Commissioner, a couple of times and, though he was no dove when it came to Pakistan, we became friends. In 1991, the Indian Foreign Secretary Muchkund Dubey visited Islamabad and Mani took advantage of this relationship to invite me, then the head of the ISI, to a reception at his house. As an exception, I agreed. Making the best of this scoop, India's super-diplomat, who had earned the unofficial title of "Viceroy" when representing his country in Sri Lanka and Bangladesh, handed me over to his daughter, Abha, who was working on Sindh. It alerted me to the Indian interest in our "soft underbelly". A brief one-on-one meeting with the Indian Foreign Secretary rounded up a useful evening. Soon after that, Dixit went back to Delhi to succeed Dubey as Foreign Secretary.

India was indeed an important issue for me during my MI and ISI days, which coincided with the eruption of the uprising in Kashmir in 1989–90. During Dubey's visit, a member of his team asked me about the ISI's main focus. In those days, we were more involved on the western borders, but I still said "India" to put the fear of the ISI into Delhi's South Block. Of course, the hardboiled diplomat was too seasoned to show any reaction. Dixit and I met many times after that at Track Two meetings, the last time being in February 2004 at a conference organised by Pugwash in Delhi. It was just before the Indian national elections and Mani told me, "Asad Bhai, I am now the foreign policy advisor of the Congress Party. We could do better than before, but not well enough to win". Like all the ISI's election forecasts, Dixit's too was proved wrong, though happily so, and he went on to become the National Security Advisor. He died before I could ask him what tricks the scholar-statesman now had up his sleeve to fox his naïve Pakistani counterpart, whose area of expertise was taxation. (Tariq Aziz, Musharraf's trouble-shooter on India was from the Revenue Service.) As if India did not have enough advantages over its breakaway twin already!

On servicing our bilateral relations, a remark that made a deep impression on me was one made by the Indian Defence Attaché in Islamabad in the early 90s. Brigadier (later Lt.-General) G K Duggal, when asked about his mission in Islamabad said, "بس دشمنی نبھا رہے ہیں" (managing animosity, sanely)." Indeed, this is a more challenging call than handling a friendly relationship. A minor accident when I was heading the ISI must have provided the Indian Air Attaché with something to write home about. Close to where the Serena Hotel now is, my car had a scrape with some other vehicle. Some delay was inevitable in order to take care of the formalities and, since I was in a hurry (and there was no follow-up car), I got out to look for a taxi. Just at that time, along came the Indian Group-Captain and offered me a lift. I asked him to drop me at the Presidency.

The years after the 1971 war saw Pakistan cut to size. Two developments set the course for our bilateral relations: India's nuclear test of 1973 and the Soviet withdrawal from Afghanistan in 1989. Since the former happened soon after the debacle of 1971, Pakistan took the nuclear path largely for psychological reasons, but we soon discovered that this acquisition could also deter a conventional war and provide space for sub-conventional and limited conflicts. Paradoxically, Moscow's exit from Afghanistan, for which Pakistan had worked hard, and the subsequent demise of the Soviet Union, tilted the Indo-Pak balance against us. As the Cold War was winding down, the USA once again started wooing its first love on the subcontinent, India.

Yet another factor that went in Delhi's favour was the economic revival masterminded by Prime Minister Narasimha Rao and Finance Minister Manmohan Singh in 1991. It coincided with the financial pain inflicted on Pakistan by its elected elite and the US-led sanctions for our refusal to roll back our nuclear programme. Two factors still helped Pakistan stand its ground: its perceived nuclear capability, and some sound management by its civil-military leadership in order to withstand American pressure. The resistance in Kashmir grew in the meantime, although the Sikh unrest, that had peaked around the time just after the Indian Army stormed the Golden Temple in 1984, was petering out.

Pakistan's decision to send infiltrators into IHK before the 1965 War had not been thought through. The assumption that it would not lead to an all-out war with India turned out to be a miscalculation. The real damage, however, was the Kashmiris' loss of faith in Pakistan's ability to help their freedom struggle. In the aftermath of the 1971 debacle, and later due to the war in Afghanistan, Pakistan was neither keen nor in a position to pursue the Kashmir cause. After the Shimla Accord signed by Indira Gandhi and Zulfiqar Ali Bhutto in 1973, the Kashmir issue remained on ice. The uprising in January 1990, therefore, took us by surprise (I was the DGMI at that time), perhaps also because the unrest was atypically led by urban youth, educated but unemployed. By the time we realised its seriousness, Prime Minister Benazir Bhutto was still convalescing after the birth of her second child, and the first presentation on the subject was made to President Ghulam Ishaq Khan. The PM was represented by her mother Nusrat Bhutto, a Senior Minister. At that nascent stage, except for the need to watch further developments, no major decision was advised.

Back in office, Ms. Bhutto tasked the Foreign Office, the ISI, and the MI, to brief representatives of all political parties on the uprising. Some deliberations took place behind closed doors. The broad consensus was that the turbulence would soon fizzle out and, except for some diplomatic activity, no other action was warranted. Of course, the intelligence agencies were to keep watch and maintain contact with those who had crossed over from Indian-held Kashmir, some of them for military hardware and training. In the absence of any Government directive, it was up to the GHQ to manage the situation as best as it could. The unrest, however, picked up pace and became a mass movement. The Indian crackdown in the valley was accompanied by a military build-up on the Pakistan borders. Since most of the heavy ordnance had been left behind in cantonments where the Indian formations were stationed in peacetime, it was clear that India was not mobilising for war and the move was more of a political act to demonstrate strong action. We consequently decided to keep our own forces in their barracks.

In June 1990, Robert Gates, the then Deputy National Security Advisor in the US (later Director of the CIA and Secretary for Defence) visited both the countries to plead restraint. He did not quite expect the relaxed atmosphere in Pakistan. The Prime Minister was visiting North Africa and the President, who knew better, did not take Gates's concerns about the likelihood of a nuclear holocaust seriously. The Indians, however, obliged him by pulling back from the borders and as a *quid pro quo* demanded that the US dissuade Pakistan from providing any support to the militancy in Kashmir, and to even consider declaring Pakistan a state sponsoring terrorism. Now that the Cold War was over and Pakistan no longer a frontline state, the US agreed and faithfully followed up. In fact, this fitted nicely with the United States' new Pakistan Policy.

Some time in early September 1991, I, as the head of the ISI, received a call from the American Embassy to inform me that Ambassador Oakley, on home leave at that time, was being rushed back to Islamabad for a day to deliver an important message. He came to my home after midnight, accompanied by a very sleepy Deputy Head of Mission, Beth Jones, and told me that the Pressler Amendment would be revoked on 1 October 1990. We took it sportingly, as it was only intended to provide a temporary relief during the Soviet occupation of Afghanistan. However, when it was followed by charges of abetting terrorism, it became obvious that the new bilateral relationship would not only be about our nuclear programme. The next three years saw a remarkable low in Pak-US relations. It was essentially President Khan's great experience and the resolute support of the civil-military establishment that helped Pakistan tide over those difficult times. All this while, the resistance in Kashmir continued to intensify, and, because of that, so much pressure was generated on both sides of the LOC that the ISI could no longer be kept out of it, primarily to ensure that the turmoil did not spin out of control and ignite a war with unpredictable consequences.

A people's movement seldom finds united leadership right at the outset. There were over a hundred groups in Afghanistan during the initial years of the Jihad against the Soviets. The ISI reduced them to seven and subsequently brought them under the political umbrella of the AIG. Having learnt from Vietnam that Giap needed a Ho Chi Minh, and from Afghanistan that an armed struggle must ultimately find an agreed political focus, the ISI persuaded the Kashmiri resistance to form a supreme council. So the *Tahreek-e-Hurriyat-e-Kashmir* was born. Like the AIG, the *Hurriyat* did not quite serve the purpose either. A few groups remained outside its fold and some who had joined it left. Micromanaging a liberation movement is a tough call, and this one was a particularly tall order. The Indo-US nexus was powerful and Pakistan suffered from institutional instability and a lack of political cohesion. Consequently, under pressure, it committed a cardinal sin: it left the resistance to its own devices.

Fighting the state is a complex undertaking. If it was directed against a hard state like Russia, or if the stakes were high and humanitarian considerations low, like for India in Kashmir or for Israel in Palestine, the reprisals can be brutal. The resistance must therefore be prepared for the long haul. Left to eager or fanatic elements, it does not pay enough attention to non-military means—which eventually matter more—and the resistance soon burns itself out. The Mujahedeen and the Taliban survived for decades because they staggered their military operations in time and space. On the other hand, the attrition rate of the Punjabi Taliban, always on the go in Afghanistan, was very high. The same fate befell the Kashmiri resistance. It might have lasted longer than we expected, but it failed to consolidate on a political front and in due course its armed element lost momentum. It still served a purpose in that it persuaded both India and Pakistan to be serious about finding ways to manage their chronic relationship.

In the summer of 1997, the two Prime Ministers, I K Gujral and Nawaz Sharif, asked their foreign secretaries, Salman Haider and Shamshad Ahmed, to develop a framework to resolve, or at least to contain, our bilateral conflicts. The design logic of their blueprint, called the "composite and integrated dialogue", was sound even if the nomenclature was not. Since the idea was to resolve the simpler issues first and, then, in the improved environment, to start addressing the more complex ones, dealing with all of them in tandem (as implied by "integrated") would mean no movement unless there was reasonable progress on intractable issues like Kashmir. The "integrated" part was therefore quietly dropped (but not from the official text). The process was now more like moving on parallel tracks with our disputes and getting them out of the way as and when possible. No longer strictly "composite", the dialogue still retained that politically correct adjective. What we now had was a multiple-track and multiple-speed formula.

The evolution of this concept was purely a civilian enterprise. All the same, since it is the military that claims primacy in the study and development of strategic thought, it may be gratifying to note that a defence strategist too would have been impressed by the formulation. When operating along multiple axes, the forces that meet less resistance continue their momentum. That helps movement on other fronts as well. When the situation is right, some fronts are reinforced to affect the breakthrough needed to capture the main objective, in this case durable peace in the subcontinent. One of the architects, Salman Haider, recalled that during the brainstorming sessions, someone mentioned Liddell Hart's theory of "expanding torrents", which is precisely about building on small gains.

Good concepts, brilliant designs, and even sound strategies, have never been enough. For their success, we make certain assumptions and lay down conditions that must be fulfilled. It must be assumed for example that an agreement, no matter how favourable to one or the other side, is not to be touted as a unilateral victory. Eager to make political capital out of the accord, some Pakistani officials went to town claiming they had made the Indians *finally* agree to discuss Kashmir. India reacted predictably and clarified that the only aspect of Kashmir it ever intended to discuss was Pakistan's support to the insurgency. The composite dialogue, and along with that the peace process, was put on hold.

The following year, in 1998, the archrivals brought their nukes out of the basement. The celebrations that followed in India and Pakistan, and not only on the streets, were accompanied by plenty of chest thumping and bellicosity towards each other. Obviously, there were also concerns both inside and outside the region: how would the two nascent nuclear powers adjust to the new, potentially dangerous, nuclear environment? At the very least, some measures were necessary to prevent a situation in which one side or the other was to fire a nuclear weapon in panic or because it misread a signal, such as a missile test by the other.

Since it was a matter of grave concern for both the countries, a hotline between the two DGMOs was quickly established. Indeed, the basic issue to be addressed was the conflict-ridden relationship that might lead to a nuclear exchange. If that required a spectacular step, then Vajpayee was the man to take it. In February 1999, he undertook his famous Bus Yatra (journey) to Lahore. The Declaration that he signed on 21 February with his Pakistani counterpart, Nawaz Sharif, went beyond nuclear confidence-building measures and attempted to revive the peace process. The composite dialogue once again formed the bedrock of the agreement. Once again, it had to be shelved before it got a fair chance when, in early May 1999, Pakistan-backed troops and militia were found occupying heights on the Indian side of the LOC in the Kargil sector. (I have discussed the details in Chapter 7).

Indo-Pak relations suffered another setback when, later in the year, the Pakistani army chief, General Pervez Musharraf, took over in a military putsch. Since the General was the architect of Kargil, India was obviously reluctant to resume the peace process as long as he was in power. But when Musharraf was found to be firmly in the saddle,

Vajpayee invited him to give peace another chance. Musharraf, who had, in the meantime, assumed the office of the President, visited India in July 2001 and met the Indian Prime Minister in what became known as the Agra Summit. It failed because the hawks in Delhi led by LK Advani, the Indian Home Minister, scuttled the process.

In the aftermath of 9/11, events took a further dip. When America decided to invade Afghanistan to flush out Al-Qaeda, the group suspected of having masterminded this enormity, it sought cooperation from Pakistan. India was obviously unhappy with the prospects of Pakistan once again becoming a frontline ally of what was now the sole superpower. It offered its own services instead. Pakistan got the role as it was better located. Already sulking for being upstaged by Pakistan, India mobilised for war when its Parliament was attacked, probably by members of a banned Pakistani militant outfit. For most of 2002, the armed forces of the two countries remained in a state of high alert. There were, however, good reasons that it did not escalate into war, even a limited one.

Some of the reasons are well known: the risk of nuclear conflagration, because of which third parties were eager to restrain both sides before they went over the brink. Another, perhaps the more potent constraint, is less known. An all-out conventional war between the two countries was very likely to end in a stalemate. Since countries do not normally start wars without a reasonable chance of achieving a strategic objective, India and Pakistan after 1971 did not take their conflicts beyond a build-up on the border and skirmishes across the LOC. Another factor that led to the disengagement of forces was the vested interest of the resurgent Indian economy.

India still could have initiated a war in 2002, either in frustration or in the belief that the US presence in the area would deny Pakistan its nuclear option. But then there were other implications to consider. With active hostilities removing all constraints on Pakistan from supporting the insurgency in Kashmir, the insurgency could become more intense and durable. More importantly, if the war ended without causing major damage to Pakistan, it would have deprived India of a potent card that it had so far used to good effect: the threat of war. Even though Pakistan had a reasonable chance of preventing India from achieving a decisive military victory, it was still sensitive to Indian threats of war. Being the smaller country, its economy was more vulnerable to warlike tensions. After thirty years of high economic growth, it had gone through its worst recession in the 1990s. Now that there was some promise of recovery as an important ally of the US, tensions with India were an unwelcome development. Paradoxically, when the drums of war receded, both the countries found that their threat cards had been played out, seemingly for the last time.

Pakistan had, time and again, warned that if India did not agree to resolve the Kashmir problem, the region could be blown apart in a nuclear holocaust. In the absence of any desperate resolve in Pakistan to follow up on these threats, this argument was fast losing its effectiveness. I believe, by 2002, India's threat of a major conventional war too had run its course. Now that the two countries had manoeuvred each other into a deadlock, it was time to revive their on-again off-again peace process. The 2004 SAARC Summit in Islamabad seemed to be the right moment. Before that, the stumbling blocks that had caused the failure at Agra had to be removed.

The very fact that the framework evolved in 1997 had survived nuclear tests, the Kargil episode, a military coup, 9/11, and the stand-off of 2002, proved that it was a robust construct. One of its best features was that it could accommodate the preferences of both the parties and prevent concerns, even serious ones like Kashmir, from scuttling the process. In Agra, this potential for an understanding was not best used because the two sides insisted that their respective interests be recognized as "the core issue": Kashmir for Pakistan; and cross-border infiltration for India. To resolve this conflict in the spirit of the original concept, all one had to do was to make both the concerns part of the process.

Two extracts from the joint press statement of 6 January after Vajpayee met Musharraf to seal the agreement show how smoothly it could be done.

> President Musharraf reassured Prime Minister Vajpayee that he would not permit territory under Pakistan's control to be used to support terrorism in any manner. ...

> The two leaders are confident that the resumption of composite dialogue will lead to peaceful settlement of all bilateral issues, including Jammu & Kashmir, to the satisfaction of both sides.

The plan was now perfect, but to start the process some movement had to take place on ground, for example, with a round of meetings on mundane issues to establish a good beginning. It had, however, been the thinking in some quarters that a gesture on Kashmir, even a symbolic one, might be the best way to kick start the process. Kashmir after all was not only the "core issue" for Pakistan, having sucked in hundreds of thousands of Indian troops, it was also a "multi-corps" problem for India.

The gesture had to meet some essential criteria: it was to be without prejudice to the declared Kashmir policies of India and Pakistan; it had to provide some hope that a resolution of the dispute was seriously sought; and it had to sufficiently engage the Kashmiris to let the two countries work on their less intractable issues. The meeting of the leadership on both sides of the Kashmir divide seemed to meet these criteria adequately. Ultimately, it was decided to start a bus service between the two parts of Kashmir from 7 April 2005. The idea must have been that not only the leaders but divided families too could be brought together. The bus was also bound to make a bigger and better all-round impact than meetings between a few individuals, which, in any case, were not expected to show immediate results. There was, however, a risk involved: if the odd bus were to be blown up by any of the many detractors of the peace process, it would be a serious setback at this nascent state. That, mercifully, did not happen, and nor did much else after the initial euphoria over the bus trips and some high-profile visits by the Hurryiat leaders to Pakistan. The symbolism was still helpful.

Musharraf was a man in a hurry. Instead of letting the improvement in the environment guide an evolutionary peace process, he wanted to force the pace, and that too on the thorniest path. He started bombarding India with proposals on Kashmir in rapid succession. Delhi responded with deafening silence for any of the following reasons. First, if the ideas were coming from the other side, they could not benefit India. Next, even if they were reasonable, why give Pakistan the credit? If one waited a bit longer, Musharraf might concede some more. There was no compulsion to change tack, and, since the things were now under control, why risk a course which might go out of hand? The Indian rationale for non-response, that Musharraf was, at that time, losing ground in Pakistan, was therefore at best disingenuous. All the same, I have reason to believe that Musharraf's famous four-point formula held plenty of resonance for the Indian part of

Kashmir. Maybe they too, having suffered for decades, were now running out of patience.

In 2007, Musharraf did run into problems at home, and after he was removed from power in September 2008, his plans for the resolution of the Kashmir issue, at least under his label, were obsolete, as was the Composite Dialogue two months later when, on 26 November, Mumbai was subjected to a four-day carnage, allegedly by a Pakistan-based militant group.

Obviously, business as usual was now out of question, and for the rest of his tenure the Indian Prime Minister Manmohan Singh was more or less managing the fallout of Mumbai. His security establishment, in the meantime, did not do too badly in refining the Limited War doctrine. Under the nuclear overhang, "war is no option" is a self-serving (Pakistani) argument. Kargil did take place after 1998. It remained limited and under any actual or perceived nuclear threshold. Having failed to adequately respond to the 2001 attack on the Indian Parliament and 26/11 Mumbai, a quickie war limited in time and space, as envisaged by India's Cold Start Doctrine, could adequately fit the bill. This might even become an attractive option in the well-grounded belief that it would remain limited.

In a purely conventional setting, the doctrine was unlikely to help India affect a strategic breakthrough. There may even be serious imbalances during the short time that such a war was expected to last. In a nuclear environment, however, quick and limited gains are the only desired objective. And if that were to serve the political aim of sending the right message, especially to its own people, that mighty India did have options when hit by terrorist attacks, the Cold Start Doctrine was eminently suited to accomplish it. Pakistan responded by threatening to induct tactical nuclear weapons (TNWs). The fact that in our environment they could create strategic effects is not relevant. Both the CSD and TNWs are primarily to serve a political, perhaps even a psychological, purpose.

*The Peace Process*

The logic of the composite dialogue was prudently based on resolving contentious issues at a deliberate pace. It is essentially a slow pace, but considering our poor track record and cautious bureaucratic culture, quite realistic. The problem was that neither our two peoples nor the political leaders were known for the patience needed to keep faith in a process that did not show tangible results on regular basis. For a while, it was possible to keep them in good humour with brave pronouncements and cultural exchanges, but soon they would be demanding the increased economic and trade benefits that the process promised to deliver.

In addition, there was always the threat of sabotage, not only by the militants who would find periods of no progress ripe for their activity, but also from any other quarter, external or internal, that was not in favour of an Indo-Pak rapprochement. Even though some very heroic statements were once made in the two capitals that acts of terror could not derail the peace process, and there were reasons to believe that both countries understood that the control over peace was not to be yielded to its detractors, some well-planned and well-timed acts of sabotage could seriously set the whole process back. Mumbai was proof of this, if any were needed.

Kashmir can also be counted upon as an issue needing constant care. Though contained for a while, it had the potential to erupt if its people were not taken on board (as happened in the middle of 2016). Even if the two sides abided by the spirit of the "composite dialogue", there were bound to be problems. Pakistanis, for example, could become impatient because the "favourable environment" that was supposed to help resolve the issue was taking too long to establish. Indians, on the other hand, might start getting nervous if the Muslim majority from their part of Kashmir found greater affinity with their co-religionists in Pakistan.

The conduct of a peace process is, therefore, too complex an affair to be left to any one organ of the state. Bureaucrats are required to point out the technical aspects of an issue. When they are stuck, their political bosses have to take decisions to break the logjam and, if needed, exercise leadership to garner public support. Occasionally, however, it might be political compulsions that become the stumbling block. After Mumbai, any Indian government with an election looming would have had a hard time trying not to yield to public sentiment. At times like these, some sane minds working behind the scenes could make an invaluable contribution, not only by advising a pause when necessary or a breakthrough when stuck, but also by seeking fresh grounds for cooperation. After the Mumbai attack, for example, not a single voice from the establishment on either side supported the implementation of the "Joint Anti-Terror Mechanism" an idea which the two Prime Ministers, Manmohan Singh and Yousaf Raza Gillani, had approved in Havana in 2006, precisely to handle such incidents. The peace strategists could have used the JATM to build mutual confidence. If selected carefully, this group could even come up with ideas of how best the two countries could work together to help Afghanistan in this hour of great distress. Unless some Indians thought it was a Pakistani ploy to lure them into the Afghan quagmire or the Pakistanis saw it leading to their "encirclement" by India, cooperation on Afghanistan might become the first regional initiative to get the foreign forces out of our area. The story of the monkey grabbing the whole cheese from quarrelling cats is after all a classic South Asian fable.

Let us concede that—despite the arguments I previously listed which are primarily based on a rational model—the possibility of a limited armed conflict spinning out of control cannot be completely ruled out. What if not everyone acted rationally or someone panicked? These are all valid concerns, but do not address a live issue, which is India's political and psychological compulsion to find a satisfying response, in case incidents like 26/11 recur. The matter becomes more complex when we realise that there is no way to ensure that they do not. Once again taking the cue from military principles, the strategy of the indirect approach, which is superior to forcing an issue, would be useful. Since resuming the existing peace process was politically or technically problematic, or in case one side was uncomfortable with the subjects already on the table, there would be no harm in taking up fresh issues, especially if they were of more immediate concern. Luckily, both countries are faced with a sufficient number of them and even have the luxury of being able to choose which one to prioritise. Water and the problem of Afghanistan are two themes that could engage both India and Pakistan gainfully, and might even provide some distraction from their mundane feuds.

Kashmir was always a sensitive and a complex issue. In the meantime, it has become, for both the countries, a matter of prestige, ego, and political survival. It could still become a model of cooperation. Its waterways have been the subject of much heartburn between the two countries, but water being an increasingly scarce commodity and such an essential one, this resource could provide an incentive to find a modus vivendi. I have reasons to believe that the idea of joint hydro-projects had once gained currency on both sides of the divide. I have no idea how it could be implemented, but just imagine the effect it could create: India's ability to utilise Kashmir waters to benefit the local population, and Pakistan being able to claim it had a share in this noble undertaking.

Afghanistan was as near a level playing field as any that the two countries could find. Pakistan has the advantage of geography, shared ethnicity, inter-dependence and even a bit of history. India too has a few assets: greater finances and less of the baggage of proximity. Both so far seem to have vied for competing influence. In due course, both will be granted their due share by the Afghans. Better cooperation amongst them would not only help the Afghans when they need it most, it might also provide the two largest countries in South Asia yet another opportunity to promote regional solidarity.

*Intelligence Cooperation*

During the Cold War, the USA was less than generous when sharing information with its NATO allies. This only changed after the horror of 11 September 2001. If that was the case amongst allies, what were the prospects that India and Pakistan, with their long-standing ill will, would cooperate meaningfully in this field? One could nevertheless envision conditions where it became thinkable. When countries are faced with common external or internal threats, the exchange of mutually beneficial information might not only be desirable but also prudent. Intelligence services could provide an ideal back channel to pave the way for political dialogue, with the added advantage of discre-tion and deniability. If the Governments concerned are not in a posi-tion to embark upon a peace process due to political constraints, they might ask their premier agencies to establish links. (In rare cases, the agencies may even do so on their own initiative.) By the time the envi-ronment becomes favourable for the dialogue to be brought out of the basement, the secret channel would have prepared the necessary ground, identified contacts, and even recommend an approach. If war is not a desirable option, dialogue away from the public glare makes plenty of sense.

Secret channels can also help to prevent panic reactions, such as the hasty mobilisation of forces or nuclear alerts. For these and other reasons, it is advisable to establish a preventive mechanism, with intelligence cooperation being its lynchpin. Even in the worst days of the Cold War, the CIA and KGB never ceased to maintain contact. Nor did we. Both the countries in fact took covert as well as overt measures to prevent unintended reactions. During the Pakistan Army's multi-corps exercise in 1989, Zarb-e-Momin, India did not move its troops to the borders since its Ambassador and military attachés in Islamabad were informed and observers invited. Similarly, when India mobilised its troops in Punjab at the end of 1992 to ensure that there was no revival of Sikh militancy, Pakistan was duly informed, perhaps even invited, to do ground checks. Post-nuclearisation, to prevent false alarms over their nuclear alert statuses, both Islamabad and Delhi developed a reasonably functional system of exchanging information, including prior warnings on missile testing. Some of our ISI Chiefs have also met their Indian counterparts to assess the chances of Intelligence cooperation.

The JATM, though not operationalised as mentioned above, could be improved to ensure the sharing of intelligence, at least on groups operating from either side of the international border. In case of an incident, it could provide for joint actions like investigation and the interrogation of suspects. Bureaucratic and political reservations are expected, some of which might even be legitimate, such as concerns about "sovereignty" and intrusion into sensitive matters. However, if these are not overcome, the endless exchange of dossiers, à la post-Mumbai, becomes unavoidable. Even if it were established, the system would work primarily, if not solely, on the basis of the threat being mutual. Initially, we could be content with this. As the two sides develop trust and rapport, its canvas would expand. One day, even joint trials might become possible.

*Track Two: Circuit or Circus?*

Soon after I retired from the Army, I was involved with a few Track Two circuits. This was partially due to my stint in Intelligence, but essentially because of our toxic relationship with India. I could therefore be counted amongst the beneficiaries of this circus that performs around the globe. After the two National Security Advisors, Ajit Doval of India and Naseer Janjua of Pakistan, met in Bangkok in December 2015, some of our prominent colleagues from one of these tracks had reason to feel gratified. Only a few weeks earlier, they were charged with conveying to their respective sides that a covert channel between the two Governments was strongly advised. Their role might have made a difference, but one would do well to remember that the establishment was not holding its breath for some wiseacres to return from a Track Two *Yatra* to enlighten it on issues that the incumbents in office believed was their turf. At times, they might actually gang up against these spent cartridges who, having royally messed up under their own watch, were now pretending to know better. Those of us who have access to the decision makers or have a voice in the public domain (through media or open discourse) could still contribute by sharing their Track Two experience. Even the most stubborn of the governments, when it has exhausted all options or come to a dead end, might recall an odd piece of advice given by an old timer, who himself might have learnt a thing or two from his former adversary, now a worthy colleague in this confessional league.

The real benefit of this track accrues when a participant is willing to shed some of his prejudices and admit mistakes. Of course, these tracks also facilitate the formation of new "old boys' clubs", transnational in their composition. I too gained by reflecting deeply on my service experience and from some exchanges with my counterparts, even writing joint papers with them, and coming up with what seemed to be "breakthrough" strategies.

## *An Afterthought*

I did not come to the conclusions right away. Rather, as events unfolded, one tried to make some sense of them and adjusted one's assessment accordingly. Some things seemed to make sense in theory, but when there was no movement even on the most mundane of matters, like the easing of visa and trade regimes, then I was forced to reflect again. The conclusion was that the Indo-Pak relationship was frozen in time, and that there were good reasons for that.

The status quo, if not too inconvenient, is the establishment's preferred option. If it proved to be of advantage vis-à-vis the adversary, so much the better. If the price one has to pay to improve relations seemed to be more than the cost of conflict, one would do one's best, or worst, to prevent change. Since India has, during the last two decades, achieved a greater level of comfort compared to Pakistan, it would rather manage the present state than risk a transformation whose dynamics it may not be able to control. Pakistan might like to break the stalemate in its own favour but has, in the meantime, become reconciled to the situation in the belief that it can not only live with the present state of affairs but can also deal with any aggravation.

It is too soon to assess how Modi will handle the Indo-Pak relationship. All the steps he has taken so far—inviting Nawaz Sharif to his oath-taking, and then reading him the riot act; heating up the Line of Control between the two countries; calling off the Foreign Secretaries' symbolic meeting on a fabricated pretext (our High Commissioners used to routinely meet the Hurriyat leaders, including before such visits); the Ufa non-event; the 167-second huddle in Paris; melodramatically crash-landing in Lahore after giving a mouthful to Pakistan in Kabul; the "nuanced" reaction to Pathankot—each of these can be rationalised in an individual context. Taken together, they reflect a persona that loves to keep others guessing and basks in the media glare, both traits that are politically helpful but are inimical to stable relations, especially in the fragile Indo-Pak equation.

Indeed, I had believed that India would defend the status quo at all cost, but must admit that I had not considered including a caveat: what if there was a revolt in Kashmir that India was unable to contain with the methods that had worked in the past? When that happened in the "post-Wani awakening" of 2016, even the status quo became tenuous. Considering that such events could recur, we have to be prepared for more explosive times. I still think that all our earlier efforts to service this relationship were useful and conflict management efforts will be resumed in due course. If the lessons we learnt, some of them "on the job", were only kept in mind and the urge to find "final solutions" checked, then the next rounds of negotiation could be more productive.

# 15

# THE AMERICAN CONNECTION

## DANGEROUS OR FATAL?

America was once a very popular country in Pakistan. Even though we were not the first choice from the region when it was looking for allies to contain the Soviet threat, after its overtures to woo India were rebuffed by an anti-imperialist Nehru, it had to settle for second best. The relationship did Pakistan plenty of good. It had its military and economic rewards, and it helped us develop the much-needed confidence to stand up to our arch-rival to our east. But what actually won our people over to the new make-believe world was what was once seen as the American Way of Life. Hollywood must have played a role, like Bollywood does in Afghanistan. The spontaneity of American culture indeed had its own winning ways. As students we used to skip classes to watch the latest Westerns and save money to buy American thrillers. Ayub Khan's putsch in 1958 was generally welcomed in our own country and when he struck all the right notes with his American counterparts, Eisenhower and Kennedy, we wanted to believe that this marriage was made in heaven.

The first unit that I joined after I got my commission in the Army was entirely equipped by the Americans. Our barracks too were built by them. We were given to understand that since the supply chain was assured, we could fire our guns to our heart's content. That mind set cost us dearly—and continues to do so. There were not enough reserves when we went to war in 1965, and indeed no further supplies. The American arsenal, we were told, was only to be used against a Communist threat. If it was meant to be mothballed when fighting any other other enemy, no one told us. The fault still was all ours. Preparing for the worst was the part of our tradition that we had ignored, and also that the onus of managing an alliance was on the weaker side, which stood to lose more when the arrangement did not work.

It was expected to work a bit better during the 1971 war, because in the meantime we had done the US a few favours and had taken risks in the process. A base near Peshawar was used by the American Air Force to fly spy missions over Soviet territory. The city was now in the crosswire of the other superpower. More significantly, just before the war, we had facilitated contacts between Washington and Peking. We could not have done this without also building a special relationship with China. Until we took Kissinger "over the hump"(literally helping him fly over the Himalaya to China in 1971), this was not only resented but also vehemently opposed by our American allies. Taiwan in those days was the only China the US ever wanted to know. I have no idea if Washington had made any firm commitment to send its Seventh Fleet to save our forces on the eastern front, which were desperately in need of help during the Bangladesh War, but when it did not arrive, the lesson was clear. This was that resisting external (that is, American) pressure in pursuit of internal interests may have had its rewards, but doing a good turn to an upstart power had none.

When India exploded a nuclear device in 1974, it was obvious, as argued elsewhere in this book, that Pakistan would follow suit. It was equally obvious that the US, the leading proponent of nuclear exclusiveness, could do precious little to restrain India but would do its utmost to prevent Pakistan from developing nuclear weapons. It not only did so, but also made it very clear that American relations with Pakistan were transactional. Soon thereafter, the event that defined our bilateral ties was the Soviet invasion of Afghanistan. It was proclaimed as a defining moment in global power politics. America still hedged for two years, but when the Afghan resistance with whatever modest support Pakistan could give showed the potential to bog down the rival superpower, the US jumped into the arena. And when it did, it not only turned a blind eye to our nuclear ambitions but also pampered us in all possible ways.

A special legislative provision, the Pressler Amendment, circumvented an American law that banned military aid to Pakistan. We could now get what at that time was one of the best combat aircrafts in the US inventory, the F16. The ISI was generously helped to steer the Afghan resistance. Pakistan could pursue its nuclear programme while the US would look the other way. As Defence Attaché in Germany, I was given an exclusive briefing by a CIA team. I have reason to believe that it was not an intelligence ploy (I had never seen such elaborate maps). Two points were especially telling: those briefing me stated that it was America's chance to do a Vietnam on its nemesis, and, in their assessment, the Soviet Union could not sustain the war. Considering that this was the early 1980s, just the beginning of the conflict, I not only appreciated the gesture but, in due course, also their judgment as well. That still did not mean that Pakistan was now America's "strategic partner".

Perhaps the first country to suspect that the Soviet Union was in terminal decline was China. It also seemed to have foreseen that when it came to pass, India would have no compunction reaching out to the still surviving superpower. The US's infatuation with India, despite the latter's neutrality during the Cold War, was well known. To provide India an option other than putting all its eggs in Washington's basket, Beijing started to woo Delhi in 1986–87. The foresight proved useful. In due course, eighty billion dollars in mutual trade was likely to dissuade India from confronting China, even if the US so desired. India, however, could not be prevented from exploiting the emerging unipolar environment. It helped that the US sent clear signals that, with no more threat from the Soviets, it was ready to mend fences with Delhi.

After the uprising in Kashmir in early 1990, India moved some of its military formations close to its western borders—more to soothe domestic concerns than to threaten Pakistan. Robert Gates, the then Deputy National Security Advisor under the senior President Bush, visited the subcontinent in May 1990 to bring both adversaries back from the brink. India obliged, but in return asked the US to prove that it was sincere in its desire to turn a new page in bilateral relations.

Once the Soviets withdrew from Afghanistan, some regression in the Pak-US special relationship was only to be expected, as was, in all fairness, Washington's resumed efforts to deter Pakistan from going down the nuclear path. What surprised us, nonetheless, was the harshness with which Washington threatened to declare us a "state sponsoring terrorism" if we did not stop providing arms to the Kashmiri resistance. That was not the only charge either. In the early 1990s, we used to label the weeks in a month according to the threat-card that the US would focus on: if it was the fourth week, it must be Narcotics. Nuclear arms, Fundamentalism, and Terrorism were the other labels rotated on a weekly basis. Mercifully, Pakistan at that time was blessed with leadership, both civil and military, that understood the game. With the passage of time, despite irritants like our stance during the Kuwait crisis of 1990–91, differences over Afghanistan, and the American concerns about the ISI's competence (the details are in the relevant chapters), we managed to gain time and create a space for the restoration of near normal ties.

When Pakistan went overtly nuclear in May 1998, some displeasure from Washington was indeed on the cards. However, since India had led the way we were reasonably sure that this phase would soon be over. Besides, we had friends like China and Saudi Arabia who offered us the political and financial support that helped us keep our cool. In due course, our nuclearised status offered fresh impetus to engage the US constructively. Nevertheless, the Kargil misadventure (details in Chapter 5) provided India with yet another opportunity to play the American card to its advantage. The US, ever so eager to please India, prevailed upon Pakistani Prime Minister Nawaz Sharif to withdraw from the captured heights, thus adding to our self-inflicted humiliation and facilitating the regime in Delhi to sweep the ensuing polls. What still proved to be beyond American power, despite Sharif's appeal for help, was to prevent the coup that he suspected was likely, because after Kargil, relations between the civil and military leadership were on the boil.

The argument that America is usually more comfortable with dictatorial regimes that can be manipulated a little more easily may not be too off the mark, but I do not think the US reluctance to condemn the Musharraf-led coup on 12 October 1999 was due to its preference for military rule. The US clout to bring about regime changes in Pakistan is limited and while Washington issues pro forma statements when the reins change hands in Islamabad, its Ambassador gets ready to be amongst the first to be called by the new ruler, civil or military.

It was fortuitous for the US, that two years down the line, when it needed Pakistan's help to invade Afghanistan, it was better served by the one-window operation offered by Musharraf than it would have been by an elected regime that might have dithered because it had to consult Parliament. Indeed, a collective decision-making body, elected or even created, helps to postpone or avoid difficult choices or try to negotiate a better deal. When the US assaulted Iraq in 2003 and asked for certain facilities from its NATO partner, Turkey, the latter could legitimately regret that its Parliament did not agree. Even the OIC, probably the least effective of all multinational clubs, found some use for its existence. The few times that the US suggested Pakistan would benefit from recognising Israel, we evaded the issue by arguing that such questions were best decided by the OIC. Our own Parliament also came to our rescue in 2015, when we were asked to help our most valued friend, Saudi Arabia, in its disastrous decision to attack Yemen. It unanimously voted against sending troops into another quagmire like Afghanistan, and helped us to continue building bridges with Iran. (Earlier such unity amongst our lawmakers was only seen when their own perquisites and privileges were at stake.)

This gambit is also available to those who need not consult anyone. In September 1990, I went to meet the famous Afghan leader, Ahmed Shah Massoud, in his base camp a few kilometres inside our borders. I invited him to accompany me to Peshawar to meet some other prominent Jihadi figures. When he said that he had to take permission from his *shura* (advisory council), the message was quite clear, "Just because you are the DGISI, don't think I will jump whenever you whistle". How much he was bound by his *shura*'s advice I do not know, but the next day he was in Peshawar. Musharraf too would have gained by following this principle. Of course, he was not expected to take such vital decisions on his own. Even if the decision conveyed a day or so later was to be essentially the same, that of a willingness to cooperate with the US, the message that he had to take many others along with him would have helped Pakistan negotiate a better deal, and Musharraf would have learnt some basic rules about how to be tough in international relations. When he later tried to justify his prompt capitulation, there were no takers. عزرے گناہ بدتر از گناہ—rationalising a sin was worse than committing it.

Though pressurised a great deal, no one had threatened to bomb Pakistan into the Stone Age if it did not fall in line, nor was it expected that we would accept all the infamous seven demands. Once we did, more were bound to follow. In due course, some were resisted, but as another Persian saying goes: گربا کشتن روز ے اول (the best impressions were made right at the outset). Plenty of damage was already in the pipeline. Granting uncontrolled access to the US military and its secret services inevitably caused friction within the country and consequently with the US as well.

For a while we even believed that we were allies again, this time the major one outside the NATO system. That, however, was an illusion, and not only because the power differential between the two countries was too large for Pakistan to qualify for this honour. Allies share in decision-making and pursue common objectives through compatible means. A coerced partner that was more interested in getting paid for its services was unlikely to be too fussy when ignored, or protest against disproportionate military means that the US employed against the Afghan population. Of course, even a hired hand can refuse to act against its vital interests, regardless of the stick wielded or the carrot dangled. It did not take long before we realised the actual cost of this Faustian deal.

Since the two countries had divergent interests and conflicting policies, Pak-US relations drifted to such a low that in 2011 some of us were openly talking about the two so-called allies now waging a "low-intensity war". It was not too inaccurate a description. American Drones and its paid agents were killing our citizens and many Pakistan-based Afghan Taliban and their sympathisers were attacking Americans and their allies in Afghanistan. It was only when Pakistan suspended all support to the allied forces in Afghanistan for seven months that the two countries reviewed the rules of engagement, and by the middle of 2012 it looked as if both would now begin to coordinate their efforts to restore peace in Afghanistan. That too turned out to be a deception. The contradictions between the interests of the US in the region and the interests of the countries bordering Afghanistan are so stark that there seemed no way that these could be reconciled.

Why the American military presence in Afghanistan seems so open-ended is a question that cannot be easily answered. Is it to retain a foothold in a strategically significant area, or because it does not want to abandon the country in chaos and thus add another failure to the long list of Iraq, Syria, Yemen and Libya? Or is it because the regime it has installed in Kabul cannot sustain itself politically, economically and militarily without the American forces staying within striking distance? These are all questions that can be discussed ad nauseam. The fact is that even after sixteen years of occupation, combat troops from the US and some of its allies show no signs of leaving, thus ensuring that some Afghans continue to target them and their local partners. Pakistan will thus remain under pressure from Washington and Kabul to undertake action against the Afghan insurgents to prevent them from moving across its frontiers. This is a demand that Pakistan cannot fulfil even if it had the capacity to do so. Afghan resistance has sympathisers on both sides of the borders and Pakistan cannot afford to make new enemies— it is still suffering the blowback from its 2004 military action in South Waziristan, and as a policy, it does not use force against any Afghan group except in self-defence, not only because it has to live with them long after the foreigners are gone, but also because it believes that it must one day bring all of them to the negotiating table. That again is a mission that cannot be aligned with the American interests and those of its clients in Kabul.

Ever since the US became the sole superpower, it has led military invasions—into Iraq in 1991 and 2003, and Afghanistan in 2001. It has abetted allies who did the same, in Libya and Yemen for example, or supported militants to destabilise unfriendly regimes like in Syria and Ukraine. None of these interventions brought peace and stability in the target country or in its neighbourhood. In fact, the ensuing turmoil not only continues, but there have been no signs that it will abate anytime soon. Some hypotheses therefore suggest that this was all by design, because stability in some areas was not in America's interest. It helps the US better than any other power to play off one country against the other and thus retain leverage. Armaments being one of its major industries, the US can sell more weapons when there are conflicts. And unity in certain regions may lead to developments that would be detrimental to the US or Western interests, such as the emergence of an Islamic block, a nexus led by Russia and China, or in resource-rich Central Asia where the US was not as competitive as some regional powers.

For a long time, one was reluctant to accept this line of thinking, not just because it sounded so much like the conspiracy theories that have been spun so often that they have lost traction, but because to follow up on such designs—demolishing an existing order through destructive intervention and then managing the resultant chaos—demanded a steering ability that was nowhere in sight in the US corridors of power. Some of respected European intellectuals would talk, in bilateral exchanges, about ignorance and confusion in Washington's decision-making circles. Churchill's famous quote, "Americans can always be counted on to do the right thing, after they have exhausted all the alternatives", was his way to describe the gung-ho culture of a conceited and arrogant power.

Whatever else might be said about the conduct of the American Afghan policy, no one ever denied that the three pillars of state power in Washington—the State Department, the Pentagon, and the CIA—acted more or less independently of the Presidency. One was, therefore, inclined to believe that the turmoil in areas visited by the US armed forces was more likely to be an "unintended consequence" of the massive use of military power (the primary instrument of the American policy) without adequate thought or concern about how to put Humpty Dumpty together again. It may not sound very flattering to the most powerful country on the globe, or provide much consolation to the victims of its trigger-happy actions, but it at least absolves it of malevolence. Nevertheless, it is too serious a matter to ignore the opposing view.

In the heyday of the Soviet Union, Moscow used to justify building a mighty war machine and having expansionist policies by arguing that it was surrounded by hostile powers. At that time, some sceptics rightly mused, had Russia become the largest country on earth merely by deterring foreign aggression? Similarly, a legitimate question to ask today would be, has America reached its present unrivalled status by just acting like a bull in a china shop? I was still inclined to give some benefit of the doubt to what was once seen as a benign superpower (and probably the largest giver of humanitarian relief), if it were not for the nagging pattern in which the US not only persisted with the military option, but also rejected or subverted all efforts to peacefully resolve conflicts. That this was almost the norm in the post-Cold War period suggests that there just might have been a method in this absurdity.

The only institution created in Europe during the days of *Détente* that was to rely entirely on persuasion to address contentious issues was the CSCE, the executive arm of the Helsinki Process, upgraded to the OSCE after the Soviet Union disintegrated. Its rationale was to disarm (where the force of arms would not work, try something else). It also had the sanction of all the European countries from both sides of the East-West Divide of that time and, more importantly, enjoyed the essential mandate. It could, for example, meddle in a member country's internal affairs if they were to impact the region. The first instrument that was made irrelevant when the US took charge after the Europeans made no headway with the Yugoslavian crisis was the OSCE. Of course, the Bosnians, and later the Kosovars, were grateful because all the relevant institutions—the UN, the EU, the NATO, and indeed the OSCE—had failed, and the US-led war did end what was seen as ethnic cleansing, even genocide. This military operation may not have had UN cover, but then force is the instrument of last resort, when no other option proved viable. However, one also knows that the post-war debris can only be cleaned up by non-military means, for which the OSCE was best suited.

Some of the other cases of American intervention suggest that *not* using force at any stage might be anathema to this hyper-power. When Iraq occupied Kuwait in August 1990 (as the DGISI, I had to watch this crisis) some of my American interlocutors seemed nervous: what if Saddam did agree to withdraw before the deadline of 16 January 1991 set by the UN? It was, for them, the worst-case scenario. (General Schwarzkopf, as I have mentioned in Chapter 3, thought differently.) Of course, if the idea was to establish a long-term foothold in this region, then only a military action, appropriately planned and conducted, could achieve that aim. The Saudis, after overcoming their initial jitters, were having second thoughts about a war that was likely to create more problems in the region than it might solve. As implicitly conceded by General Scowcroft, it was necessary to frighten them further about the growing Iraqi threat. (The CIA was to do this again in 2003.) Whether Saddam was spared after Kuwait was liberated in order to justify the continued US military presence or to resume the war at a more opportune time, is a matter of personal perspective, also taking into consideration their subsequent actions, like imposing No-fly Zones and embargos without bothering about the fig-leaf of UN support or about any humanitarian considerations. (It is ironic that a decade later the US rationalised its wars as "humanitarian intervention".) The resumption of war in 2003 has been condemned and criticised on many accounts, but I am not sure if anyone noticed how carefully it was prepared for, by weakening Iraq through prolonged sanctions and ensuring that it had no WMDs when it was invaded. Even though a lasting military presence was initially thwarted by Obama's review of the US's role, it was gratefully reinstated by ISIL (what a coincidence that the emergence of this scourge was celebrated by Ashraf Ghani's regime because it ensured that the American forces would not abandon Afghanistan). If perpetual chaos was the aim, groups like Daesh can indeed be very helpful.

Closer to home, the US has so regularly undermined peace efforts in Afghanistan and Pakistan that the longest war in American history can best be described—to paraphrase Clausewitz—as "the policy which must be sustained by all other means".

Soon after 9/11, when the US rejected Pakistan's offer to get Osama Bin Laden and his gang out of Afghanistan without recourse to war, we understood, even though unhappily, that a furious people demand blood at all cost. In 2002, the Taliban took the first peace initiative and offered reconciliation. Donald Rumsfeld, the US Secretary of Defence, who was virtually in charge, not only refused but persisted with the use of aerial weapons against anything that moved in areas suspected of harbouring Al-Qaida or Taliban sympathisers. Anyone remotely familiar with Pashtun history would have warned that it was a perfect recipe to incite a war of resistance. Pakistan during this period had also provoked its own tribesmen by sending the military into South Waziristan in 2004. However, it soon realised its blunder and embarked upon making peace with its alienated people. In their commander, Nek Mohammad, Pakistan found a person it could make a settlement with. He became the first victim of an American drone. A similar fate awaited our peace efforts in the Bajaur Agency, north of Peshawar. The day Pakistani officials were to meet the local tribal Jirga, another drone struck a compound in the area killing nearly ninety children. Thereafter, if it was the militants themselves who refused to take our peace offers seriously or the foreign agents (of course there are always some in such circumstances) who subverted the efforts, is easy to judge but difficult to prove.

The insurgency in Afghanistan, in the meantime, had acquired such dimensions that Obama, after assuming the Presidency, revisited the suggestion of starting a dialogue with the Taliban. If his decision was sabotaged by his own military, or the latter actually believed that the Taliban had to be put in the right frame of mind by some massive fire-power before any negotiations, could be the subject of much academic discussion, but the result was that the failure of military means boosted the Taliban's confidence to the extent that any settlement now may have to be on their own terms.

Hamid Karzai, the former Afghan President, was the target of much criticism not only by Pakistan but also from his patrons in Washington. I used to wonder how someone who wholly depended on external support for money and security, and on the numerous warlords not under his control, could be blamed for anything in Afghanistan except for clinging to the presidential post. I still admired him for hanging in for thirteen long years despite falling out with the American line rather early. In May 2012, I called on him in his palace and he invited me for a walk in the royal courtyard. His stated reason was that he needed some fresh air after long sessions sitting in a chair. I believe he wanted to get away from the heavily bugged environment inside. What he said during our afternoon exercise turned out to be of immense value for me, "President Obama was here a few days back. We have signed a strategic agreement, but I have postponed the 'bilateral security' part for one year". Thereafter, we talked about the implications of foreign forces remaining on the Afghan soil for too long, as well as the wisdom of gaining a year in view of elections in America later that year and to gauge domestic reaction. What impressed me most during his remaining period in power were the pre-conditions he insisted had to be met before he signed the BSA. That the US was to help start a meaningful dialogue between Kabul and the Taliban was the most significant.

The US, on the other hand, was more interested in getting the BSA signed. Before the matter was to be decided by an Afghan Jirga late in 2013, Philip Hammond, the British Defence Secretary, came to

Islamabad via Kabul. He asked me during the reception hosted by their High Commissioner what I thought of the prospects. "Not terribly good, you British should know how allergic the Afghans are to the presence of foreign troops on their soil, and, in any case, in the understated Afghan way, you have already been asked to leave, by a Jirga earlier this year", was my response. But the Defence Secretary thought he knew better. "Not to worry, the new Jirga has been hand-picked to do the needful", said Britain's Foreign Secretary in waiting, with a smile. I may not have liked what I heard, but am ever so grateful that even some British officials trusted me with important information. Not so gratifying, was America's disdain for Karzai's key recommendation.

There were a number of initiatives around that period, all intended to bring various Afghan factions to the negotiating table. European countries sponsored a few rounds, but these were mostly away from the media glare and primarily to assess the possibility of an open discourse. (Only Pugwash succeeded in holding a high-profile conference in 2015.) The two rounds at Doha became better known because of the key role of Qatar, the active support of Pakistan, and, most important, the participation of the Taliban. Obama's Af-Pak team was also engaged with the process. Proceedings at the first round were chaotic, and it was aborted on the pretext that both Karzai and the Taliban had played their parts badly. Doha 2 was better conducted but, as conceded by an important American participant, the US did not have its heart in the process. What ultimately made the whole game much clearer was how the Murree Process unfolded. It started after Ashraf Ghani, soon after assuming the Presidency in Afghanistan, dared Pakistan to fulfil its role and offered to address any reservations Islamabad might have had. Pakistan did manage to bring important members of the Taliban to the table and the result was a fairly credible meeting on 7 July, 2015. The second round scheduled for 31 July had to be called off because, just the day before, Kabul leaked the news of Mullah Omar's death, which the Taliban had been keeping under wraps to maintain unity within their ranks. Just as it appeared that Omar's successor, Mullah Akhtar Mansoor—who had ensured that the Taliban participate in all the meetings mentioned above—had regained his authority, an American Drone eliminated him in May 2016. It was just four days after the Quadrilateral Coordination Group or the "Quartet" (Afghanistan,

Pakistan, the USA, and China), with full American backing, had resolved to renew efforts to bring the Taliban back to the table. If anyone still believed that the US wanted a peaceful settlement in Afghanistan, now was the time to shed that illusion.

Henry Kissinger had warned us that the enmity of the US was merely dangerous, but its friendship was fatal. Pakistan has had its own experience of succeeding every time it pursued an objective against American desires: developing close ties with China in the 1960s, refusing to break with Iran after the hostage crisis of 1980s, and, of course, persisting with its nuclear programme. What is more, there are many examples that show the US has no inclination to save its other friends, besides Pakistan, such as, the Shah of Iran, Mubarak of Egypt, and even Saddam of the bipolar era. If countries like Pakistan still seek American help or can be coerced to cooperate, one must concede that some very clever hands steer American policies. Indeed, they are ably helped by us who vainly believe that once we have gained our pound of flesh or ridden through the storm, we will be able to disengage with minimum harm. Obviously, we have not taken Kissinger's warning seriously enough. The real success of American policies is that, despite all the experience to the contrary, many of our rulers still implore the US for help when in trouble. Our people's perception is that these leaders were not saved, in fact some of them were eliminated, once they had served their purpose.

Ayub Khan, Zulfiqar Ali Bhutto, and Zia-ul-Haq all benefited from American help, but they also understood the cost. Khan wrote about it in his book, *Friends not Masters*. Bhutto believed that the street movement against him was financed by the US, because of his nuclear programme. As for Zia, he ensured that it was he, and not the US, who drove the agenda on Pakistan's Afghan policy. None of them called for American help when their personal power was threatened. Whether Washington had any role in their eventual fall cannot be proven but a good many in Pakistan still believe that the US was involved in eliminating Bhutto and Zia. The plight of their successors, however, is better known and makes for a pathetic narrative.

In August 1990, President Ghulam Ishaq Khan sacked the first government headed by Benazir Bhutto, who had more faith in George Bush Sr, Stephen Solarz, and Peter Galbraith than in any other earthly or heavenly entity. She, therefore, sought their help. Robert Oakley was, at that time, the US Ambassador in Islamabad and, because of BB's infatuation with all things American, he had been dubbed the "Viceroy". He learnt about the President's decision when her dismissal was announced by the media. He grumbled that if he had not been alerted in time to send a message to his headquarters, then perhaps he could have lived up to his appellation. His counterpart in the US was Zulfiqar Ali Khan, a respected former Chief of our Air Force. He once told me that though Mark Siegel, our lobbyist in Washington, worked primarily for America, we had to retain him because BB believed that he would protect her interest. All that Mr Siegel could do after her government was sacked was collect signatures from a few members of Congress to register a symbolic protest.

When Nawaz Sharif was in the saddle for the second time (1997–99), he was under the impression that, although he had displeased President Clinton by going ahead with the nuclear tests in May 1998, he had made up for that, as the latter had released the money Pakistan had paid for the F-16 aircraft (which had not been delivered when Pressler was invoked in 1990), and then helped Sharif wriggle out of the Kargil crisis. Consequently, when civil-military relations at home were nose-diving in September 1999, Sharif sent his brother, Shehbaz, to get American help to foil the anticipated coup. However, when Musharraf did topple the Sharif government, there was not even a symbolic reprimand from Washington. But then this was not the first time nor the last that those at the helm deluded themselves that the mightiest power on earth would come to their rescue if they sent out an SOS, just because they had cosied up to them.

When sacked for the second time, by President Leghari in 1996, BB had learnt that there was no point in calling for help, but could not resist the temptation to grab power again, with some external broker-age. I do not know if the Americans or Musharraf had any part in her murder, or if BB herself was having second thoughts about fulfilling her part of the bargain in the deal she made with the Western intermediaries in exchange for another term in office. If this was the case, of course she was not going to get away with it. Nor was Musharraf going to get away with his fake re-election and dubious deals after losing control over his own constituency, the Army. There was no surprise when the politial forces, who had bounced back after their sins and were white-washed by the infamous National Reconciliation Ordinance (NRO), ganged up to remove him. One still did not quite expect that a person of his background and experience would seek American help to stay in office. When was it they last threw a lifeline to anyone in trouble, an elected leader or a ictator, even if it was someone who had loyally served them? That should have settled the debate in this country about the limits of US influence and whether its preference lay in civil or military rule. I am not, however, sure it has been settled yet.

# PART THREE

# THE OVERVIEW

16

## ADRIFT

*"Lazily drifting downstream, and occasionally putting out a boat hook to avoid collision"*

That was how Lord Salisbury, Britain's foreign minister in the 1890s, described the foreign policy of his country, which at that time was the world's only superpower. It may sound like a classic British understatement, but it is not too far wide of the mark. I was discussing the theme of this book with Marika Vicziany, Professor of Asian Political Economy at the Monash University of who, Australia, though not much impressed with my "drift" argument, did make a remark that not only reinforced Lord Salisbury's wry description, but also strengthened my resolve to further pursue this thesis. "Even the British Empire they say was created in a fit of absent-mindedness", said the scholar, who believes that all countries have policies and priorities that guide their responses. Indeed they do, but if a single, if rather unusual, incident like 9/11 could set back the policies and priorities of the mightiest powers, like the US and the UK, and even upset their core values, there just might be something else that determines the course of events.

It was September 1991, and the event was, an annual joint-services exercise of the Pakistani armed forces called the Triple-X. With the country's civil and military top brass present, it started with a review of the big picture: the collapse of the Soviet Union and the emergence of the United States as the sole superpower. We all agreed that though America too was one day destined to lose its pre-eminence—a certainty of history, as someone said—it would be prudent to assume that, for the next ten years, it would call all the important shots. There was nothing profound about this projected time frame. A decade is usually a reasonable period to plan for the future. Little did we really know that in ten years, the Pax Americana would start to wane.

When Saddam invaded Kuwait in August 1990, the US seized the opportunity to test the emerging new order. The UN Security Council was asked to sanction the use of force to evict the Iraqi forces. It readily obliged, with both the Soviet Union, now in its death throes and China—the two countries that might have demurred in the bygone bipolar era—meekly falling in line. Having evicted the occupation force and proven who was boss, the US ignored the world body when imposing sanctions or No-fly Zones over Iraq.

Europe too remained pathetically dependent on the American leadership to put out fires in its own backyard. It needed the USA, who in turn did not need the UNSC approval to bomb the Serbs in Bosnia and Kosovo. But then, no worldly power is omnipotent. Cuba and Iran could defy the US and survive (making up with them must go down in history as Obama's masterstroke—turning enemies into friends is a sign of wisdom); India and Pakistan got away with their nuclear impertinence; and China continued on its long march towards posing a serious challenge to American hegemony.

Post 9/11, the Security Council was once again needed to sanction the use of force to bring the perpetrators of this outrage to book, and was once again ignored afterwards. It did grant ex-post-facto sanction when the US ordered its NATO underlings to the Afghan front, but when it showed its reluctance to rubber-stamp the invasion of Iraq, the US and its allies went charging in regardless. The difference this time was that this unrelenting approach cost the superpower dearly. The only consolation it can savour is that there was precious little it could do to avert the great fall. A mathematics virtuoso once said, "Before an event one could talk about its probability; after it has happened one must concede its inevitability".

If the aim was to round up the Al Qaeda leadership, a little more persuasion with the Taliban, or the use of covert means with the war option held in reserve, might have paid better dividends. But the thought never crossed the American mind. A people snug in their sanctuary for so long were enraged at its violation and could only be appeased by a swift and spectacular response. Why else had they created this expensive war machine? The problem was that, once created, the infernal machine takes on a life of its own.

Capturing Kabul or securing big cities in Afghanistan was never a big deal for the invading armies (though what happened after that was another matter). That the Taliban regime could be toppled in short order was, therefore, no surprise. What surprised or dismayed many of us was the extension of the war to Iraq. Considering, however, that all empires, when intoxicated with power, overextend and meet the fate of their predecessors, this too had to happen. If it came too soon in case of the US, it was because the US itself forced the pace, though one could argue the acceleration of the process was a joint venture with Al Qaeda.

Osama bin Laden's claim that he would exhaust America by making it run around in circles could not have been accomplished without some inside help from those who benefit from wars. Their greed may be one reason that the US sank billions of dollars to train the Afghan Army for a role that it never could and never will fulfil. The predilection of the powerful to exhaust all options before doing the right thing led the US to dig itself deeper into the Afghan hole, and to enter into a state of war—a low intensity one, but still a war—with what was once its one-time frontline ally, Pakistan.

This low-intensity war was also on the cards, with both sides pursuing divergent objectives and different strategies. It does not really matter what the US's initial, subsequent, or evolving interests were. They could not be reconciled with those of Pakistan. Wars in Afghanistan inevitably spill over the Durand Line, for demographic, topographic, and perhaps historic reasons. Pakistan initially pleaded against the use of force for this reason, but later succumbed to US pressure and virtually committed Hara-kiri in 2004 when it started a military operation in its tribal areas.

The major divergence in the two interests was indeed strategic. Pakistan has to live next to the Afghans, the Iranians and the Chinese, and so we defied the American diktat on all three where it conflicted with our policy options. If the regional countries view NATO's out-of-area missions with growing trepidation, and some of us in the neighbourhood are not enthusiastic about a US-led military victory in Afghanistan, one may delve a little deeper into the concept of strategic defiance.

And what about Al-Qaeda, who started it all? It is possible that it no longer exists as a coherent entity, but it has certainly been replaced or supplemented by another by-product of American misadventures, the so-called Islamic State. Any militant group can now claim to be their affiliate and strike terror in the hearts of their enemies. Their units can be moved to Yemen, Somalia, Nigeria or Syria to keep us all chasing shadows. That makes them superpowers, even if of a different kind: nebulous, perceived, even make-believe, but superpowers nonetheless. The US no longer has an uncontested claim to that honour.

The British ruled the waves for a couple of centuries. Their successors, the Americans, also unrivalled in status in due course, were in a hurry and ran out of steam more or less within a decade. Ironically, one of the wiser maxims I have heard from the lore of the Wild West was, "If you walk a horse it will do 40 miles in a day, but on a gallop less than five".

The first time I heard "drift" used in the context of policy-making was during the very Triple-X exercise I mentioned earlier in this chapter. True to his calling, our Foreign Secretary appealed to the brass hats to intently deliberate over the changed environment before formulating the country's post-Cold War policies, otherwise we would find ourselves drifting again rather than following a well-charted course. We all agreed, probably because the thought that we might end up directionless—like the ones who float with every fast current (this is Ghalib's pearl of wisdom, and this book's epigraph)—was not very appealing. Of course, it would have been satisfying to define our own path and to maintain it, but then we have learnt from experience that even the best plans, whilst in execution, need constant evaluation and modification. That may not be the same as drifting, but more like being flexible or planning for contingencies, nonetheless it still suggests that flowing with the tide provided a better chance of success than being stuck in a groove.

Indeed, there are countries that set their aims high and have the ability to achieve them (China may be one of those few). For some others, the environment may be less favourable, the capacity might be inadequate, or, as in the case of the US, they might be under the illusion that they could get away with any misadventure, a phenomenon described by the CIA veteran, Michael Scheuer, as imperial hubris. Many others mentioned in this book also suffered from this syndrome, Musharraf during the judicial crisis (Chapter 7), and I myself for much of the time (as conceded in the next chapter). Given the odds Pakistan had to face right from its inception, we may not have done too badly if we have, in fact, managed to muddle through. On this subject, I have often recalled a statement made to me by a Bedouin prince, who was seldom sober, "There is no need for a strategy". He did not elaborate, and perhaps thinking that he had had one too many, I did not ask him to. But there was no way anyone trained in the military art could take such a brazen decree seriously. As one who had once headed the NDC, an institution that breathes and oozes strategy, for me the Prince's assertion was blasphemous. A few years later, when I had to reflect on my days in the corridors of power, I wished I had drunk from the same fountain of knowledge. I think what the wise man from the desert was trying to convey to me was that, even if we had a strategy, our actions would still be dictated by the totality of the environment, one's ability indeed being an important part of it. How did Pakistan fare on that account?

All our Bonapartes were different in their disposition and their putsches occurred in different circumstances. If they took similar paths to gain legitimacy and acceptance—such as hiring a legal wizard and assembling a bunch of political opportunists—one could have understood their compulsion, but if they did not have a strategy, in fact, a grand strategy, to live up to the greatness thrust upon them, one could only bow one's head in deference to the drunken prince. All of them were convinced that they had found the "scarlet thread", the idea around which a strategic web was woven, and followed it more or less diligently. For Ayub Khan, the focus was on economy; Zia believed in the centrality of religion, even if was only as an expedient tool of politics; and whenever Musharraf talked of strategy—and he did that all the time—he actually meant stratagem.

Strategy is indeed all-embracing. Economic development, ideological moorings, and "enlightened moderation", which was Musharraf's proclaimed recipe to achieve our Nirvana, might all be essential elements of nation-building, but they are only parts of a strategic whole.

Since our uniformed rulers did not have the time, the patience, or the vision to follow a comprehensive course, the gains they made in their selected fields did not endure. (Though Ayub Khan's achievements were spectacular: the country sustained an economic growth rate of six per cent or more, for three decades—the only country at that time to do so.) If, when exercising total control over all the instruments of state, the military could not come up with a grand design, it would be foolish to expect that while only playing a role from the side-lines, it could do any better than have hit-and-miss success.

Aslam Beg initially wanted to be the guardian angel for Benazir Bhutto in her first incarnation. When it became clear that she was not interested, the Army Chief shifted his support to Nawaz Sharif, only to regret the choice soon after. Asif Nawaz was obliged to Sharif for backing his nomination to the coveted appointment and was all set to remain out of palace politics, but once sucked into it, he went for the Prime Minister's jugular. Both Waheed Kakar and Jahangir Karamat believed that their role was essentially supportive and they had no deeper plans if their services were declined, as was the latter's on the creation of an NSC. Musharraf indeed shifted from extreme obedience to the ultimate defiance. So if the Military, in or out of power, had no strategic designs, would it not be reasonable to assume that our politicos, with their nose close to the ground, were sensible enough to play it by ear? I do not think I know enough to give a good answer. I suspect though that they were well familiar with the art of strategic survival: the hard-core politicians always bounced back, often against great odds.

In the late 1980s, Benazir returned from exile and snatched power from all the legatees, military or civilian, of the man who had hanged her father. After her dismissal and a couple of years in the political wilderness, she regained power, despite her dismal first stint and the sympathy wave her rival Nawaz Sharif enjoyed for his suspected persecution by whatever passes as the 'establishment'. Perceived support from the Army and a favourable electoral line-up (as I have explained in Chapter 3) may explain that particular outcome but does not negate the notion that patience in politics was a greater virtue than performance. Nawaz Sharif may have been elected thrice as the country's Prime Minister due to the mess made by the regimes he succeeded, but the fact that the last time around he descended on the throne from a death cell and banishment, only confirms that this creed was immortal. No wonder that in 2015, Zardari could mock Raheel Sharif with the jibe that, despite all the power the latter enjoyed at that time, the politicians were forever. And the Zardari phenomenon, either in jail or at the helm, would also bear out the foresight of Faiz Ahmed Faiz, one of our greatest names in literature: مقام فیض کوئ راہ میں جچا ہئ نہیں جو کوے یار سے نکلے تو سوے دار چلے (Except for my beloved's place and the gallows, no other destination was good enough for me).

Indeed, our political leadership had no grand designs for the country's future, but they did have a way to ensure their own lasting political relevance, whether it was their faith in the inability of their adversaries, be they in uniform or in "civvies", to keep them out of power for too long, or in their own ability to keep their core constituency intact until they could capture power. Either way, as long as they managed to hang in there and not be hanged, our career politicians kept themselves in the reckoning. Marking time is for civilians what the militaries define as the scarlet thread of a strategy.

On the foreign front, too, Lord Salisbury's dictum guided our conduct, even though it was, perhaps, more than a lazy drift; we often changed tack as the tide of events were read, or misread.

To start with, our relations with the US were never "strategic". These were circumstantial alliances of convenience, at best tactical moves to tide over an event. The fact that they broke down whenever we differed on issues, like our nuclear programme or the resolution of the Afghan imbroglio, implied that they were transient. All the same, the relationship did have its benefits: Pakistan developed economically, created a potent war machine, and, as an ally of sorts of the world's mightiest power, gained a high profile. In due course, we realised that our patron could not help us to resolve our core issue, that of Kashmir. Since the UN too could not help us, despite the many resolutions passed, the onus of doing something was on ourselves, and that inspired the military efforts of 1965. After the fiasco of 1971, the dispute was virtually dormant till the unrest that started in Kashmir after the rigged elections of 1987 turned into an insurgency. Unlike our launching of raids in 1965 or capturing the Kargil heights in 1999, our decision to support the resistance in the 1990s was not a deliberate one—we drifted into it. It just so happens that since it was essentially an indigenous movement, it caused more trouble for the Indians than all the efforts initiated by us, and it still simmers, despite the fact that we have virtually left it to its own devices. The thinking now seems to be that the issue could be better addressed if the relations with India improved, or the situation in Kashmir drastically deteriorated, which it did in early 2016. Pakistan tried its best not to get involved but, of course, there is no doubt that if the unrest were to continue along this arc we would be sucked into it again.

On Afghanistan too, our choices more or less followed the same pattern. Surprised by the Soviet invasion in 1979, the decision to support the Afghan resistance was, inter alia, to gain time till some help arrived, as all we had to sustain us up to that point was faith. Even when it did, led by the US, there was no certainty that it would lead to the liberation of Afghanistan. We were unsure which of the two myths: that the Soviets never abandon a territory they have once held or that the Afghans have never lost a war of resistance, would be proven wrong. The result was that we were not quite prepared for the consequences of the Soviet withdrawal. In the course of time, a policy did emerge, which was to facilitate reconciliation among as many Afghan factions as possible. But our plans to accomplish that aim could not keep pace with events, as the collapse of the PDPA regime, emergence of the Taliban, and the US-led invasion of Afghanistan overtook them. Post 9/11, again, Pakistan has had to adapt its responses to various developments, such as, the Bonn and Istanbul processes, the Doha initiative, the Chinese involvement, and, as in the case of Kashmir, we must now wait for some other fast current on which to ride.

The main argument of this book is that, having taken a decision, even sometimes a provisional one because of a contingency, we tried to calibrate our responses to the developments, some outside of our control and others resulting from our own actions. This has not been accepted by most of whatever passes as our "strategic community". The thesis may make sense and even bear close scrutiny, but since the results of our decisions were often not very agreeable, or the issues remain unresolved, academic experts are not prepared to concede that the state did attempt to act as best it could, given its limited ability, and to adapt to an evolving situation, though not always perfectly.

It is, indeed, the right of scholars to express their opinion, which would be very helpful to decision makers if they were also to suggest alternative courses of action and their implications. But most of the commentators or opinion makers are no more than "well-meaning dreamers", who have never had to take a decision in a crisis and can therefore hardly contribute constructively. They excel at making wish lists of what should be done—always by others, but never by themselves. Some even add a caveat, warning us what fate awaits us if their particular list is not taken seriously. If anyone mustered the courage to argue that these wishes are not likely to be fulfilled, he or she would be seen by these commentators as a naysayer. Except for keeping the noise level high, this group does no harm, unless it is taken seriously.

Drifting with the tide may have its conceptual and practical benefits, but there are a good number who do not believe that things happen without someone, usually an invisible hand, pulling the strings. There are good reasons for this belief. Newton's first Law of Motion, which argues that "every object in a state of uniform motion tends to remain in that state of motion unless an external force was is to it", could be seen as apposite here. Since all of them (the state, the non-state, and the supra-state actor) hardly ever come clean, or remain in the shadows, some deep thinkers use their skill and abundant imagination to unlock the algorithm of events. In this role, they are expected not only to decode developments but also situate them in a context. The trouble is that since they usually have little or no information to fulfil their mission, they select facts and figures that best fit the big picture they have in mind, and "sex up" the evidence to convert the disbelievers.

And then there are other problems.

Life is complex, but the masses want a simple cut-and-dried explanation. For them, nothing is more plausible than some divine entity who steers the wheels of our destiny. That also makes it easy for the conspiracy theorists. There are enough of the "usual suspects" around to fit the bill: the ISI, the establishment, the vested interests, and, indeed, the US and any of our many ill-wishers abroad. It is also very convenient. Since the reins were held by some other, very powerful, actors, there was little for us to do, so let us be resigned to our fate.

The most damaging consequence of this exercise is that if done too often it loses traction, as it seems to have done. As soon as one suspects that some conspiracy theory was being woven, one switches off or mocks the inventor. That has provided optimum space to the real conspirators. Yes, they also exist, and their activities range from espionage to sponsoring anti-regime elements in countries of their interest. They can now wreak any amount of mischief and get away with it. Hardly anyone would believe that there might still be conspirators around. In the Pakistani context, a good example of this phenomenon is the TTP, its genesis and what we think of it.

Its roots may well lie in our military operation of 2004 in South Waziristan. Some tribesmen took up arms against the state because we had violated their traditions and our agreements with them. In due course, they were joined by many others, some for our alliance with the US and others in pursuit of their ideological or political motives. In this environment, it was obvious that some forces, mostly foreign, who were unhappy with our policies, internal or external, or who were looking for an opportunity to punish us for past grievances, would infiltrate this body or support the elements waging a war on the state of Pakistan. The TTP is now a coalition of nearly forty groups with diverse origins and different agendas. But the common belief is that it is a product of our support for the Mujahedeen against the Soviet occupation and the Afghan Taliban, old and new. Admittedly, the onus of handling this insurgency, regardless of how it started and developed, is entirely on us, but the perception about its emergence does place our state policies in a poor light, and that too in the eyes of our own people.

There is also a more universal dimension to this dilemma. Wars led, encouraged or supported by the US—be they in Afghanistan, Iraq, Libya, Syria, or Yemen—have all failed to realise the declared objectives of America or its allies, caused great loss to life and property, and have destabilised many regions. Is this simply because the US and its allies, such as the UK, France, and Saudi Arabia, were incompetent, and the disasters were therefore inevitable, if unintended? Or, since there seems to be a pattern to it, is the real objective to create chaos in certain regions, or to nip potential adversaries in the bud? Another explanation is more popular: the US and its coalition partners may suffer losses, including economic ones, but those who benefit from war, primarily the military industrial complex and the oil syndicates, are powerful enough to trap these countries in conflicts in which everyone loses but themselves.

Arguments exist in favour of all these hypotheses. The incompetence theory is borne out by the reliance mainly or solely on the massive use of conventional military power which is unsuited to asymmetric wars, and the near consensus that the major organs of the American state (the CIA, the Pentagon and the State Department) have chronically failed to coordinate their war effort. Chaos in certain areas certainly has some benefits for the US (former Vice-President Dick Cheney even said as much) as it provides the space to play one regional power against the other and thus retain relevance, and also to sell weapons to warring parties. If there were real or potentially hostile powers in that region (and there is enough pervasive anti-Americanism to find a few), instability in the region would help to erode them from within. The defence industry in America is still one of the surviving big businesses (many others have now been outsourced to China). Keeping it in good health must be the compulsion of any government, and therefore war at all cost must be a primary principle of American policy.

The discussion could go on endlessly. The common denominator in all these possibilities is that the combination of regional issues and the interests of big powers ensure that certain areas in particular, and the world in general, keep drifting into turmoil.

# 17

# MEA CULPA

Anyone who has risen to the exalted rank of a three-star General, held some prized appointments on the way, retired as the head of the topmost training institution of the armed forces, and, after retirement, was twice the country's Ambassador, should be expected to be reasonably sane. But when I reflect on my past, some of my actions were so outlandish that there must have been an invisible hand that kept pulling me out of all the trouble I got myself into. I entered the corridors of power soon after Zia passed away in August 1988. This was one of the reasons that made me often ponder the role of Destiny. Fate certainly did intervene repeatedly in the late General's favour and, you could even say, it finally came to his rescue when he had run out of all worldly options.

In his address at the Command and Staff College, Quetta in 1979, General Zia narrated an incident that occurred at the fag end of the Second World War, when he almost drowned on the beaches of Rangoon. Where Zia and his unit were disgorged from the landing craft, the water was too deep for his height. The two-metre tall Risaldar-Major, who happened to be close by, caught hold of his shoulder straps and pulled him out like a "bucket of water", in Zia's own words. Zia did not do well in the crucial staff course, but a guardian angel helped him recover from this setback. His part in the notorious "Black September" anti-Palestinian operation in the early 1970s might have earned him the Jordanian King's gratitude, but his force commander, Major-General Nawazish Ali, was raring to have him cashiered—the Major-General died just in time, however. Zia went on to get his second star when Prime Minister Zulfikar Ali Bhutto decided to oblige King Hussain. Bhutto made his future hangman the Army Chief, over the heads of six senior Generals. As Moses grew up in the house of the Pharaohs, Zia was nurtured by the man he was to go on to execute. We all know that both the superpowers of the Cold War era effectively joined hands to provide Zia with legitimacy and victory in Afghanistan.

No comparison with myself is intended, nor would it be proper. Moreover, there was no event as spectacular in my own case. Considering, however, the indiscretion and, occasionally, outright folly of which I have been guilty, I must reluctantly concede that I too have had more than my share of deliverance. My escapades began even before I joined the Army.

While doing my Bachelor's studies at the Lahore Government College, I got into an argument with a lecturer, but instead of settling it within the room I started a demonstration in the corridor. The man was an angel. He could have had me expelled from the college, but he told the class that he did not wish to ruin my career. I felt ashamed, apologised, and have believed ever since that, more than my career, he saved my soul, though I went on to sometimes lose my head.

In the referendum of 1984, we were given a (Hobson's) choice: if we voted for an Islamic system in Pakistan, Zia would continue to be the President, a nominally elected one, for five more years. The swindle was perfect. It deceived no one but there was nothing that anyone could do about it. I tried to be clever, by writing in our formation's monthly report that because of his services to the country, Zia could just as well have been elected had there been a direct question in the referendum. A friend at the Headquarters had more sense than I did and deleted that part. This time, it did save my career. I still learnt nothing.

Soon after this, I was at the NDC lecturing Zia on the merits of undiluted democracy and was understandably consigned to the sidelines (the episode is also mentioned in the Preface). This time, the rescue came from across the borders. When the Indians undertook the exercise Operation Brasstacks in 1986, one of the Army's reserve brigades needed a commander. I came back into the mainstream but had sense enough not to write a letter of thanks to General Sundarji, the Indian Army Chief. Zia's exit from the scene did land me the high-profile job of the DGMI, but I did not acquire the gift of sensing when to pull back when prudence so demanded.

General Aslam Beg was an effective Army Chief and a trusting boss. As Defence Attaché at the Embassy, I had organised his visit to Germany when he was the CGS, and he was my Corps Commander when I was commanding the brigade at Kohat. He got me over to head MI soon after becoming the COAS—the position that took most of his attention. He still found time for the Army's traditional role in foreign policy and for his self-assigned charge to guide the nascent democracy of Pakistan. The problem was that though sincere in helping the recruit regime, he wanted things to move on a fast track and was susceptible to bad advice. When BB appointed a retired General to head the ISI, General Beg started toying with the idea, probably prompted by some of his informal aides, to mobilise the MI to do some political work as well.

In the middle of 1989, BB decided to bring the power struggle within the establishment to a head (the details are in Chapter 2). Beg did not seem too happy that the DGMI was not proactive. And that is where I faltered. To appease the boss, I volunteered to play ball. Benazir, by that time, may have spurned all efforts to be reconciled with the other pillars of power, and I may have hinted to Beg, even though mildly, that his cronies had some other agenda. The fact is that when I told the Chief we had a chance of making the No-confidence motion of September 1989 a success, it was to win back his favour. A more serious mistake was to induct a few street-smart operatives into my team who did deliver at that time, but subsequently became a liability. I not only met some politicians to give them the necessary message but also brought some high-profile personalities into contact with Beg. The motion failed, but I had my first lesson in politics, which was that these politicos were just too smart for us naïve soldiers. One of the old foxes alerted me in July 1990 that the President was quietly preparing to dismiss the Government.

General Beg, still in two minds about whether the powers he had inherited from a military dictator struck the right note in a democratic order, was nevertheless impressed by my connections in the right places. He made up his mind that once Bhutto was sent packing, I would be the right man to head the ISI. My efforts to get back into the Chief's good books were bearing fruit. Although both Beg and I were to come to regret this power play soon after its success and for years afterwards, at that time, the thought never crossed our minds.

I have given a detailed account in Chapter 8 of what became known in our political lexicon as the Asghar Khan Case. Since the affidavit that I gave to Mr Rehman Malik led to this ignominy, I have often been asked: "Why did you have to?" For more than the last two decades, I have tried to tell myself that there were good reasons: I was merely stating facts, and as many others were involved, one day the truth was bound to come out. Since the Interior Minister had taken the Army Chief on board, some military in-house investigation must have taken place. The affidavit was for a discreet judicial inquiry, and, as some students of history used to say, by stating facts I had done them a favour. Frankly, none of that was the prime motive, and making history was certainly not on my mind. I may not be able to precisely reconstruct my thinking process, but I believe it was a combination of some unflattering factors: obliging a regime that had rehabilitated me after my early retirement, the fear of losing another job, and perhaps also a fear of being found guilty of hiding facts from the law.

None of this is very complimentary to myself, and actually reflects my appalling judgment. I have cursed myself the most for having believed that a document with my signature would never become public, despite the fact that it had considerable potential for blackmail. I may have pleaded for discretion, and that too in an "For Your Eyes Only" (the highest military classification) letter to the Prime Minister, but it only goes to prove that, despite my many years of experience, which included dealing with politicians, I had no idea about the ways of the world.

So many of us who have tasted power suffer from hubris. It is not only countries, like the US, or heads of state, like Musharraf, who believed he could get away with the murder of the Baloch chieftain, Bugti's murder, but also lesser individuals like myself who develop illusions of immunity. Had I picked up the courage to say a firm 'No' to Beg when he asked me to organise the distribution of funds, I would not have been involved in this unprofitable business. I have rationalised my actions by arguing, as I have done in this book, that I did it out of conviction, having some experience of BB's many gaffes, but someone more shrewd would have handled the episode better.

After falling out with Nawaz Sharif, I had no qualms about hobnobbing with Benazir Bhutto, against whom we had all ganged up only a couple of years previously. To justify this somersault, I had made myself believe that she had learnt her lesson—and of course BB agreed, and why would she not? It was only much later that it dawned on me that all she had learnt was to posture a little more convincingly. Since the new Army Chief, Asif Nawaz Janjua, was no more a Sharif fan than I, I actually believed I was on a holy mission. Primed by Farooq Leghari, who said my word would be more effective than his, I threw all caution to the wind and called Ms Bhutto from my cell phone when she was in London. When Asif Nawaz died a week later, I lost my immunity. When Bhutto came back to tell the new Chief about our exchanges, I lost my job.

Indeed, there were occasions when I got away lightly, despite acts of imprudence. As DGMI, emboldened by Beg's *glasnost* and encouraged to be proactive, I decided to talk to some people who had connections in high places. Most of them went right back to their patrons, both within the country and abroad, and spilled the beans. An odd couple of times, I even violated the convention of keeping a distance from foreign missions. If a Marine at the US Embassy did not extend me the courtesy due, it was only I who was to be blamed. I learnt a little too late that such meetings, especially with American diplomats, carried a risk. His or her reports back home would, of course, quote you, and if you happened to be someone significant like an intelligence bigwig, the report would annotate your name with "protect source". If such documents were ever leaked or captured—as they were from the US Embassy after it was occupied by the Iranian revolutionaries—this remark, though not intended to identify one as their agent, could prove very embarrassing, to say the least.

I did not like old-fashioned constraints and suffered from the illusion that I could hold my own against the rest of the world. In fact, the others proved cleverer. They massaged my ego, prodded me to talk more, and were not taken in. We still feel elated when told that ours is a more open society than the Indian. I suggest we make others work hard to read our lips, and harder still to fathom our thoughts.

I suppose when a DGISI of the early 1990s recounts his blunders, some may legitimately expect a few confessions on the foreign policy front. But this account is about my personal experience and not the right place to judge the decisions or policies of the state. My views on how we handled the crises in Afghanistan and Kashmir, in any case, have been adequately covered under the relevant chapters. A few regrets that I have because of my personal contribution could be recounted, so as to get them off my chest. All of them concern the Kashmir uprising which started in February 1990.

When I took over the ISI in August that year, the interim government led by the late Mustafa Jatoi was fully involved in electioneering. Important decisions of the state were, therefore, in the domain of the Presidency. GIK's experience, as well as his team, which consisted of some of our best bureaucratic brains, such as his Secretary, Fazl-ur-Rehman, two retired federal Secretaries, Ijlal Haider Zaidi and Roedad Khan, and a former advisor to Zulfikar Ali Bhutto, Rafi Raza, amply qualified the Hill for this role. IHK at that time, as one recalls it, was fired up.

In early September, the President's office asked me to help form a "unity government" in Azad Kashmir so that it could better handle the fallout of the turmoil from across the LOC. In operational terms, it meant that the incumbent Prime Minister, Mumtaz Rathore from the PPP, should accept the veteran Kashmiri leader, Sardar Qayyum of the Muslim Conference, as the President. Rathore agreed, Qayyum was accommodated, but as soon as Nawaz Sharif formed the government in Islamabad, the old fox got rid of Rathore, probably the only chief executive of Azad Kashmir who had never been accused of financial or political corruption. I, as the underwriter of the arrangement, felt embarrassed and joined the group that believed Sardar Qayyum would be the last man standing against the liberation of IHK, because that would bring an end to his own political career.

In the absence of any clear guidelines from the political leadership, it was practically up to the ISI to decide how best to handle those who came over from the IHK to get support against the Indian occupation. We did what we could, which was primarily to keep a handle on them and to contain the militancy below a certain threshold. It turned out to be impossible, despite our efforts to provide them with a political umbrella, the *Hurriyat*. The armed resistance lasted longer than expected, creating immense anxiety amongst the Indian establishment, but also took a heavy toll of Kashmiri lives. If there was any other way of handling it—refusing to arm them, diverting most of their efforts to wage an *intifada*, or controlling their tempo—I do not know, but because the whole thing eventually drifted out of our control, I do feel that some other model might have been better.

I also often felt sorry for not having given Amanullah Khan (Gilgiti) his proper due. He headed the Pakistani chapter of the JKLF that strived for an independent Kashmir, not a very popular stance on either side of the border. Personally, I was not averse to using this option as a tactical or a bargaining tool, even as the second preferred option, if accession to Pakistan was not possible. My regret is that, though Khan was the initiator of the movement and was more committed to the Kashmir cause than all the others, against my own better judgment I did not pick up the courage to give him his rightful place. When I heard that he had passed away, I recalled how seriously he organised his rallies at the border town of Chakoti on 27 October every year to remember the martyrs of the massacre of 1947. These days, when so many polls in IHK indicate majority support for the independence option, one must admire, even if regretfully, Gilgiti's foresight.

At times one gets one's comeuppance right here on earth, and does not have to wait till the life hereafter. In the early years of the post 9/11 decade, when our angry countrymen were targeting the military top brass, our star-studded convoys used to travel at breakneck speed and they expected all other road users to keep the fast lane free. I must have taken some extra time moving left after I spotted in my rear-view a four-star fleet with lights flashing and heard sirens blowing. The military policeman in the lead vehicle gave me a dirty look as he zoomed past. It took me back to my service days. Though I carried only a one-star plate at that time, the military pointsman spoke harshly to a cyclist who came in my way. The man pleaded to be spoken to politely. I should have apologised for the behaviour of the uniformed sentry, who used my rank to bully the poor chap. This was a lack of courage on my part again. Retribution took two decades coming, and it came through the agency of someone of my own uniformed clan.

18

## REFLECTIONS

Much of what I have written in Part One of this book is from the perspective of a practitioner. I like to believe, furthermore, that the observations and assessments in the later parts are also based upon some introspection. Of course, it is possible that these too are coloured by my experience in the field. Even so, while talking to a military audience after my retirement, I was at times politely reproved for philosophising issues, which actually meant that I was not stating things as clearly as expected from someone who was once in active service. It must have happened because, on reflection, I often realised that things had not been as they had first appeared and, at times, not even seemed to be after they had unravelled. Of course, one also understood that, at any given stage, the response to the situation had to be commensurate with the way a development was perceived. The best one could do was to take interim decisions and then adjust the course of action as and when the events unfolded—a "constructive drift", if you like. All the same, let me muse a bit on where I think I may have learnt to look beyond the obvious.

I do not recall when I first heard the edict, "perceptions are more important than reality", but after I started dealing with amorphous threats, it become my favourite quote. At the tactical level, when the picture of the enemy was reasonably clear, we in the military carried out what was called "threat assessment". Faced with a country like India, which has a range of resources that could be employed against us in any number of combinations, the same task was better described as threat perception. It actually implied perceiving how India perceived the threat from Pakistan. I was once so carried away by this mantra that I cited it to Benazir Bhutto when she was the Prime Minister. The smart lady reminded me of this on a later occasion to rebut an argument that she did not like. In due course, I got so obsessed with the power of perception that I no longer believed that reality was anything but our perception of reality. I may have come to that conclusion when so many "truths" about the same episode were being propounded that I had to admit that the only truth was what one believed to be the truth.

This process of abstract learning continued.

During a discussion I was getting quite frustrated because my version was not getting through, even though all those present knew that I had been a witness to that particular event. I was reflecting over this when someone asked me to "change my narrative". Arguments indeed have no chance against belief systems: religious, political, or historical. These are built over a long period of time, through a chain of narratives. That reminded me of another pearl from Ghalib: پہلے تو اپنے دل کی رضا جان جلے پھر جو مزاج یار کہے مان جلے (once you have made up your mind, accepting the right argument will inevitably follow). We all have our villains of the piece. If they were the US or India, all the turmoil in the country could be conveniently placed at their door. Often these are internal actors. If one was upset with the military's role in politics, our tensions with the neighbours could readily be rationalised as the Army's desire to protect its special status in the country's polity. Indeed, according to some, but for the Madrassas or the ISI's proxies, the country would never have suffered from the curse of terrorism. Notwithstanding the part played by all these suspects, hardly anyone who was convinced of their culpability would consider the conflicting evidence, even when it was supported by statistics, like the ratio of "terrorists" trained by the seminaries to those who came from the universities in the West.

We have repeatedly been reminded that, whereas all the others who count in our strategic calculus, the Americans, the Indians, the Taliban, even the detractors within, have their narratives all firmed up, Pakistan has not. One is, of course, aware of the power of narrative but the notion that all of us must agree on a single account was neither possible nor desirable. Some despotic regimes tried this in the past, by shielding their people from dissenting views, but the gains were short-lived. America has been more successful (even our mainstream opinion makers buy the versions made in the US), but only after sustained and subtle efforts, and then, too, because the country has provided sufficient succour to its citizens to earn their more or less unthinking loyalty. In our case, the official narrative triggers more scepticism than conviction. We may win any war, including the disingenuously coined "war on terror". But we lost the war of narratives long ago.

The power of narrative is so awe-inspiring that it can even make us believe in myths—the myth of power, for example.

A part of that myth, nonetheless, has already been exploded. Not many now believe that brute military power, even such as that at the disposal of the US, could prevail upon a genuine armed resistance. No one described it better than Rosa Brooks, Professor of Law at Georgetown University, in her article published on 4 April 2013 in *Foreign Policy*, "Why sticks and stones will beat our drones". We have also, in the meantime, admitted that going nuclear did not make Pakistan an "invincible fortress". The bluster after the nuclear tests in May 1998 was essentially to fulfil the desire of a people who had not heard much good news in a long time. The Soviet Union had collapsed only a few years before despite its colossal arsenal.

There were times that our presidents enjoyed unusual powers, such as those of dismissing governments and dissolving assemblies, but they could seldom do anything less. If the mischief was contained below a certain threshold, their powers were limited to writing letters. Our Army, too, is believed to have wielded amazing powers in national affairs. At times, only a handful of its soldiers turned the course of the country's history. Once in power, its collective might failed in the most trivial matters. Soon after taking over the ISI, I learnt about the limits of its clout. A police station in Islamabad would not even register a report after one of our vans had an accident. The man at the desk made it very clear that the other vehicle belonged to the Customs, for him a more important customer than our mighty agency. And when the Assistant Commissioner of Pishin, then a sub-district near the Afghan border, refused to issue a routine permit to our trucks carrying wheat for the Mujahedeen, it was obvious that he was prepared to challenge our powers.

And what about the power of the much-feared clerics? Of course, each one of them can move a mass of humanity to wreak havoc in a town, but all of them, even if they ever got together, could not persuade a single man to remove rubbish from the street. They have the power to tyrannise a whole community through the loud speaker, but cannot sway anyone by simple word of mouth. When I took up the pen after my retirement, for some time I deluded myself that it was mightier than the sword I had just sheathed. I am not sure if my writing impressed even the few who could read, but the man wielding the gun continued to strike terror into the hearts of all who got on the wrong side of him.

One of the most enduring beliefs in Pakistan is that education is one of the country's major problems. If this implied that most, if not all, of our problems were because of our educated classes, I might have agreed. But I cannot think of any of our chronic ailments, such as, corruption, inefficiency, and apathy, that can be blamed on our illiterate masses. They have, in fact, sustained us through their hard work, primarily because they remained outside the stranglehold of our highly literate establishment. They can only be faulted for having kept the country afloat and thus sparing our leadership the urgent need to mend its ways. "Lack of education" is yet another cover that we use to avoid addressing a bigger malaise—elitism. There is also the pervasive belief that our democratic system would reform itself. I have never heard that the beneficiaries of a dispensation—in this case, those who get elected because the system favours the crooks—ever worked to bring about the changes that would weaken their own oligarchic hold. Talking of the beneficiaries, have we not noticed that those who ride on the coat tails of military dictators plead with their patrons to hang on to power by hook or by crook?

The power brokers in uniform have often been asked why they picked the likes of the Bhuttos, the Sharifs and (Altaf) Hussain to do their bidding, and then regretted these choices afterwards. I cannot think of a good answer, except that, most of the time, it was to get rid of a known evil, in the belief that if the next one proved no better, he or she might at least be more pliable. It never worked. When looking at the most likely option after Benazir Bhutto was dismissed in 1990, no one had any illusions about Nawaz Sharif's skills, but we all deluded ourselves into believing that he would play the establishment's game. The MQM was indeed created as a counterweight to the PPP's stranglehold over our "soft underbelly", but also because its military godfathers believed that the Muhajirs could be kept on a leash. Despite all these lessons, Musharraf still went ahead and created a "Quisling" League, which at the first available opportunity subverted its patron's flagship project, the Devolution, by effectively denuding the local governments of any financial and administrative autonomy. Bad judgment, imperial hubris, or Realpolitik? Perhaps it was all of these rolled into one.

Some of us were foolish enough to believe that our main role in Afghanistan was to maintain leverage with the Taliban in order to bring them to the negotiating table. It dawned on us rather late that the resistance to a negotiated settlement came from those in Kabul who would lose their perks (perhaps even their lives) if this were achieved, and it came also from their benefactors, the US, who, if there were peace, might be denied a military foothold in Afghanistan. The beneficiaries of the status quo—as in the Indo-Pak equation—were naturally unwilling to rock the boat.

Having believed for the last quarter of a century that Pakistan should be proud of its role in the defeat of the Soviet forces in Afghanistan, one was initially a little surprised when some representatives of the Kabul regime started asking the surprising question: had it not all been a mistake? On reflection, it started making sense. They might be the beneficiaries of that "mistake", but if this intervention repeated, this time they would be the sufferers. On reflection, the thought was not that unusual. Germans had made good use of cheap energy from coal. Now that they had better sources available, we were often advised to find some other more environmentally friendly means, whatever the the cost. And, of course, both India and Pakistan used to be warned that the West might have been lucky to have escaped nuclear accidents, but we had better not take the risk and should abandon the quest for this dangerous acquisition.

It seems there is no end to the illusions that we have created merely to avoid coming to grips with reality. "If only we could improve our image", was one of them.

The image is a reflection of reality, distorted by the perspective—at least, that was what I had believed for a long time. Pakistan, for example, could be "imagined" differently by a sociologist, an archaeologist, a geo-politician, or a strategist. I have known cultural historians from Germany who remained enthralled with our country, even when all others were preparing to write it off. But the criteria in these Kafkaesque times are indeed complex.

In the 1950s and early 1960s, the image of America's "most allied ally" was symbolised by the over six-feet tall, uniformed Ayub Khan with his clipped moustache. Zia, though also in uniform, did not have Ayub's frame and wore a moustache more befitting of a rustic villain. He still won for us the image of a bulwark against the "evil empire". Benazir could not wear a uniform or a moustache but was hailed as the *Darling of the West* when she postured as the *Daughter of the East*. Musharraf looked comical in his fatigues, with the trousers tucked into his boots, but he won back for us the label of a frontline ally—till he decided to salvage a bit of his own reputation and some autonomy for the country. Since then, Pakistan's image is in tatters.

The country certainly has changed in the last half century, and not always for the better, but its image rose and fell in direct proportion to its role as the front-loading or back-stabbing ally of the mightiest of powers on earth. The most lasting impression is indeed made by how we behave at home and abroad. In principle, building images which contrast with the situation on the ground is an illusory exercise. If anyone seriously believed that we could fool the world, he was living in a make-believe one.

If the power of the media, too, was an illusion, I would be a very happy man. But to my great discomfiture, it is not.

"The insurgents can only kill a few of us but the media will slow-poison the whole society", said a young woman with a doctorate in strategic studies, who is no fan of the Taliban. Since the pen was always deemed to be more powerful than the sword, the media's soft power could indeed be more effective than the brute force of the militants. But if one looks at the trajectory that the media has taken over the past few hundred years, its toxic fallout was almost inevitable.

In 18th century Europe, the press, after the church, the nobility and the townsmen, was the fourth estate. In due course, it was exalted enough to be regarded the fourth pillar of the state, after the executive, the legislature and the judiciary. As it grew in power, it was at times diffidently called the fourth force. Since, in Pakistan, it is now more effective than the state in shaping perceptions—more important than reality, as already suggested—it may well have become the first force. If the charges of poisoning still seem a bit over the top, please remember that when the state abdicates the business of hearts and minds, the media, or for that matter the Taliban, will fill the void and acquire noxious powers.

One of our former Prime Ministers actually believed that statecraft was all about "space in the media". He would not even release relief goods unless a good many cameras were present to showcase his compassion for the poor. Essentially a PR man, his infatuation with publicity was understandable. As the country's Ambassador to Saudi Arabia, I was also accredited to the OIC, known for its masterly inactivity. Before the first session, an experienced diplomat briefed me on my role, which was to "deliver a hard-hitting speech and ensure that it makes headlines back home". If media puff is now the measure of performance, at times even a substitute for action, no wonder that it has turned the head of the media. In the meantime, the situation has only got worse.

I remember that in our military schools of instruction we were told that information was best conveyed through audio-visual aids, since they mobilised most of our knowledge-acquiring tools: seeing, hearing, and reading. I am not sure if that was the sole reason that made the television the most favoured arm of the media. I think we no longer have the time or the patience to get our daily dose of news and views from print. I also suspect that TV has helped us switch off the most taxing of our learning faculties, which is thinking for ourselves. It creates such a sense of fulfilment that we feel we are being programmed to absorb all wisdom with very little effort on our part.

A respected journalist of the old school once enlightened me on the curse of the TV ratings that has led to this rat race in which one-upmanship is the name of the game. Concocting or "sexing up" stories was bad enough, though still this was not solely a Pakistani affliction. But the way our TV channels have gone haywire with the circus that goes under the label of "talk shows"—this must be an indigenous phenomenon! Indeed, there are many issues to discuss and our people are curious. In search of clues, they surf the media, but what they get in return is recycled banalities. It usually starts with some seemingly end-less rant about the sins of the past, and depending on whom one dis-likes the most, the US, the Army, the politicians, or the Mullahs are blamed for all the mess. The "historical perspective" at times is certainly useful, provided it also leads to a logical course for the future. Instead, what we get from experts and analysts is a wish list of platitudes. Even more distressing are the canned questions that are essentially intended to needle guests who were once in the decision-making loop: why was something not done sooner, or what did you do when you could make a difference?

By their own admission, the first and the foremost duty of the media is to inform. Anyone halfway familiar with their antics knows better than to take their scoops seriously, and awaits confirmation or, more likely, denial. The cynics use a simple device, "if it is on the media, it must be wrong". There is a good chance that they might be proven right. But a large number of people, even though they have been duped before, swallow whatever the media dish out. In my opinion, these people are beyond help.

The problem is that the only means available to reform the media must come from the media. We often seek cure from the cause. "تمہیں نے درد دیا ہے تمہیں دوا دینا" (you caused the pain, and only you can provide the cure), is part of our folk wisdom. "You broke it, you fix it", in other words. This homeopathic principle must be a vintage belief. Long ago, I read somewhere that the best antidote to snakebite comes from its own poison. This monster, the media, however, is not going to detoxify itself. When intoxicated with power, no institution does. But if we think that they do more harm than good, then the onus of sanitising or even defanging the media is on us.

The prevalent perception in the country is that we are not in control of our destiny and an external hand steers what happens here. It pro-vides an expedient excuse to do nothing. We may have had our way on a number of major issues—witness the China policy of the 1960s, our relations with the post-revolutionary Iran, and our nuclear pro-gramme—but the obsession with the foreign factor is endemic. A threat by an American non-entity or some doomsday prediction, hurls our media in the overdrive. Their 'nefarious agenda' will be discussed for days on end till the instigator becomes a household name. If some turmoil follows, whatever be the reason (and, in our case, there are always many), the notion that a hidden power is calling the shots is reinforced. Resignation and apathy loom larger than before.

To hold the media responsible for this depressing state would be giving them too much credit, nor can they stand in for a state that has the credibility to line the nation up behind its narrative. At best, the media can help air a few well-reasoned narratives and let the people come to their own conclusions. Over time, people would learn not to fall for these infernal designs. The idea is to stimulate a spirit of enquiry rather than conditioning the audience to swallow formulated knowledge. As in countries where the smug arrogance of the big media houses has driven people increasingly to rely on social media networks for an alternative outlook, in Pakistan, too, the mainstream media would lose their primacy as opinion makers. I have no idea if it was this sort of new rage that brought millions to Tehrir Square in Cairo to topple a military dictator, or assisted the elected Prime Minister in Turkey to thwart a coup. I do not know if alternate media would help us understand the world a little better, but they do, at least, provide an outlet for those whose views never had a chance to be expressed.

A few years ago, I met a bright young lady full of fervour and very optimistic about the future of Pakistan. She had her reasons to be so, but one factor seemed particularly exciting. There were quite a few like her who exchange views on social media. As a firm believer of the value of networking, I wished her all the best. A word of caution was still in order. I have no idea how long our youth will remain exuberant before the harsh realities of life bring them crashing down to earth. Invited to the Herat Security Dialogue in September 2015, I came across a similar group imported by the Kabul Regime. All of them were young, Western-educated, articulate and determined, as one of them stated, to "change the face of Afghanistan". The only problem was that they never had a chance to know anything about their own country. I doubt if they would be humble enough to learn from a young woman in a remote village, who probably asked the most pertinent question at an event organised by BBC in Kabul, "Why do we have to seek Pakistan's help to talk to the Taliban—can't we do it ourselves?" That indeed is the Afghan way, especially of the tribesmen. Of course, it was not the occasion to explain why the whiz kids of Kabul were so averse to negotiations with a group that had its feet on the ground.

I, too, was one day taught the ultimate truth by a humble teacher. Some of us believe that all a nation-state strives for is about economics, until we are reminded that there were times when Pakistan had consistently shown a growth rate of six per cent or more for three decades. Why do we think this growth passed virtually without a trace? Representing the security establishment, I indeed concede that, at the best of times, the defence forces provided only limited space for the country's grassroots development to be ensured by non-military means. The basic bricks to build the nation, said the wise man, was therefore something more robust—the character of the people and the society.

# NOTES

INTRODUCTION

1. The two courses, the National Defence Course and the Armed Forces War Course, that it used to conduct for the selected senior officers from the Civil and Military establishment had a strong research component.
2. The 111 Brigade stationed in Rawalpindi has earned a place in Pakistan's political lexicon. Its march on Islamabad signals that yet another military intervention is on its way.

6. IN THE HOLY LAND

3. Pushing the tribesmen is not a good idea. I learnt that on the job, first with the Afghans and then with the Saudis. On Musharraf's first visit, when I badgered the Royal Protocol officials to confirm the programme for the visit expeditiously, I was told not to worry and all would be well. And so it was. The same advice I gave to my Austrian colleague because his ministry was chasing him before the visit of their lady-chancellor and he was not making any headway in Riyadh. I said all he had to do was to assure his headquarters that "everything would be just fine", and of course get his chancellor a good abaya. That visit too went like clockwork.

7. POST 9/11: PARTNERS OR PAWNS IN THE "GLOBAL WAR ON TERROR"?

4. Kayani's successor, Raheel Sharif, decided that the situation was too critical to wait for a political decision, and that the Army would go ahead regardless. People indeed heaved a sigh of relief, but considering

that non-military measures were not in place, a blowback anywhere from Peshawar to Karachi was a foregone conclusion.

5. It seldom does. Besides the two examples in this chapter, President Kennedy went back on his promise not to sell arms to India if Ayub Khan were to facilitate US covert operations in Tibet.

## 12. TERRORISM: A POLITICAL TOOL, OR A TECHNIQUE OF WAR?

6. See https://groups.google.com/d/msg/virtual-artists-collective/.../M2Z4jD4CCQAJ

7. From here on, I shall use the terms "terrorist" and "terrorism" only for NSAs and acts committed by them.

# INDEX

# INDEX

# INDEX

Glasnost, 125; Invasion of Afghanistan (1979–89), 15, 17, 45–6, 57, 124, 134, 136, 140, 166–7, 173, 187–8, 195, 197, 212–14, 236, 246, 253; Moscow, 15, 171, 182, 195, 218; Red Army, 51; Siberia, 2

Spain: Madrid, 103

Spanta, Rangeen Dadfar: Afghan Foreign Minister, 110

Sri Lanka: 84; Colombo, 79

Staff College, Quetta: 56, 63, 72, 124, 149, 241; graduates of, 51

Straits of Hormuz: 150, 183

Sundarji, General: Indian Army Chief, 243

Supreme Court: 9–10, 44, 70, 114–15

Swati Taliban: 105

Switzerland: Geneva, 170

Synot, Sir Hillary: British High Commissioner in Pakistan, 157

Syria: 217, 232; Civil War (2011–), 238

tactical nuclear weapons (TNWs): 203

Tahir-ul-Qadri: 87

Tahreek-e-Hurriyat-e-Kashmir: 197

Tajikistan: 182

Tajiks (ethnic group): 176

Taliban (Afghan): 98–9, 136–7, 178–9, 183–4, 188, 190, 198, 216, 220, 222–3, 238; diplomacy efforts, 181, 184; growth of, 176–7; members of, 185; regime of (1996–2001), 91, 98, 177–8, 231, 253; removed from power (2001), 177

Taliban (Pakistani): 105, 152, 198, 257; efforts to counter, 126; insurgency activity of, xiv

Tehreek-e-Taliban Pakistan (TTP): 106, 238

terrorism: 105, 109, 160–3; counterterrorism, 158, 162; cyber, 156; international, 159; origin of, term 109; state, 157; watch lists, 155

Thailand: Bangkok, 208

Third Reich (1933–45): 57

Toynbee, Arnold: 165

Triple-X (1991): 229–30, 232

Turkey: 215

Ukraine: Russian Annexation of Crimea (2014), 182

*Ummah*: 83, 88, 92

United Arab Emirates (UAE): Abu Dhabi, 108–9; government of, 108

United Kingdom (UK): 103, 138, 152, 166, 186, 238; government of, 157; London, 49

United Nations (UN): 37, 54, 94, 163, 172, 174, 219, 235; Geneva Conventions, 161; Military Observer Group in India and Pakistan (UNMOGIP), 121; personnel of, 172; Security Council (UNSC), 46, 56, 97, 230

United States of America (USA): xv, xx, 54, 57, 71, 73–4, 76, 98, 100–1, 138, 155–6, 169, 175, 179, 186, 201, 211, 215, 217–18, 223, 225, 230, 235, 237, 244, 251, 253, 256; 9/11 Attacks, 64, 85, 87, 91–5, 135–7, 151, 157, 163, 177–8, 181, 186, 189, 191, 200, 206, 220, 229, 236, 247; Central Intelligence Agency (CIA), 22, 100, 135–6, 138, 185, 196, 207, 213, 218–19, 233, 239;

INDEX

Hollywood, 211; military of,
133, 137, 151–2, 216–17, 220;
New York, 104; Pentagon, 100,
177–9, 185, 218, 239; Pressler
Amendment, 167, 213; State
Department, 104, 156, 185,
218, 239; US Central Command
(CENTCOM), 32; Washington
DC, 32, 49, 78, 91, 98, 104,
178, 185, 213–15, 217–18,
223–4
University of Berlin: students of,
61
University of Erlangen: students
of, 61
UNOCAL: pipeline construction
interests of, 176–7
Urdu (language): 19, 143; poetry,
20

Vajpayee, Atal Bihari: 77, 200–2;
Bus Yatra to Lahore (1999), 75,
199; electoral victory of (1998),
71; Leader of BJP, 71
Velayati, Ali Akbar: 173
Vicziany, Marika: 229
Vietnam: 197, 213
Vogel, Hans-Joachim: 54

Warsaw Pact: 57
Wayn, Ghulam Haider: Chief
Minister of Punjab, 37
Wazir, Nek Mohammad: 100
von Weizsäcker, Richard: 54
Wikileaks: 22

Wimmer, Willy: German
Parliamentary Secretary of
Defence, 63
World Bank: xiii; personnel of, 46

Yakunin, Viktor: Soviet Ambassador
to Pakistan, 15
Yaqubi, Colonel General Ghulam
Faruq: Head of Afghan Ministry
of State Security, 170
Yemen: 93, 217, 232, 238; Civil
War (2015–), 217, 238
Yugoslav Wars (1991–2001): 57,
219

Zahir Shah, King: 166, 169
Zaidi, Ijlal Haider: 26; Advisor on
Defence Affairs, 31, 33
Zaki, Akram: Secretary-General in
MFA, 173
Zarb-e-Momin (1989): 207
Zardari, Asif Ali: 43–4, 104,
106–7, 126, 147, 235; electoral
victory of (2008), 102; family of,
20, 102
Zhirinovsky, Vladimir: 62
Zia-ul-Haq: 3, 16, 21, 31, 34, 84,
125, 146, 223, 233, 242, 254;
address to Staff College, Quetta
(1979), 241; death of (1988), 2,
5, 9–10, 12, 132, 241, 243; foreign policy of, 167–8; regime of,
xiii, 1–2, 9–10, 26, 43, 66, 134;
rise to power (1977), 4–5, 124